CONTENTS

Introduction   v

Chapter 1   The Outsider   1
             Chris Boardman, 1994

Chapter 2   Beware of the Badger   19
             Bernard Hinault, 1980

Chapter 3   The Bulldog   35
             Wilfried Nelissen, 1994

Chapter 4   The Sculptor   51
             Joël Pelier, 1989

Chapter 5   The Boy with Fire in His Eyes   63
             Mark Cavendish, 2009

Chapter 6   For Fabio   77
             Lance Armstrong, 1995

Chapter 7   Dutch Cold War   91
             Marc Sergeant, Frans Maassen, 1992

Chapter 8   Trilogy   105
             Eddy Merckx, 1971

Chapter 9   Guerrilla Warfare   123
             *Luis Herrera, Bernard Hinault,
             Laurent Fignon, 1984*

Chapter 10   Anarchy   145
              Stephen Roche, Jean-François Bernard,
              Andy Hampsten, 1987

Chapter 11   The Devil   161
              Claudio Chiappucci, 1992

Chapter 12   Shock and Awe   181
              Bobby Julich, Jörg Jaksche,
              Marco Pantani, Jan Ullrich, 1998

Chapter 13   What about Zimmy?   205
              Urs Zimmermann, 1991

Chapter 14   The Unknown Warrior   215
              José Luis Viejo, 1976

Chapter 15   Champagne Freddy   229
              Freddy Maertens, 1981

Chapter 16   Honour Among Thieves   247
              Lance Armstrong, Iban Mayo, 2003

Chapter 17   Untold Stories   269
              Mark Cavendish, Bernhard Eisel,
              David Millar, 2010

Chapter 18   Playstation Cycling   283
              Andy Schleck, 2011

Chapter 19   Redemption   301
              David Millar, 2012

Chapter 20   La Résurrection   319
              Greg LeMond, 1989

              Acknowledgements   339
              Index   340

RICHARD MOORE

ÉTAPE

THE UNTOLD STORIES OF THE TOUR DE FRANCE'S DEFINING STAGES

HarperSport
An Imprint of HarperCollins*Publishers*

By the same author:

In Search of Robert Millar
Heroes, Villains & Velodromes
Sky's the Limit
Slaying the Badger
The Dirtiest Race in History

First published in 2014 by
HarperSport
an imprint of HarperCollins*Publishers*
77–85 Fulham Palace Road
London W6 8JB

www.harpercollins.co.uk

1 3 5 7 9 10 8 6 4 2

HB ISBN 978-0-00-750010-9
TPB ISBN 978-0-00-750011-6
EB ISBN 978-0-00-750012-3

Printed and bound in Great Britain by
Clays Ltd, St Ives plc

MIX
Paper from
responsible sources
FSC www.fsc.org **FSC® C007454**

INTRODUCTION

Étape is the result of a simple idea: to tell the stories of selected stages of the Tour de France through the recollections of the protagonists. I wanted to capture and convey the mystery, beauty and madness of the great race. But new interviews were key; I didn't want to recycle already published and in some cases familiar stories. And so I sought out the heroes and villains, the stars, journeymen and one-hit wonders. I spoke to two five-time Tour winners, a three-time winner, a one-time winner, and a former seven-time winner.

On the following pages are the fruits of this labour: a collection of notable stages, some great, some obscure. They encompass extraordinary feats and diabolical deeds, heroism and deceit, farce and tragedy. Each chapter stands alone but they are interconnected since, inevitably, there are characters who reappear. One, Bernard Hinault, even manages to have a crucial influence on a stage, and a Tour, in which he wasn't riding.

The featured stages are personal favourites, drawn mainly from the Tours I have watched since my first glimpse on television in 1984. But I couldn't resist others that piqued my interest: a trilogy of remarkable stages involving Eddy Merckx and Luis Ocaña in 1971; a curious win by José Luis Viejo in 1976, which I had read about in an out-of-print cycling book; any one of the sixteen stages won by one of the sport's most endearing figures, Freddy Maertens, in the course of his bizarre career.

There were mysteries to investigate and myths to debunk – the feud between two team directors that distorted the outcome of a stage in 1992; a rest day disqualification in 1991; the untold stories of the *gruppetto*; and some classics: l'Alpe d'Huez in 1984, Paris in 1989, Sestriere in 1992, Les Deux Alpes in 1998.

There are a number of premature deaths – Ocaña, Marco Pantani, Jose María Jiménez, Laurent Fignon – but only one occurred during the Tour. That was Fabio Casartelli in 1995 and I can vividly remember the room and sofa where I sat, and how I felt, when television pictures showed him curled up on the road, a pool of blood forming by his head. One chapter focuses on an emotionally charged stage three days later, won by Casartelli's team-mate, a young American called Lance Armstrong.

The older Armstrong reappears in a later chapter, from 2003: a stage and a Tour that now have an asterisk against them and a line through the winner's name. Despite his disgrace, I wanted to include Armstrong, partly because he is difficult to ignore, partly because nobody could argue that some of his Tours (the stage I chose in particular) were not dramatic. I didn't know if he'd agree to an interview, but when I explained the project by email he responded within minutes: 'You bet.' Then I wasn't sure what he wanted out of it, other than to talk about the 2003 stage to Luz Ardiden as though it was still in the record books; as though it still mattered. 'Those Tours happened,' he said, 'despite what a bunch of dickheads say.' Of course, you might disagree ...

Mention of Armstrong raises the spectre of doping, which, as Armstrong himself is quick to point out, he did not invent, even if he has done more damage to the sport's reputation than any other rider. But doping, cheating, skulduggery: for better or worse, all are woven deeply into the fabric of the Tour.

I thought of doping in cycling as I read the American writer Roger Kahn's book, *The Boys of Summer*, in which he recalls his early days as a cub reporter in New York. His first job was to cover high school sports at a time when the coaches were striking over pay. Consequently, there was little sport. 'But if this mess doesn't get settled, what will there be to write about?' he asked his editor.

'As you say, the mess.'

Perhaps in recent years 'the mess' of doping has overshadowed the sport to an unhealthy degree. Of course it is an important, dare I say interesting, subject. But there is so much more: the deeply fascinating – often fascinatingly deep – people who make up the peloton; the complexity of road racing, with its teamwork and tactics; the courage and skill of a stage winner, whether a journeyman like Joël Pelier, a winner in 1989 (and now a sculptor), or Mark Cavendish, arguably the greatest sprinter of all time. I hope that the following tales illustrate all of this, and do convey at least some of the mystery, the beauty and the madness.

CHRIS BOARDMAN

Chapter 1

THE OUTSIDER

2 July 1994. Prologue: Lille
7.2km. Flat

'At the 1994 Tour, everybody went for a three-week race,' says Chris Boardman. 'I went for seven minutes.'

Chris Boardman was, and remains, unique. In the history of the Tour de France, at least since the prologue time trial was introduced in 1967, he is the only rider ever to go there specifically, and exclusively, targeting the *hors d'œuvre* to the race, the prologue.

Like some other *hors d'œuvre*, the prologue time trial is an acquired taste. 'As pageantry goes in so beautiful a sport, ho hum,' was the verdict of the American journalist Samuel Abt. 'No long lines of riders flashing by, no desperate early break-aways, no sprinters tearing for the finish line, no climbers struggling to drop one another as the road rises.'

It isn't even a proper stage – that is the whole point. The prologue was conceived as a way of adding an extra day to the Tour without falling foul of the regulations governing how many days the riders were allowed to race. And the motivation for its inclusion was financial. Don't hold that against it, however, because in this it is no different to the race itself, set up to market the newspaper *L'Auto*. The Tour has always been nakedly commercial. But the commercial imperative intensified after 1962, when Félix Lévitan was appointed co-director, alongside Jacques Goddet. Goddet and Lévitan, both journalists, remained in charge until 1987, with Goddet looking after the sporting side, Lévitan responsible for the money. After Goddet and Lévitan, there were two short-term replacements, Jean-François Naquet-Radiguet, a cognac salesman, and Jean-Pierre Courcol, a former professional tennis player. Each lasted only one Tour before, in 1989, it passed once more into the safe hands of another journalist (and former professional rider), Jean-Marie Leblanc, who in turn handed it on to another ex-journalist, Christian Prudhomme, in 2005. In 110 years, the Tour de France has had only seven directors. And five of them have been journalists by profession.

The latest incumbent, Prudhomme, is no great fan of the prologue. For the first time since 1967, he opted not to include one in 2008 – then did the same in 2011, 2013 and 2014. It isn't just a question of taste: this is also commercial. Prudhomme (formerly a television journalist) points to statistics that show the television audience is at its lowest when the Tour opens with a prologue time trial. It might be better for those who are there to watch – with the action spread over many hours, and the chance to see the riders individually and up close – but there is another and increasingly important audience to think of: TV. Like Sam Abt, and arguably most others, they prefer the spectacle of a road race.

Lévitan's motivation for adding the prologue was to increase the Tour's earning potential. Back then, the main source of income was the money paid by cities and towns along the route. They paid to host a start, even more to host a finish, and so Lévitan began to add what he called split-stages: more than one stage in a day. On occasion, he even managed to squeeze three stages into one day. The riders hated it.

The prologue time trial was a marginally more popular innovation than split-stages, and it was Lévitan's way around the rule, from cycling's world governing body the Union Cycliste Internationale (UCI), that stated a race could not last more than twenty-two days. Just as an *hors d'œuvre* is not considered a proper course in a meal, the prologue, which must be less than 8km, does not count as a proper stage. Thus it exploited a loophole in the UCI rules. And yet the first prologue, on a Thursday evening in Angers in 1967, was not actually called a prologue. It was called stage 1a (1b followed the next day). Two years later, the name 'prologue' was adopted.

That first one was won by an unheralded Spaniard, José María Errandonea, who held the yellow jersey only until the next day. Including stage 1a, the 1967 Tour comprised twenty-five stages over twenty-three days and 4,780km (the 2013 race was 3,400km over twenty-one stages). But the 1967 Tour is mainly remembered for tragedy. This was the Tour that saw the introduction of a new, short stage to add another day's racing to an already packed schedule, and which saw the death of a rider, Tom Simpson, on the barren slopes of Mont Ventoux. If the two events were linked, little heed was taken – the Tour was again run over twenty-three days and 4,684km in 1968.

*   *   *

There are fans of the prologue, too. Thierry Marie in the 1980s, Boardman in the '90s, Fabian Cancellara in the 2000s. Its appeal lies in its simplicity: it's as pure a test of speed as you can get in professional cycling.

The prologue to the 1994 Tour de France was a classic. Held in the centre of Lille over a pan-flat 7.2km course, with wide boulevards and only a few sweeping bends, it was the perfect test. It was perfect in other ways, too, since it served up a tantalising confrontation between two masters in quite different fields.

It pitched the three-time Tour winner, Miguel Indurain, against a novice, Chris Boardman, whose only experience of the Tour had been as a spectator twelve months earlier. In terms of their background, they couldn't have been more different. Indurain was steeped in the traditions of road racing on the continent, slowly ascending the hierarchy of his team until emerging as leader in 1991, the year of his first Tour victory. The twenty-five-year-old Boardman had arrived on the continent fully formed, as the finished article – but a complete contrast to Indurain, given that he came from a very different tradition. His apprenticeship was served in the obscure backwater of British time trialling.

Boardman felt like a fraud. 'I felt like I cheated my way into this game,' he says.

The Indurain–Boardman match-up was a little like the annual shinty–hurling international between Scotland and Ireland. They are essentially the same sport, but they exist in isolation, one quite separate from the other. When one tradition takes on another, there is always fascination and intrigue, in the same way that there might be with twins who are separated at birth and brought up in different families, in different countries. What, if anything, do they have in common?

Continental road racing and British time trialling appeared to have nothing in common, other than that both involved people riding bikes. One took place on the closed roads of Europe, often against the backdrop of the Alps and Pyrenees, and involved tactics, teams, courage and panache. The other was held in the early morning on fast, busy roads, against a backdrop of speeding lorries and cars, and involved calculation and pacing.

The British scene had never produced a champion able to convert his talent to continental road racing. But by 1994 Boardman had showcased his talent in shop windows more glamorous than dual carriageways in Britain; at the 1992 Olympic Games in Barcelona, where he won the pursuit, and then a year later at the Bordeaux Velodrome, where he went for the ultimate time trial, arguably the only one that resonated on the continent: the world hour record.

It was in July 1993 that Boardman took on the hour record in Bordeaux, 24 hours before a stage of the Tour de France finished in the French city. The timing was both deliberate and ingenious, because it allowed for a kind of cross-pollination. 'The Hour', already a big deal in the cycling world, became even bigger: it was amplified by its proximity to the Tour, not least because so many journalists were able to attend. At least one team manager was able to take it in, too. Roger Legeay, who ran the French Gan team, was more open to Anglophones than most, since his team, previously sponsored by Peugeot Cycles, had a history of having English-speaking riders, from Tom Simpson and Shay Elliott, through Graham Jones, Robert Millar, Phil Anderson and Stephen Roche, to his current star (albeit a fading one), the American three-time Tour de France winner, Greg LeMond.

Boardman had gone as far as he could in Britain. The only place for him to go now was the continent's professional scene. Yet it was a step he was reluctant to take. 'I was an outsider,' he says. 'I was a time triallist from Britain. The Olympics were amateur, so you either wait for someone to knock you off the top step, or you turn pro.'

The hour record that Boardman set out to break was held by the Italian road racing star of the 1980s, Francesco Moser. But by the time he came to tackle it, it no longer belonged to Moser. A week before Boardman's attempt it was beaten by his domestic rival, the Scotsman Graeme Obree, on a track in Norway. 'I'm disappointed not to be breaking Moser's record,' said Boardman at the time. He feared that Obree's astonishing feat might remove some of the gloss from the record. He needn't have worried. If anything, it raised interest. It meant Boardman had much to gain, but perhaps even more to lose.

He beat Obree's mark, and with that, as Ed Pickering notes in his book, *The Race Against Time*, 'The first part of Boardman's PR ambush on the Tour was complete.' The Tour reciprocated, staging their own 'ambush' as they invited Boardman to the podium in Bordeaux at the end of the next day's stage, to share the platform with the man in the yellow jersey, Miguel Indurain, on his way to his third successive overall victory.

Tellingly, Boardman stood on the lower step, grinning like a schoolboy as 'Big Mig', in the yellow jersey, waved at the crowds with the bearing of a member of the Spanish royal family. It should also be noted that, although Indurain himself was gracious and humble, Boardman's achievement did not meet with universal respect in the professional peloton. Luc Leblanc, the leading French rider, expressed his view that, if they put their minds to it, most members of the Tour peloton could better Boardman's distance.

Less than a year later, in Lille, Boardman and Indurain met again, this time on the road. Indurain had built the foundations of his three Tour de France wins on his domination of time trials. He then rode defensively in the mountains, rather than with the attacking flair and panache of some previous Tour winners. If that didn't fire the passions of many fans, it was impossible not to admire his prowess against the clock. He was a machine, most obviously in Luxembourg in 1992, when he averaged 49kph (30mph) over 65km and finished three minutes ahead of his closest challenger. 'I thought I was having a good day and I lost four minutes,' said a bewildered LeMond at the finish. 'I thought for a moment I must have taken the wrong course.' LeMond's last Tour win had come in 1990; the speed of his decline, or Indurain's improvement, or both, was staggering.

Boardman, meanwhile, had indeed been able to use his hour record as a springboard into the professional ranks, joining Legeay's Gan team. 'Roger had come to see the hour record and Pete Woodworth [Boardman's manager] had spoken to him,' Boardman tells me. 'I wasn't super enthusiastic or excited at the idea of turning pro. I was more intimidated ... No, trepidation would be the right word. We went to see him at the Tour of Britain [in August] expecting him to say, "This is the pro team; this is where you'll fit in," but instead he asked me: "What do you want to do?"

'It was bizarre,' Boardman continues. 'I said, "Well, I'd quite like to go to the Tour de France, but only to ride ten days." Roger just laughed and said: "First-year pros don't often get to ride the Tour. But we'll see."'

Boardman guested for Gan before the end of the 1993 season, in a time trial, the GP Eddy Merckx. 'I wore one of Greg LeMond's skinsuits,' he says. He won it. 'I had no idea what to expect because you were segregated. Although I'd won an Olympic gold medal, the fact was that if you asked any pro bike rider who had won the gold medal at the pursuit in the Olympics, they possibly wouldn't have known.'

The GP Eddy Merckx really offered few clues to Boardman's potential. Although he was surprised to win, he was operating safely in his comfort zone in a time trial. The real test came the following year, with his induction to the peloton. Not that there was any formal induction: he was expected to know how to ride in a bunch, where to position himself, and be familiar with the unwritten rules and etiquette. Most riders graduated from the European amateur peloton, which operated to similar rules – but of course Boardman was different. He might as well have come from Mars.

'It was always about managing my nervousness,' he says. 'I really struggled at first. For three months I thought, I'm not going to cut it. I don't like it. It's scary. It's painful. It's highly stressful.

'In the bunch I was at the pointy end or the blunt end' – the front or the back. 'The problem with this is that at both ends you end up fighting: at the front to stay there, at the back to move up. It was terrible. Greg helped a lot, he gave me tips. Things like, "All you can see is a mass of riders in front of you, but if you're going round a right-hand bend there will always be a space that appears on the left; so you can accelerate into a space that isn't there yet." Or, "Overlap your bars with someone else's in the middle of the bunch and they'll automatically want to move away." Greg gave me tonnes of little tips that really helped. But it was all cerebral consciousness stuff so it was hard, hard work.'

Boardman made a breakthrough at the Tour of Murcia in March. 'It used to be that people who were unfit or sick went to Murcia, while everyone else went to Paris–Nice. I won the prologue there and it was my first time in a leader's jersey.' It meant more than his Olympic gold medal or hour record. 'The jersey was a passport to the front. I hadn't experienced that before. It was a pivotal moment. If you were a neo-pro you got battered: you're the softest target, people just push you out the way. But when you've done something in the race, you've got a badge. Life gets a bit easier.'

What most troubled Boardman was that all his old certainties counted for little. Up to now, his career had been built on calculation and measurement – to the nth degree; all that had mattered, through training and aerodynamics and working with his coach, Peter Keen, was making himself fast. Adding another 150-plus riders to the equation complicated things.

*   *   *

Boardman's place in the Gan team for the Tour was still undecided when he rode the Dauphiné Libéré, the week-long French stage race, in late May. He guaranteed his selection by winning three stages, the haul including the prologue, the time trial and, more surprisingly, a road stage, on a 157km loop around the Alpine town of Chambéry. For that one he broke away alone – and time trialled to the finish.

But as the Tour got closer, he began to feel unwell. He suffered terribly with nerves, which led him to work with a psychologist, John Syer, in the run-up to the Barcelona Olympics. The stress would force Boardman to think himself ill, or falling ill, even when he wasn't.

His preparation, after his triumphant Dauphiné, was typical Boardman – on the face of it, idiosyncratic, but meticulously planned and thought out. While his peers were doing warm-up road races in Europe, he rode and won a 10-mile time trial for amateurs in north Wales. Looking ahead from north Wales to Lille and the Tour prologue, he said: 'The podium is a possibility. It's difficult to know who will be up there. Specialists like Thierry Marie seem to be fading. Indurain has been very quiet … Rominger is lying low.'

'Chris is very close to his best form,' said his coach, Peter Keen. 'He still has a slight problem with a chest infection that we're trying to clear up. A sputum sample enabled us to find the type of microbe and he is now on antibiotics.'

Boardman kept talking about this illness, too. Now, how-ever, he says he can't remember being unwell. He thinks it might have been a case of getting his excuses in first. 'I used to need mental crutches like that, like many athletes do. You're hypersensitive to any sensation or the slightest twitch or any-thing. It's a bit childish, but it's a crutch, in case it goes wrong. You don't just say, "I couldn't go any faster and I wasn't good enough." You weren't secure enough in those days to think like that.'

In the days before the prologue, Boardman carried on doing his own thing, as strange as it seemed to his team-mates. He had his routine for coping with the nerves. 'What I used to do was read and sleep. They were my two escapes.' To assist the 'escape' he liked science fiction – Iain M. Banks was a favourite. 'It was a way to not be there, while you were still there. And I slept under pressure. A lot. Which is quite a handy trait.'

He didn't do what his team-mates did, what professional riders had always done, which was to go out for easy rides in the week before the race, recce-ing the prologue course at a gentle pace to get a feel for it. 'They used to go out and ride the course if it was open and have a chat,' Boardman says. 'I went out on my own and I could probably tell you now where all the grids were, where there was a bump on the road. I memorised it.' Most importantly, he memorised it at the same speed as he would tackle it on race day. 'They put the team car in front of me; I had to do it at race speed. So I had the car in front, it would take me up to speed, then get out of the way before the corners. I thought I could get round the whole course without braking, but that was the only way to find out. So I had it all mapped out. That was two days before. From that point forward, we got all the information we could.'

Boardman habitually uses 'we' instead of 'I', meaning his team – not his professional team-mates, who were mere colleagues, but his far more important support team, led by Keen. But Keen wasn't there – he 'felt like a fish out of water', says Boardman, and rarely went to continental races.

Boardman's wife, Sally, was in Lille. 'I used to resent Sally being there,' says Boardman, with a smile to suggest he is joking. Only, he isn't really. 'She used to have a good time, a party, and her friends came over. I'd see them, they'd come to the hotel, all in happy spirits. They were going to have a good day. And I'm thinking, I'm crapping myself here. I've got seven minutes that decide my salary for the next year. It used to, reasonably or not, make me quite angry.'

Did he dream of becoming only the second Brit after Tom Simpson to wear the yellow jersey? 'I did, yeah. But you just go out there and try and win. That's the beauty of the time trial. You do your thing. It was the psychologist who got me to realise that you can only do what you can.'

Prior to the Barcelona Olympics, Boardman spilled out his fears to John Syer. 'What if this goes wrong? What if I can't go fast enough? What if the other guy's faster? What if I puncture?'

Boardman expected Syer to offer words of reassurance. Instead, he said: 'Yeah, well those things could happen.' Boardman was puzzled. 'I said, "Hang on, aren't you supposed to be helping me here?" But he said, "No, this is the deal, mate – elation and despair are two sides of the same coin, in equal and opposite proportion. If you want the big win, you've got to risk the big low. So instead of trying to deny that, why don't we stare it in the face?"

'I sat on the start line at the Olympics and thought, fuck it, I'll just be as good as I can. And when I cross the line I'll look at the board and see what I've done. He taught me that you can't affect what others are doing, or let them affect you.'

Now, when it came to the 'others', there was only really one. Indurain. 'He was a brick,' Boardman says. 'However he did it, it was pretty amazing.' He had never raced Indurain before the start of the 1994 Tour, so predictions were difficult. While Indurain had won the last two prologues, Boardman was the Olympic pursuit champion and hour record holder. Indurain might confirm what many suspected – that continental road pros were a different breed, even a superior species. Then again, Boardman, although he came from a small pond, clearly had a special talent. The contrast between the pair was striking in almost every way. Indurain was tall and rangy, six foot two and twelve and a half stone; Boardman was compact and stocky, five foot nine but solid at eleven stone. On a bike, the differences were more marked: Indurain was a jumbo jet, Boardman a fighter plane.

'It was really, really hot,' Boardman recalls of the day. He didn't have a special routine before the race. 'Most of it was having the courage to do nothing. I learned that from my pursuiting days. Because when people are nervous, they go out for a ride. We were staying in a hotel just out of town. On the morning I went out on my bike for an hour. Just really easy. The others went for a couple of hours. The days before, too, they went out, and said, "Are you coming?" I said, "No, I'm going out on my own with two sprints."

'My routine was worked back from the time of the start: I want to be on the start line with three minutes to go, so how far is it, to walk from the bus to the start house? When am I going to warm up – because that had to be really close to the event. Where's the signing on? When am I going to put my numbers on? When am I going to eat? It's incredibly detailed. But the day is mainly waiting, until it's time to act.'

While Boardman's day was 'dialled', others' were more flexible – or shambolic. 'I remember riders getting their time trial bikes and getting their tools out, adjusting their saddles and bars.' It was inconceivable to Boardman that this would not have been taken care of in advance. 'This was my office; this was where I went to work. You don't plug in a new piece of equipment before the most important meeting, do you?'

Boardman's bike, a new Lotus 'Superbike', essentially a road version of the machine he'd ridden at the Olympics, attracted attention. LeMond, always interested in equipment, was spellbound. He warmed up facing Boardman outside the Gan team's campervan. 'Greg was like, "Oh, a shiny new piece of kit!" He was genuinely fascinated, and he picked your brains about equipment a lot. He was like a very, very intelligent kid.'

As he waited to start his effort, Boardman tried to take his psychologist's advice and embrace the challenge ahead – which meant embracing his fear. 'I thought, right, this is going to be the hardest thing I've ever done. And there's no escaping that. There's no pretending I'm going to have an easy day. It is going to be the most unpleasant thing I've ever done and I accept that.

'It was quite liberating.'

The scale of the Tour was something new, even compared with the Olympics. 'But I had to accept that all these people lining the road ahead of me, and the size of this event, and the millions of people watching. I can't affect that and that doesn't affect me. Put it to one side. It was all about my performance.'

Boardman was among the last starters, along with the young world road race champion, Lance Armstrong; finally, Indurain, in the yellow jersey as the previous year's winner, would be the last man to go.

In the start house, Boardman was held up by an official and the TV camera lingered – the commentator Phil Liggett described it as 'a tense but marvellous moment' – before the countdown began, the official holding out five fingers and folding them over:

'*Cinq ... Quatre ... Trois ... Deux ... Un ...*'

Boardman shot into a corridor of people: there was a huge crowd, six deep, lining the straight, pouring over the barriers, leaning into the road. Boardman sprinted, out of the saddle, before settling into his extreme position: arms stretching over the front wheel, head down, like a bullet. He remembers little of the ride. He doesn't recall it being painful. 'They tend not to hurt if you've got it right and you're fresh, which I was.'

The rider who started a minute in front of Boardman was Luc Leblanc, who had been so dismissive of his hour record a year earlier. The contrast in styles was remarkable: the bare-headed Leblanc, his brown hair blowing in the wind, on a bike on which he didn't look comfortable, shifting in the saddle, frequently standing up for more power – which, as Boardman knew, came at the cost of aerodynamics. Boardman had clocked Leblanc as he waited in front of him, 'on a bike you could quite literally go and buy in [the sports shop] Decathlon. Probably 44cm [wide] bars.

'Even if he'd been producing the same power as me, he'd have lost at least a minute ...'

There was something else that Boardman knew, though he doesn't say whether he derived any special advantage from the knowledge. Having the team car behind you could serve as an aerodynamic aid: 'People don't realise that having a car up your butt makes a bloody big difference. Because turbulence goes behind you and sucks you backwards, having a car behind you is beneficial. It's 20 watts difference.'

All the riders had cars behind them, but perhaps Boardman's was closer (it was certainly close the following year, when Boardman fell in the rain at Saint-Brieuc, and was almost run over, ending his second Tour within a few minutes of it starting).

In Lille, Boardman knew he was on a good day, but didn't know how he was going relative to anyone else. For those watching on television, too, there was scant information; the action was mainly transmitted from a fixed camera on the finish line, which tracked the riders as they sprinted up the long, wide, gently rising finishing straight – all of them fighting, weaving from one side to the other in search of a smoother surface or the most sheltered spot, getting out of the saddle to try and generate more power.

Boardman was careful not to start too fast. He was wary of getting carried away by the occasion; the people cheering, the realisation that he was riding the Tour de France – *the Tour de France!* The knack to riding a good time trial is always the same: it's all about pacing, judgement, calculation. Things that Boardman is good at. 'The equation in my head, in any time trial, was: how far is it to go; how hard am I trying; is it sustainable?

'And that changes depending on how far you have to go. If the answer is "Yes, it is sustainable," then you're not trying hard enough. If the answer is "No, I can't sustain it," then it's too late.

'So the answer you're looking for is: "Maybe."'

For the entirety of his ride, Boardman remains in his aerodynamic position: bum up, head down, only shifting slightly for corners. He knows where he has to touch the brakes, where he doesn't. And as he enters the long finishing straight, he can see, in front of him, his minute-man, Leblanc.

'Look at this!' says Liggett on commentary. 'The arrival of Chris Boardman! He has almost caught Luc Leblanc!'

'I thought that was perfect,' says Boardman, a wry smile playing on his lips. 'After Bordeaux, he says that half the peloton could break the hour record. And next year, I catch him for a minute ...'

Leblanc gives Boardman a target to aim at in the final kilometre: a big, 44cm-wide, off-the-peg bike-shaped target, hair billowing in the wind. Now it is impossible not to be struck by the contrast. Leblanc is a diminutive climber but he looks twice the size of Boardman.

Boardman aimed for his back wheel. 'The straight was long, and seeing Leblanc allowed me to change strategy slightly.' This was where the answer to the question always in his mind – 'Can I sustain this effort?' – went from 'maybe' to 'no'. But it didn't matter. It would be over soon. 'When you see something coming up and think, "I can push on a bit more and get a 'reward' before the end..."' The reward being the catch. 'That helped quite a bit.'

Leblanc, riding up the right-hand gutter, becomes aware of the Exocet missile behind him, turns around to glance over his shoulder, then moves over as Boardman, who had seemed to be toying with which side to pass him on, rockets up the inside. The time to beat is 8 minutes, 13 seconds, by Armand de Las Cuevas. Boardman speeds through the line: 7:49. The fastest time by 24 seconds. And at 55kph, the fastest time trial the Tour has ever seen.

Boardman already knew it had been a good ride. 'It was one of the very few moments in my entire career where I could not have done anything differently. It was perfect. They don't hurt, you just can't go any faster.'

He looks a little wistful as he adds: 'I never got those conditions again.'

There's no time to linger on Boardman in the aftermath of his ride; we see him freewheeling into a mass of bodies and disappearing. The camera flashes instead to an expressionless, yellow-jerseyed Indurain in the start house. Three seconds later, his countdown begins. Eight seconds after Boardman finishes, he starts.

Indurain, the last of the 189 riders, hammers around the course. His time trialling had let him down at the recent Tour of Italy, where he finished second to Evgeni Berzin. But now he looks formidable. Whereas Boardman was compact and bullet-like, Indurain is a blunt instrument: he bludgeons his way through Lille's broad boulevards. He gets out of the saddle: a rare sight. His mouth is open, gasping for air: also a rare spectacle. He's usually so cool, so impassive. Finally he appears, swinging around the final bend, on the brink of his third consecutive prologue victory – or is he? The clock reads 7:40. 'It's a long, long way to go, Miguel,' Liggett's voice crackles with emotion.

The clock counts on: 7.44 ... 45 ... 46 ... 47 ... 48 ... 49 ... And still Indurain powers up the finishing straight. Liggett again: 'Boardman is the leader of the Tour de France! He's done it!'

Indurain lunges across the line and the clock stops at 8:04: a full 15 seconds slower than Boardman.

Boardman remembers little of that eight-minute wait. 'It's a blur. You do something, there's loads of noise, then people say: "You've done it!" And that's the first time you start to have self-belief.'

Boardman is perhaps not as impassive as Indurain, but he is not exactly emotional, or sentimental. 'I was happy,' he says. Then corrects himself: '*Relieved*. That there had been this opportunity and I'd taken it. I had done what I came for.'

Classement

1 Chris Boardman, Great Britain, Gan, 7 minutes,
   49 secs
2 Miguel Indurain, Spain, Banesto, at 15 secs
3 Tony Rominger, Switzerland, Mapei-Clas, at 19 secs
4 Alex Zülle, Switzerland, ONCE, at 22 secs
5 Armand de Las Cuevas, France, Castorama, at 24 secs
6 Thierry Marie, France, Castorama, at 29 secs

BERNARD HINAULT LEADS OVER THE *PAVÉ* EARLY IN THE STAGE

Chapter 2

BEWARE OF THE BADGER

1 July 1980. Stage Five: Liège to Lille
236.5km. Flat, cobbles

The French call it *pavé*. It sounds exotic and benign – it could be a succulent cut of beef – but for cyclists it has a different meaning. It is the *pavé* that defines Paris–Roubaix, the 'Hell of the North' one-day classic that includes twenty-odd sections of cobbles, or *pavé*; hell because these cobbles are not the small stones polished by thousands of cars in a city, but large, uneven boulders planted in mud, arranged to run in narrow strips across the plains and fields of northern France and Belgium.

They are roads, but rarely used as such these days and hardly worthy of the name. Some are maintained purely for the purpose of meting out punishment once a year, around Easter time, to the cyclists of Paris–Roubaix.

Every decade or so, the *pavé* features not only in Paris–Roubaix but also in the Tour de France. In 2004 it was the *pavé* that destroyed the hopes of the Basque climber, Iban Mayo. In 2010 it did the same to another stick-thin climber, Fränk Schleck. On that occasion, even Lance Armstrong, who had capitalised on Mayo's misfortune six years earlier, was a diminished figure, caught behind the carnage and reduced to chasing shadows, or younger, faster versions of himself, over the bone-jarring stones. 'Sometimes you're the hammer and sometimes you're the nail,' said Armstrong after the stage. 'Today, I was the nail.'

Paris–Roubaix lends itself to great suffering and great quotes. Arguably the best is Theo de Rooy's following the 1985 race, when he crashed, withdrew, and vented: 'It's bollocks, this race. You're working like an animal, you don't have time to piss, you wet your pants; you're riding in mud like this, you're slipping. It's a piece of shit …'

'Will you ride it again?' asked the reporter.

'Of course. It's the most beautiful race in the world.'

It's dangerous, the *pavé*. In 1998 Johan Museeuw fell in the Arenberg forest section during Paris–Roubaix and nearly lost his leg; in 2001 Philippe Gaumont broke his femur; in 2010 Fränk Schleck broke his collarbone. The weather matters. On dry days the dust kicked up by the bikes and vehicles fills lungs and leaves riders coughing for days. But when the rain falls, the challenge and danger are of a different order. A very different order indeed.

On 1 July 1980, it poured. It was a grey, bleak day as the Tour prepared to leave the industrial Belgian city of Liège, to head west to Lille. Five days earlier, the Tour had started in Frankfurt, then dipped into France, to Metz, before crossing another border to Belgium. Bad weather dominated those early stages. But the fifth stage, to Lille, looked set to be the worst of the lot. The rain was unrelenting. The wind blew hard across the northern European plains. 'Thousands were by the roadside, sheltering under trees or huddled by their cars,' as one report put it. 'If stages two and three were purgatory, then stage five was hell.'

*   *   *

Few Tours have started with a bigger favourite than Bernard Hinault in 1980. *Le Blaireau* (The Badger) had won the previous two, including 1978, his début. That year, although only twenty-three, he rode with such impressive authority, even leading a riders' protest at the end of one stage, that an aura was already starting to develop. The timing was right. In the same year that the great Eddy Merckx retired, a new *patron* was needed, and here was Hinault, waiting in the wings, poised to stride confidently to centre stage.

He didn't have to wait long. A year after his first Tour and first win, Hinault returned and dominated. To underline his superiority, he even claimed the traditional sprinters' finish on the Champs-Élysées. To win there, in the yellow jersey, showed more than strength and speed. It showed panache and defiance. It was a two-fingered salute. And it was completely unnecessary. Hinault entered Paris with a lead of three minutes over the second-placed Joop Zoetemelk (which in the record books is thirteen, after Zoetemelk was subsequently docked ten minutes for a doping offence). His win in Paris was Hinault's seventh stage of the 1979 Tour. He was at the zenith of his powers.

There was, from the beginning, more to Hinault than physical ability. Sean Kelly, the Irishman who emerged in the late 1970s as one of the best sprinters and one-day riders, is not given to exaggeration or hyperbole. Ask him about Hinault, however, and his admiration, even awe, becomes apparent. 'He was the boss,' says Kelly. 'The *patron*, as they say. In the Tour de France especially he was very much the *patron*. When you had two mountain stages then a flat stage, he'd go to the front and say, "OK, today we're going to ride slowly for the first 100km. Nobody attacks."

'If somebody did attack they would get a fucking bollocking,' Kelly continues. 'I've seen it myself: Hinault go after somebody and say, "If you do that again, you won't ever win another race."'

Graham Jones, who raced with Hinault, said that, in the main, he asserted himself 'physically on the bike rather than verbally. He would occasionally shout a bit, but usually it was because he was on a bad day, like anybody. But I remember once at the Tour de Romandie, he was getting a bit annoyed early on and he went to the front for 20km and strung it all out and then he sat up and said, "Have you had enough?" That certainly quietened everyone down for a while.

'He was the last *patron*,' Jones continues. 'Armstrong wasn't a *patron*, because he didn't ride enough races all year round to do that. A *patron* is there all year round. I can remember riding Paris–Nice or the Tour of Corsica where Hinault was there, riding to win.'

He was more than a caricature of a mafia boss, but like a mafia boss Hinault kept his friends close and his enemies closer. He could be generous to team-mates, helping them to victories in 'lesser' races, with the deal being their full commitment to his own cause when it came to the big 'appointments', to use his description. Hinault was not Merckx: his appetite for victory wasn't as voracious as the Cannibal's. He didn't care about small races. He cared about big races, and he certainly cared about the Tour de France. It was always his main appointment.

Badger-watching has been an enduring fascination of the last few decades, from when he bestrode his sport like a colossus, to his annual berating of the latest current generation of French riders for being lazy and overpaid (as the last French winner of the Tour, in 1985, Hinault occupies a special, not to say important, position). In his late fifties, he has aged well. He is dark, handsome, brooding; a fearsome presence, prone to displays of the anger and aggression that were the hallmarks of his career. Yet he can also appear relaxed, calm and friendly; he smiles often, laughs regularly, and most of the riders he raced with now speak warmly of him. The overwhelming impression is of a man who is comfortable in his own skin, who doesn't merely *appear* to not care for the approval of others, but is genuinely indifferent to either flattery or criticism. There is an authenticity about Hinault. For someone who seemed to race so often on anger, he doesn't appear to be haunted by demons. He is refreshingly black or white and perfectly comfortable being Bernard Hinault, the Badger – the nickname given to him when he was a young rider by a fellow Breton, and which hints at his wild nature and fighting qualities. Just as he did when he was a rider, Hinault exudes confidence; he radiates certainty.

These days, the Badger's job, when he has not been tending to his farm in Brittany, is to look after the podium at the Tour de France, supervising the daily jersey presentations. He is needed in this role, because on three occasions in recent years the podium has been invaded by protesters, and Hinault has appeared from off-stage, like a bouncer. Each time he attacked the younger, taller intruder (Hinault is a surprisingly diminutive five foot eight), forcing them off the podium, then glowering and snarling at the stricken figure, daring them to return. As if they would.

He used to react in the same way if somebody attacked him on a bike. One of his previous directors, Paul Köchli, has attempted to analyse the trait that made Hinault such a formidable competitor: 'What made Hinault so successful was that he would act very emotionally in a race when he is challenged.' When confronted by a podium invader, the same instinct surfaces. 'The podium is Hinault's space – he is responsible for it – and if someone is challenging him … even if the guy is two metres twenty tall, Hinault will take him on and take him down.'

It suggests some primal instinct. 'The Badger was a boxer,' says another of his former directors, Cyrille Guimard. 'He needed to be permanently squared up to someone, in opposition to someone. He needed combat.'

*   *   *

Almost every race that he started in 1980 seemed to add another chapter to the Hinault legend. There was Liège–Bastogne–Liège, the late spring classic in the Ardennes, with its succession of short but steep climbs. This year was harder than ever, on account of the weather. It snowed almost from the start. After 70km of the 260km race, 110 of the 170 starters had abandoned. Even Hinault considered abandoning. But with 80km remaining, he did the opposite: he attacked. He could barely see through the thickening snow; he raised a hand to his face to protect his eyes, to be able to decipher the road.

'My teeth were chattering and I had no protection against the cold, which was getting right inside me,' he said later. 'I decided that the only thing to do was ride as hard as I could to keep myself warm. I didn't look at anything. I saw nothing. I thought only of myself.'

He caught the two escapees who had been freezing out front, dropping them and continuing alone. By now he was riding into a blizzard. His hands were numb, making changing gear and braking difficult. Yet he ploughed on through the snow, a fleet of vehicles gathering behind – windscreen wipers swishing – and making fresh tracks in the snow, as Hinault was doing just ahead of them. The observers in their warm vehicles must have wondered, with voyeuristic curiosity, how long he could endure; when he would bow to the inevitable. But there was no question of Hinault quitting. If anything might have persuaded him to carry on, it was the thought that people were following him, awaiting his capitulation. Similarly, he seemed to derive strength from the riders who abandoned and were back in their warm hotel on the finishing straight; as though, merely by carrying on, he was making his point.

By the time he reached Liège, Hinault was ten minutes ahead of the next rider, Hennie Kuiper. But victory came at a cost to Hinault: his frostbitten hands never fully recovered.

To this day, when it is cold, he suffers discomfort in two fingers. But what made Hinault's Liège–Bastogne–Liège even more remarkable was this salient fact: despite being from France's coldest outpost, Brittany, he hated the cold.

It was another spring classic, held the week before Liège–Bastogne–Liège, that provided an important rehearsal for the 1980 Tour, given that the same *pavé* would feature in July. On 13 April, in sunny, dry conditions, Hinault was in the mix, following the likes of René Bittinger, Francesco Moser, Gilbert Duclos-Lassalle and 'Mr Paris–Roubaix', the four-time winner, Roger De Vlaeminck. Eventually, it was Moser who escaped alone to win his third title, but Hinault came in with the first group. He was fourth.

Hinault had also ridden over the cobbles in the 1979 Tour, when, unusually, they came not in the first week of the race, but on stage nine, from Amiens to Roubaix. On that occasion, he punctured and lost over two minutes to Zoetemelk. That was the problem with the *pavé*. It didn't respect strength, form, fitness or reputation. It could be a game of chance. Hinault hated it. He called Paris–Roubaix a 'nonsense', and worse, 'a race for dickheads'.

In October 1979, when the 1980 Tour route was announced, and it included two stages with *pavé*, five and six, Hinault was not happy. After leading the riders' strike at Valence d'Agen in 1978, he threatened the ultimate protest: another strike.

But in the first half of the 1980 season, he was on track. He could do no wrong. A few weeks after his win at Liège–Bastogne–Liège, Hinault rode and won the Giro d'Italia. So when he appeared in Frankfurt for the Tour de France, and won the prologue, it seemed the script was already written. There was little point in talking of other contenders.

*   *   *

Twenty-three years later, almost to the day, I am sitting
with Bernard Hinault in an outdoor café in, of all places, the
Chelsea Flower Show in London. As incongruous a setting
as any, the equivalent might be meeting the Dalai Lama at
a bare-knuckle boxing match. Refined gentlemen and wom-
en, on a break from wandering around the display gardens,
drink cream teas in the café, unaware, certainly, that there
is a Badger in their midst. A Badger sipping cappuccino from
a paper cup.

His presence is explained by the fact that Yorkshire will
host the start of the 2014 Tour de France. They have a
specially commissioned Tour-themed garden, beside which
Hinault obligingly poses alongside various dignatories, as
well as the Tour director, Christian Prudhomme. At one
point, Prudhomme spots a rucksack with the Tour de France
logo, worn by an elderly man, ambling from garden to
garden in the company of his wife. Prudhomme leaps after
him, stops the couple, then summons Hinault. Hinault strides
over, shakes hands, smiles genially – he speaks not a word
of English.

'Do you know this man?' asks Prudhomme, as the gen-
tleman whispers to his wife that it's Bernard Hinault, the
five-time Tour winner.

There are photos, smiles, and then the couple wander
off, back into the crowd, with their fanciful story. 'Yes, yes,
I'm telling you: Bernard Hinault. At the Chelsea Flower
Show!'

When we sit down, and Hinault casts his mind back to
1980 and the *pavé*, he seems to have modified his stance, a
little. 'I always say to young riders at the start of their pro
careers: "Ride Paris–Roubaix." Why? Because the day you
have to ride the cobbles during a Tour stage, you'll know how
to ride them.'

But he always said he hated Paris–Roubaix. 'I didn't like
the cobbles in Paris–Roubaix for the simple reason that if you

fall at Roubaix, and break your collarbone, you won't make it to the start of the Tour de France.'

Almost any rider can master the *pavé*, Hinault explains, but only with practice. 'Once you do it a few times, you won't be scared. I did Roubaix for the first time in 1976, then '77, '78, '79, and in 1980 I was fourth. The previous year I'd been eleventh. I had places there already.'

After 1981, Hinault would never ride Paris–Roubaix again. And the Tour did not return before his retirement in 1986. So 1980 represented his penultimate *pavé* experience.

*   *   *

Graham Jones recalls that it wasn't just the stage to Lille from Liège that made the opening week of the 1980 Tour de France so brutal. 'Look back at the distances,' he says, '260, 280km stages, and the weather was shit the whole Tour. I think it rained fifteen, sixteen days.

'The stage began into the wind, on fairly typical straight roads across the Wallonne,' Jones continues. 'It wasn't that hilly, but I was lying second in the King of the Mountains competition and chasing points, with Jean-Luc Vandenbroucke, on these very small hills.' Ahead of them loomed the *pavé*. And the rain showed no sign of abating. 'There was talk of a semi-truce,' says Jones. 'Wet cobbles could be very dangerous.'

Not surprisingly, it was Hinault who was behind this pact. He hadn't been able to organise a riders' strike – though there was still talk of this in Frankfurt on the eve of the Grand Départ – but he had tried to use his influence to take the sting out of the stage. 'I talked to all the riders,' Hinault recalls, 'and we said that because of the bad weather we weren't going to race. Then I stayed in the front five at all times.' This, too, was typical Hinault: riding at the front, asserting his authority. ('Let's just say that the Badger liked to keep watch,' said his old director, Cyrille Guimard.)

From this vantage point, continues Hinault, 'I saw the TI-Raleigh rider, Jan Raas, attack. And when that happened, I thought: "Right – this is war."

'They wanted to play?' asks Hinault. 'They were going to lose.'

Jones is not convinced that the attack by Raas was necessarily deliberate, far less a betrayal of the pact. It was more a consequence of the course, and the conditions. 'It was so dangerous that everybody wanted to be at the front. That meant it split up naturally. And gradually it turned into a full-scale race.'

Still, the initial semi-truce meant the riders fell an hour behind schedule as they headed north, into the driving rain, towards hell, where spectators huddled under trees or waited in their cars, engines running, heaters on, windows steaming up. The conditions were treacherous: on one stretch of cobbles a Swiss TV car lost control and spun off the road. The *pavé* that featured today, totalling 20km, were 'as bad as anything the Hell of the North could offer,' as the report in *Cycling Weekly* put it. 'Domed roadways, dotted with water-filled craters which, for all the riders knew, could have been one inch or six inches deep.'

Hinault, maintaining his presence in the first five, tried to enforce the truce. But Raas's team, TI-Raleigh, managed by the formidable Peter Post, also wanted to keep watch, which meant remaining at the front, out of danger; and driving up the pace if their place at the front was threatened. This was their terrain, their conditions: the driving rain, the crosswinds, the cobbles. On the flat roads of northern Europe, they dominated. Yet there was a problem. They had come to the Tour with huge ambitions: to win stages, as they always did, but also the overall prize, with their Dutch climber, Joop Zoetemelk.

Hinault followed seven riders as they broke clear. He was simply following the wheels, he says. Also in the break were

Hennie Kuiper, Michel Pollentier, Gerry Verlinden and Ludo Delcroix, and three from TI-Raleigh: Jan Raas, Leo van Vliet and Johan van der Velde. So four Dutchmen, three Belgians, and Hinault.

'At first in the break, there were five or six of us,' says Hinault. 'But there were punctures, crashes, so it kept changing.' Verlinden and Van der Velde both punctured. Hinault himself then suffered a puncture, but managed to get a quick wheel change and clawed his way back up to the lead group, now numbering five. Van der Velde made it back, only to puncture again: the front wheel this time. Raas gave him his, but neither rider made it back up to the leaders, and they were caught by the bunch. Since it was Raas who, according to Hinault, lit the touchpaper, the Badger might have been quite happy about that.

But TI-Raleigh had another problem, as Van Vliet tells me. 'We thought Zoetemelk was going well, he rode well in the time trial, so he was in a good position. But that stage, Zoetemelk was not so good. We wanted to make the stage. But when Zoetemelk couldn't hold the wheels, you have a problem.' What of the truce? 'I think for this stage Hinault was even more afraid than Zoetemelk,' says Van Vliet.

If Hinault was afraid, he was doing a good job of hiding it. And the cards were falling in his favour. 'We were riding for Zoetemelk to win,' Van Vliet says, 'so we had to wait for him.'

Once the break was established, Hinault was committed. When, with 20km to go, Kuiper attacked, opening a ten-second gap, it was Hinault who hunted him down. Delcroix was still there, and he wouldn't help, sitting on Hinault's wheel. But gradually Hinault closed the gap to Kuiper, so that all three were together with 9km to go. The bunch was now two minutes behind. It was one of those rare days at the Tour when the race was being turned on its head; where it was perhaps not being won, but could be lost.

Aware of this, TI-Raleigh, the team that had, in Hinault's description, declared war, were chasing hard. Zoetemelk sat at the back of a string of team-mates, splattered by the water and mud thrown up by their wheels, looking thoroughly dejected.

Ahead, Hinault and Kuiper worked together, sharing the pace-making, while Delcroix sat behind, ostensibly protecting the interests of his team leader, Rudy Pevenage. The driving rain continued; a thick gloom descended. Jones remembers 'the car headlights on, it was so dark. And then we did a loop at the finish in Lille. It felt like night. It was grim, and the clothing was not like it is now. We had just moved from wool to acrylic jerseys. No use in the rain.'

On the outskirts of Lille, Delcroix's hand shot up. He had suffered a rear wheel puncture. More karma. And so now there were two: Hinault and Kuiper, a shrewd all-rounder who had been Olympic road race champion in 1972, professional world champion three years later, and second overall in the Tour de France two years after that.

They entered Lille together, and began the 3.9km finishing circuit, only for Kuiper to go the wrong way when the road was split by straw bales. He corrected himself, turning around and sprinting back to rejoin Hinault. They were racing, on gloomy, rain-sodden streets, in front of a diminished and bedraggled crowd. It had taken them eight hours to ride from Liège to Lille: eight hours to do 249km. So it didn't just look like night, as Jones recalls. It was night.

Hinault describes the finish with another of his nonchalant shrugs: 'It was the two of us. I attacked in the sprint. Won quite easily.' In his book, *Memories of the Peloton*, he elaborates a little: 'My impression of hell was confirmed. I suppose that, as the winner, I shouldn't complain too much, but I really can't understand why we have to face such conditions. I think of the riders who got stuck in the mud, lost on the unmade roads, standing in the rain with a punctured wheel, waiting for the team car. I can't understand what inhuman conditions have to do with sport.'

*   *   *

The next day, with more cobbles on the road to Compiègne, the organisers relented. Hinault threatened to lead another strike and Félix Lévitan, the Tour director, agreed to change the first 20km of the stage, to cut out the worst cobbled sections. Despite that, Hinault began to experience pain in his knee. 'It hurt a lot, starting that day. It wasn't a problem at all during the first day, but the second … They thought it was small crystals in the knee.

'Twenty-five kilometres of cobbles one day, and then 25km again the next day,' he adds, shaking his head. 'Twice in two days, eh? And the rain … there was so much rain.'

This knee pain led to Hinault's darkest hour: his midnight escape from the Tour, once it reached Pau in the Pyrenees. Earlier in the day, there had been a time trial, won by Zoetemelk, with Hinault fifth, which was enough to give him the yellow jersey. He accepted the jersey on the podium, told the journalists his knee was okay, and that night fled back home to Brittany, only telling Guimard and the race organisers. In Hinault's absence, the race turned TI-Raleigh's way, which offered consolation for their failure on the *pavé*. 'We won eleven stages and Zoetemelk won yellow,' Van Vliet says. 'Raas also won the green jersey. Still, I don't think Peter Post was happy.'

Hinault returned in the autumn to win one of the greatest ever world road race titles, on the mountainous roads near Sallanches, and the following year did something almost unimaginably defiant, even by Hinault's standards. He rode Paris–Roubaix. Why? 'Because I was the world champion, and when you're world champion you have to honour the jersey,' he says now.

'When you're in such good form, you just want to take advantage of it,' Hinault adds. 'That day, I crashed or punctured seven times in total. But it was as though it was just too easy for me. And I had luck: each time I punctured, I had a team-mate there, ready to give me his wheel, so I never really lost much time.'

At the finish in Roubaix, Hinault arrived with the leaders, including specialists such as Moser, De Vlaeminck and Kuiper. And he won. 'It was the last time I rode,' Hinault says with satisfaction.[1] 'I would have gone back and won another Roubaix if Félix Lévitan had let me ride the Tour of America. But he didn't, and I said, "In that case, I'm not doing Roubaix any more." If he'd said I could have gone to the Tour of America, I would have won Roubaix again to thank him.'

So he would not just have ridden Paris–Roubaix, he would have won. At the time Hinault was adamant that he would never again ride the cobbles: 'I have no intention of riding Paris–Roubaix, or the Tour of Flanders, either this year or in the future. Roads like that have nothing to do with classic racing.'

He had made his point. And as he drains the dregs of his cappuccino, he reminds us, in his brusque but amused manner, and with a typically Hinault-esque combination of pride and contempt: 'How many riders today who are capable of winning the Tour de France even ride Paris–Roubaix?'

Hinault shrugs and answers his own question: 'None.'

---

1 Hinault is mistaken. He returned one more time, in 1982, placing 9th.

Classement

1   Bernard Hinault, France, Renault-Gitane, 236.5km,
    8 hours, 3 minutes, 22 secs
2   Hennie Kuiper, Holland, Peugeot-Esso-Michelin, same time
3   Ludo Delcroix, Belgium, IJsboerke-Gios, at 58 secs
4   Yvon Bertin, France, Renault-Gitane, at 2 minutes, 11 secs
5   Guido van Calster, Belgium, Splendor-Admiral, s.t.
6   Sean Kelly, Ireland, Splendor-Admiral, s.t.

WILFRIED NELISSEN LANDS; DJAMOLIDINE ABDOUJAPAROV,
HEAD DOWN, SPRINTS FOR THE LINE.

Chapter 3

THE BULLDOG

1 July 1994. Stage One: Lille to Armentières
234km. Flat

They are sprinting for the line in Armentières at 70kph: a heaving, jostling bunch, a slightly downhill finish, a right-hand bend with 400 metres to go, another right-hander with 150 to go; then the road kicks slightly up; all heads go down …

Phil Liggett, the TV commentator, is shouting, his voice shrill: 'We've got Ludwig up in second place … The Novemail team still trying to bring their man through, and Abdoujaparov is here! He's on the wheel of Nelissen … Abdoujaparov is swinging from left to right, this will be a shoulder-to-shoulder battle … As they come up to the line, Nelissen …

'Oh, and they've gone! They've gone! One after the other!'

There's a huge noise at the moment of impact. A collective gasp, a roar: the sound of shock.

As Liggett said, they were there, shoulder-to-shoulder, and then they were gone. They were gone.

*   *   *

Old golfers never retire. They just lose their balls. So the joke goes. A variation of this joke could be made about Belgian cyclists – that they never retire, that is. The sport of cycling is so big in Belgium, the scene so vast, that it seems to absorb all the ex-pros. Retired riders become team directors, race organisers, national selectors, they run amateur teams, or, in Freddy Maertens' case, they are employed in the Flanders Cycling Museum.

Not Wilfried Nelissen, however.

Nelissen seems to have disappeared. 'Wilfried Nelissen you want? That's a tough one. Give me a bit of time,' says one Belgian journalist. Another one first expresses surprise that I want to contact him, then admits it might not be easy.

Nelissen was the third man in a golden generation of sprinters, though he tended to be obscured by the shadows cast by the other two, the flamboyant Mario Cipollini and the lethal Djamolidine Abdoujaparov. Cipollini – 'Super Mario' as he liked to be known, 'Il Magnifico' as he liked even more to be known – was an Italian playboy and showman who became ever more outrageous, arriving at the start of one stage of the Tour, in 1999, dressed as Julius Caesar in a chariot pushed by his team-mates. (In case you were wondering, it was Caesar's birthday.) On other occasions, Cipollini wore one-off, non-regulation skinsuits: tiger-print, zebra-print, a translucent muscle-suit. In retirement, he hasn't changed much. During the 2013 Tour de France in Corsica, I drove past a fit-looking forty-six-year-old riding his bike with his top off and an impressive all-over tan. It could only be Cipollini.

Abdoujaparov was his polar opposite: a dour Ukrainian. He was the Tashkent Terror, a stern-faced warrior. While Cipollini was tall, bronzed and dashing, with his chiselled jaw and mouth full of white teeth, the dark-haired, razor-cheeked Abdoujaparov was compact, powerful and dangerous; outrageously fast but a menace in a bunch sprint. There was nothing malicious about Abdou. It was just that with elbows out and head down there was no telling where he would go; he weaved left, right, seemingly out of control.

But the main victim of Abdou's erratic sprinting was Abdou himself. He was involved in one of the most infamous crashes in Tour history, on the Champs-Élysées in 1991. Head down, he was heading for the win when he veered dramatically, and wholly unnecessarily, to the right, colliding with one of the Coca-Cola advertising bollards, which jutted out from the barriers. It was as if his bike was swiped from under him. It was stopped dead by the obstacle while the sprinter was catapulted from his bike and tossed to the road like a rag doll.

Motionless, he lay in a crumpled heap, where he was hit square-on by another rider. Robert Millar, who was in the bunch as they streamed across the line, said later that it looked as though Abdou had fallen out of a plane. It was the final stage. He was in the green jersey. He had to finish. Somehow he was helped across the line and then loaded into an ambulance, an oxygen mask strapped to his face.

Abdou had a quiet year in 1992. But in 1993 he was back, and at the top of his game. So was Cipollini. And so was Nelissen, who had more in common with Abdoujaparov than Cipollini in the looks department. Dark-haired, with thick eyebrows over pale grey-blue eyes, his mouth struggling to contain tombstone-like teeth, Nelissen resembled a boxer who had lost a few fights. He looked like a typical Belgian hard-man. He came from Tongeren, the oldest town in Belgium and, more significantly as far as cycling is concerned, located in the south-eastern corner of Flanders. Any athletic child in Flanders has little chance of not growing up to be a cyclist.

Nelissen turned professional in 1991, aged nineteen, with the Weinmann team, switching to Peter Post's Panasonic (which became Novemail) in 1992. Known as *Jerommeke*, Nelissen came to prominence during his first year under Post: a win at Paris–Bourges, two stages at the Tour of Switzerland, two at the Dauphiné Libéré. In 1993 he won the early-season semi-classic, Het Volk, to ensure his celebrity status in his native land, especially in Flanders.

Nelissen's nickname, *Jerommeke*, meant nothing to anybody outside Belgium. '*Jerommeke* is a cartoon character, with unlimited strength and speed,' explains Jan-Pieter de Vlieger, a journalist with Belgium's top daily, *Het Nieuwsblad*. 'He featured in the *Suske* and *Wiske* series, Belgium's most popular comic books, by Willy Vandersteen, the acclaimed cartoonist.' Sometimes you see the *Jerommeke* nickname suffixed with 'Woefie' – the sound a dog makes? De Vlieger isn't sure. He sends a picture of *Jerommeke*: like a Belgian Desperate Dan, without the cowboy outfit. Beyond Flanders, Nelissen acquired another name: the Bulldog. To his team-mates, meanwhile, he was Willie.

Nelissen was the fastest of the lot, faster even than Cipollini and Abdou, according to Marc Sergeant, his lead-out man in 1994. Sergeant was a team-mate to lots of good sprinters, and these days the Lotto team he directs includes André Greipel, one of the best sprinters of the current generation. Yet he says: 'Honestly, Willie was maybe the fastest guy I ever worked with. He was a real sprinter.

'Let me give you an example. Sometimes he would say, "I'm dead, I'm not good today." We'd say, "Come on Willie, you have to do it – come on." And when he saw the sign for three or four kilometres to go, at that point he turned into a beast. I don't mean in a bad way. It was an instinct he had. He wasn't arrogant or aggressive, but he could say: "I'm going to win here; nobody else," and he could beat Cipollini, Abdoujaparov – anybody. And he was a friendly guy, with no enemies. Everybody respected him.'

In his pomp, Nelissen explained this transformation: 'A sprinter has to be like that. The trick is to get me mad.' He compared it to road rage: 'There was a guy once who didn't give way and he started beeping his horn at me. When something like that happens, I'm ready to jump out of the car.

People have to hold me down or I would explode. Well, that's the feeling I get when I start a sprint. That's how I get going, get the adrenaline flowing, like fireworks going off. In the sprint, I would kill or eat somebody, but after the line the calmness returns.'

The 1993 Tour was set for a battle royal between the three supreme sprinters of this golden generation. The opening stages confirmed it. Cipollini won stage one, Nelissen won stage two, Abdoujaparov won stage three. But it was Nelissen who wore the yellow jersey for two days after his stage win, then reclaimed it for one more day after stage five. Cipollini fled when the race reached the mountains to spend the rest of July on the beach – as he always did. (The Giro represented the main dish to Cipollini; the Tour was dessert. But then he wasn't a dessert man – he never finished the Tour.) That year, there were no more bunch sprints until two days from Paris, where Abdoujaparov won the classic sprinters' finish into Bordeaux and then laid to rest the ghost of 1991 by winning on the Champs-Élysées.

It was all set for 1994, though Cipollini didn't make it to Lille for the Grand Départ; he was recovering from a horrific crash at the Vuelta a España, when he was taken across the road and into the barriers by a team-mate, landing heavily on his head (he wasn't wearing a helmet). There were fears his career could be over. It wasn't. Like Abdoujaparov, and all the rest, he would be back.

This is where sprinters are different to retired golfers. They don't lose their balls.

*   *   *

Not a lot was happening on stage one of the 1994 Tour. The riders rolled out of Lille at 10.45am; it was a warm and sunny day, in the high 20s. Chris Boardman was in the yellow jersey, having won the prologue. For Miguel Indurain, going

for his fourth overall win in a row, a flat stage in northern France posed only a little more danger than a rest day.
Boardman's Gan team, which included Greg LeMond in his
final Tour, took control in the later stages, after a three-man
break had finally escaped with 67km to go, building a lead
of almost two minutes. Until then, the bunch was fanned
across the road, only coming to life for two bonus sprints,
both won by Abdoujaparov.

The Gan team reeled in the break, then Nelissen's
Novemail took over. Typically for a Peter Post-run team, they
had strong *rouleurs* like Marc Sergeant, Gerrit de Vries and
Guy Nulens. Untypically, they also had French riders, mainly
stage race specialists and climbers – Charly Mottet, coming
towards the end of his career, Bruno Cornillet, Ronan Pensec
and Philippe Louviot – owing to the fact that the sponsor
was French.

With 50km to go, Sergeant, who would be the 'last man' in
the sprint train at the end, went back to the team car to collect a helmet for Nelissen. 'I remembered later that evening
that I had got him his helmet,' says Sergeant. 'Willie was used
to wearing a helmet because in Belgium it was an obligation.
Not in France, but in Belgium and the Netherlands.'

The Novemail team took full responsibility as they
approached Armentières, their royal blue jerseys forming the
arrowhead as they entered the town to begin a 5km loop. At
the back of the lead-out train sat Nelissen in his black, yellow
and red Belgian champion's jersey. The peloton was stretched
in a long line behind. They began the loop: 'That's where it
will get dangerous,' said the TV commentator Paul Sherwen.
'Lots of chicanes and road furniture. It's going to be very
dangerous out there, that's one thing for sure.'

There were four team-mates ahead of Nelissen. But were they
going too early? Sherwen thought so. 'Too much, too soon for
Novemail,' he said as Mottet completed his turn, swung over,
and Nelissen's team was suddenly displaced by the pale pink

jerseys of the German Telekom team, working for Olaf Ludwig. By now, Nelissen had only one team-mate left. Sergeant.

Sergeant stuck to the task. He didn't drift back too far, to be overwhelmed by the peloton. He stayed near the front, telling Nelissen not to move; to remain glued to his back wheel. 'I was his guy,' says Sergeant. 'He trusted me; he followed me everywhere.' Nelissen called Sergeant his 'guardian angel'.

Under the flamme rouge to signify one kilometre to go and there are now three Telekom riders on the front. Sergeant is fourth, Nelissen fifth. The road is narrow and twisting and the peloton, still a long, thin line, is travelling at 60kph. If you aren't in the top twenty now, forget it. Abdoujaparov is there, so is Laurent Jalabert, fresh from his seven stage wins at the Vuelta.

At 550 metres to go, Sergeant spots a gap and makes his move. He takes Nelissen up the inside as they come round a sweeping right-hand bend with 400 to go. Abdoujaparov is on Nelissen's wheel. Now Sergeant hits the front. Nelissen launches himself, sprinting up the inside. Abdou goes at the same time, drawing level. With 150 metres to go, they enter a right-hand bend. Jalabert is on Nelissen's wheel, waiting for a gap.

Nelissen is sprinting, head down. He drifts a little to his right, towards the barriers, and then he disappears. One second he's there, then he's not. The sound is an explosion; and it looks as if a bomb has gone off.

Sergeant, having sat up to drift back through the peloton, sees nothing. It is his ears that tell him what happens. 'As Willie passed me, my work was done. I was à bloc [exhausted]. But a few seconds later there was a huge noise – it sounded like two cars had hit each other. An extraordinary noise. In the next instant, there were people and bikes everywhere. I went through it, I don't know how. I didn't brake. I crossed the line, then looked back.'

In the confusion, it was thought that Nelissen had repeated Abdoujaparov's error and clipped one of the barriers. This is what the TV commentators, as shocked as anyone, tell us. But it is not what happened; a slow-motion replay makes it clear.

It shows that, as the heaving bunch raced towards the finish, there was a man standing in the road. Wearing a pale blue shirt and dark trousers, he is a gendarme. His hands are in front of his face, as though he is taking a photograph. He is taking a photograph. He doesn't move; doesn't seem aware that the riders are so close. Nelissen slams into him, throwing him into the air. Simultaneously, another gendarme, 10 metres further up the road, takes swift evasive action, leaping on to the barrier. As the riders continue to stream past, the gendarme who was hit somehow clambers back to his feet and gropes for the barriers.

The photographers, camped beyond the finishing line, scurry forward to the stricken figures of Nelissen and Jalabert. The right side of Nelissen's face is swollen and bleeding; his eyes are open and staring and his chest heaves up and down. He looks in shock. Jalabert's face is bloody and he is spitting more; he has shattered collarbones and cheekbones, and four of his teeth are somewhere on the road. Fabiano Fontanelli is the third rider seriously injured; he too is out of the Tour.

The helmet Sergeant had collected for his leader might have saved his life, but now it created a problem. 'Nobody could understand the system for releasing Willie's helmet,' Sergeant says. 'He was breathing heavily, his eyes going left, right – it was pretty scary. I was able to help. I released the helmet.'

Not only had Sergeant collected the helmet, he had also come to his leader's rescue. A guardian angel, indeed.

*   *   *

Every time you watch it, you wince. It is even more sickening than Abdoujaparov's crash in Paris, than Cipollini's at the Vuelta, because of the collision with the stationary policeman, who is upended like a skittle. You watch it and think: how did *he* survive?

'Immediately after, for ten, fifteen minutes, there was panic,' Sergeant says of the aftermath. 'Willie was conscious but couldn't remember anything from the whole race, the whole day. We all went to see him later, but he couldn't remember anything. It was a disaster for our team: we were really focused on Willie for stages and the yellow jersey. But in the evening I thought about the fact I had gone back to get him his helmet. I think that was really important.'

In hospital in Lille, Nelissen woke at one in the morning, still in the emergency department. 'What am I doing here?' he asked his wife, Anja. Then: 'Did I win?'

There was a body in the bed next to him: Jalabert. Later he was shown the TV footage of the crash, and asked: 'Is that me?' He then asked the doctor how he was still alive. 'Typical reflexes of a sprinter,' the doctor said. 'As soon as he feels something, he tenses all his muscles.' Apart from his facial injuries, Nelissen suffered three displaced discs in his back. He was lucky.

The inquest began. 'The policeman had his hand over his eyes, possibly taking a picture,' said Jean-Marie Leblanc, the Tour de France director, the next day. 'Nelissen was not looking, but he apparently did not make a mistake. It was the policeman's behaviour which caused the crash.'

The policeman, twenty-six-year-old Christophe Gendron, suffered a double leg fracture. He was arguably even luckier than Nelissen. He was taken to the same hospital. He was not allowed to speak to the media, so he couldn't deny reports that he had been taking a photograph on behalf of a little girl in the crowd. It was said that she had asked him, and he had taken her camera across the barrier.

A few months later, the recuperating Nelissen gave an interview to the Belgian journalist Noël Truyers. He was having some problems with his fingers. He had tried to assemble a wardrobe but couldn't do it, and in the end smashed it with a hammer. 'Everything about the crash I only know through

what other people told me and from what I saw on the telly,'
Nelissen said. 'The mechanic has thrown away my bike. The
forks were broken, the frame was in two pieces. The rest is
somewhere in my house: shoes that I cannot wear any more;
shirt and shorts that seem to have come out of the shredder;
my helmet broken into four pieces …

'Damn, I regret this fall,' Nelissen said, 'because I'm sure I
would have won the stage.'

It was almost overlooked, but Abdoujaparov, for once, was
blameless: he sailed past the wreckage to win the stage. That
was what seemed to irritate Nelissen most. 'Everybody says
that I couldn't get past Abdou. Come on, guys, Abdou was
dying, and I was just getting the 53x11 [gear] up to speed. It
was the first time I used this particular gear. I had tested it
a few times before, and now I wanted to score big time. You
would have seen quite something …

'They also say that if I hadn't crashed into that policeman, I
would have crashed into the barrier anyway. Everybody who
says so doesn't understand a sprinter. We have an instinct.
I can feel obstacles, I can smell a barrier. We just don't take
policemen who take pictures into account.'

Even if Nelissen couldn't remember what had happened,
his body offered a daily reminder. He called them 'souvenirs':
the scars on his knee, on his fingers and above his right eye.
But that winter he was already thinking about his comeback. He attended races, where he was a star attraction. At a
criterium in the Netherlands a young fan approached, open-
mouthed. 'Nelissen, is it really you?' In France a policeman
asked if he would pose with him for a photograph. 'Too bad I
don't speak French,' said Nelissen. 'I would have asked him if
he could make some speeding tickets go away.' He posed for
the photograph anyway.

Nelissen had no qualms about returning to the sport, he
told Truyers. 'There are always risks, but I'm not scared. I need
risks, because of the thrill. They excite me, ignite the fire.

I love to be challenged. I once bought a horse, just because it threw everybody out of the saddle. I'm a daredevil, but I'm not reckless.

'I'll never let go of the handlebars during a sprint. I never let somebody box me in. If someone pushes me, I'll return the favour.' And yet he admitted that one aspect of Armentières would influence him. 'From now on, I will look out carefully to see if there's danger on the horizon, like the Indians do, but then I will immediately look down.

'I only fear one thing actually,' Nelissen continued. 'When I see the images of Armentières, I realise that I had a lot of luck. I fear that my chances to come away like that again in a similar incident are very small.'

*   *   *

It was as though Armentières had never happened. The following season, Nelissen won two stages at Paris–Nice, one at the Four Days of Dunkirk, one at Midi Libre. He replaced his shredded Belgian champion's jersey: he won the national title again. The next year, he carried on: a stage at Paris–Nice, three at Étoile de Bessèges.

Then came Ghent–Wevelgem in March 1996 and the realisation of his one fear. It wasn't a sprint; mid-race, Nelissen collided at high speed with a concrete bollard by the side of the road. He was aware of everything this time: lying on the road screaming in agony, his right kneecap crushed, cruciate ligaments ripped apart, femur and tibia broken, pelvis cracked. He lost two litres of blood and underwent emergency surgery at Ghent University Hospital.

'As far as I'm concerned, he should never get back on a bike again,' said Anja. 'If he told me that he was going to stop cycling, I'd be happy. I admit there are crashes in this sport, but why is he so often among the victims? And why is it so serious each time?'

Nelissen returned again with a lower division team. But the after-effects of the crash were profound. The knee gave him constant pain; he could barely ride 40km. He had three more rounds of surgery, then admitted defeat. Nelissen retired in 1998, aged twenty-eight.

*   *   *

These days, Nelissen lives in Kerniel, in east Belgium. He and Anja split up but he has a new partner, Viviane. And he runs a courier company, Nama Transport.

The difficulty in contacting Nelissen owes nothing to his reluctance to speak. He is no recluse. He is simply – unusually for a Belgian ex-professional – no longer involved in the sport of cycling. He was for a while; he ran a youth team for six years. But no other door opened, partly, he thinks, because he only really worked with two team directors, Peter Post, who retired, and Jean-Luc Vandenbroucke, with whom, he says, 'I was constantly fighting.' He still follows the sport 'very closely, but if you look around my living room, you won't find any cycling memorabilia, apart from the trophy for my second victory in de Omloop [Het Volk]. Even my Belgian jerseys I gave away.'

He is still regularly asked about Armentières. It is what he is remembered for. Which is ironic, because he still remembers nothing. 'It has never come back. What I do remember now are the kilometres leading up to the finish. A lot of twisting and turning. Very fast. But the fall … nothing.

'My first memory is waking up in the hospital. I had no idea what had happened. I knew – because I was hospitalised – that something had happened to me. But I couldn't figure out what it was exactly. I had no broken bones or anything like that. How? Why? I had no idea. In the early morning, people started coming in, but I didn't really speak French back then. So it was still a bit unclear. There was a television in the hospital that you had to keep going by putting coins in it. Believe it or not, that started showing the images of the race, and just when the sprint was about to happen I ran out of money! So even then I didn't see the crash.

'I didn't see Jalabert in the hospital. I saw a man on a stretcher, but had no idea it was Jalabert. I just saw a lot of blood.'

Nelissen didn't see the policeman, either. Nor did he hear from him. In his interview with Truyers in the winter of 1994, Nelissen said: 'People say he was given a camera by a girl behind the barrier and he took the picture to do her a favour.' Even if that were true – and it was never proven – Nelissen remarked that it was 'very sweet of him, but not allowed. He was there to secure our safety, which didn't happen.

'It's unfortunate, but he didn't do it deliberately. Therefore I didn't want to press charges, even though there was a lot of pressure from the team. That would just have caused a lot of misery and pain. For him, it would have been terrible; he would have lost his job, his house. That, I would have never wanted. I don't want him to pay for the rest of his life.'

Gendron, the gendarme, worked for the French army unit CRS-3 in Quincy-sous-Sénart, though Nelissen understood that he moved – or was moved, perhaps – to the south of France with his wife and young child after the incident. The crash in Armentières was the subject of a subsequent police investigation, but Gendron was cleared of any wrongdoing.

At the time, would Nelissen have wanted to see him? 'Huh,' he says. 'An apology would have been nice … I did hear stories later on that he lost his house … But what do you make of stories like that?'

Peter Post estimated that the cost to Nelissen in lost earnings was around £2 million. And although, as Nelissen told Truyers, the rider did not want to pursue Gendron through the courts, Post felt differently. 'Peter Post didn't want to leave it,' Nelissen says now. 'But what happened in court exactly, I don't know. I personally got 65,000 Belgian Francs [about 1,500 Euros]. That's what the policeman had to pay me. But what he had to pay to Peter Post, to the team, I don't know. There was a legal case; I had to deposit my [medical] expenses, my bills. But I never appeared in court. I was just given this compensation.'

Nelissen recalls that he was back on his bike just two weeks after the crash. Really, he says, his injuries were not that bad. It was a miracle. It could also be partly why he harbours no ill feeling towards the policeman. On the contrary, he is remarkably generous. 'If you hear what happened, that he took a picture for a little child,' he says now, 'well, everybody makes mistakes in life. He has been punished very hard for it. But I don't really know what happened to him; I heard so many stories, it's impossible for me to figure out what is true and what is not.'

The legacy of the crash for Nelissen is a scar above his eye and problems with his back: 'I had three hernias that go back to the crash. My spine was damaged, but the helmet took the blow, that's for sure. You need some luck in life.' But he is known for his bad luck. 'Yeah, but I was still lucky in a way. It could have been worse. That's how I see it. I can be grateful for still being here. After my last accident [at Ghent–Wevelgem], I'm lucky to still have a right leg.

'People have often told me I was born unlucky, but that's not how I see it. The young rider in the Tour [Fabio Casartelli, who died in a crash in 1995], then [Andrei] Kivilev [who died in a crash in 2003], these riders didn't have my luck. I have to see the positive.'

He still follows the sport, he says. But he doesn't ride a bike. 'Let me put it this way: if I do ride on two wheels, it's on a motorbike. Nothing else. I drive a Harley-Davidson now, which I bought last year. I had one before, but now I changed it for a heavier model. A bit easier, more comfortable. Bike riding, no. No time and no motivation.'

And no fear of speed? 'No, not at all. But I know the dangers of riding on two wheels. I take everything into account: rain, road surface, if there are small stones … I try to anticipate, because that's when it's dangerous. If you've ridden on two wheels so many times in the past, and you've fallen so many times, then you know what can happen.'

Nelissen appears content. The only experience that can induce anxiety is the place itself: Armentières. 'I still get goosebumps when I pass through that neighbourhood. Which happens quite often, riding home from Calais. Same for Lovendegem [where he crashed at Ghent–Wevelgem]; you realise, this is where I fell. Lovendegem is worse, because that was *fin de carrière*. When I enter that town now, it's strange. I deliver there, so I am there often. It's not fear, just a strange feeling. This is where it all turned into shit.'

Armentières doesn't quite hold the same memories. As Nelissen puts it: 'There is nothing for me to forget, because I don't remember anything.'

Classement

1 Djamolidine Abdoujaparov, Uzbekistan, Polti, 5 hours, 46 minutes, 16 secs
2 Olaf Ludwig, Germany, Panasonic, same time
3 Johan Museeuw, Belgium, Mapei, s.t.
4 Silvio Martinello, Italy, Mercatone Uno, s.t.
5 Andrei Tchmil, Russia, Lotto, s.t.
6 Ján Svorada, Czech, Lampre, s.t.

JOËL PELIER

Chapter 4

THE SCULPTOR

7 July 1989. Stage Six: Rennes to Futuroscope. 259km. Flat.

On the morning of the first road stage of the 1989 Tour de France, Joël Pelier told his team director, Javier Mínguez: 'I would like to attack today.'

'Joël, you know why you're paid,' Mínguez replied. 'To protect Cubino.'

'I was an *équipier*,' Pelier explains, 'so I worked for my team leader.' Laudelino Cubino was a typical Spanish climber. 'Forty kilogrammes soaking wet and he couldn't ride at 60kph on the flat. I was his guardian angel.

'When you're an *équipier*,' Pelier continues, 'you don't have any possibilities for yourself.' But five days later, during stage six, Mínguez had a change of heart. 'I don't know why,' Pelier says, 'but he gave me *carte blanche*. During the stage, I went back to the car to get a rain jacket and *bidons*. There were about 180km left, and he asked me why I didn't attack. It was like he was challenging me. He told me he didn't think I had the balls to attack because there were too many kilometres left. He was laughing, but it was like a bet, or a challenge.'

It was the longest stage of the 1989 Tour: a grey, dreary slog south from Rennes, the capital of Brittany, down to Futuroscope, the futuristic but still unfinished theme park on the outskirts of Poitiers in western France. It was overcast and the stage, a bit like the theme park, promised little in the way of excitement. An unseasonably chilly wind blew directly into the faces of the riders, and they huddled together for shelter. The conditions did not suit a breakaway, the headwind favouring a large pack of riders over any small group. It was a day when there was strength in numbers.

After 31km, Søren Lilholt won an intermediate sprint. Sean Kelly won the second at 58km. John Talen took a third after 75km. Still the peloton was all together. In the lull that followed the third sprint, Pelier dropped back to the team car for his rain jacket and some bottles. And Mínguez joked, 'Why don't you attack?'

Pelier rode back up to the peloton, gave the bottles to his team-mates, the rain cape to Cubino, and made his way to the front. Then he proved to Mínguez that he did have balls. He attacked. 'I thought there were others following me, but the peloton seemed surprised. So I used the surprise to go on my own. And I built a minute's lead really quickly. But there were 180km left. On your own, that's suicidal. You know that, because it's such a long way, a breakaway is going to be destined for failure.'

Only one rider had ever stayed out in front on his own for longer in a Tour stage. Albert Bourlon, in 1947, was away for the best part of 253km after attacking near the start of the fourteenth stage in Carcassonne. Nobody else had gone close.

For Pelier, there were two choices. To sit up and go back to the peloton, tail between his legs, and face some gentle mocking from Mínguez, who would be unlikely to give him *carte blanche* to leave Cubino's side again. Or carry on.

He carried on, bending his back and elbows to get low over his handlebars and cut into the wind.

There was something Pelier did not realise as he began his lonely effort. Waiting at the finish in Futuroscope were his parents. That was noteworthy because Pelier's brother was severely handicapped and required twenty-four-hour care. Consequently, although his father had been able to attend a handful of events in his four and a half years as a professional, his mother had never seen him race. They hadn't planned to travel the 700km from their home in eastern France. But Joël's brother was in a residential centre for a few days. On the spur of the moment, they decided to drive the six hours from one side of the country to the other, to see their twenty-seven-year-old son in the Tour de France. They didn't say anything. They wanted to surprise him.

*   *   *

'I carried on and my lead kept increasing.' When it went past nine and a half minutes, Pelier was yellow jersey on the road. But it kept growing, to ten, fifteen, eighteen minutes ... 'It was twenty-five minutes at one point,' Pelier says. 'But even then, your mood is changing all the time. You believe, you don't believe, you believe, you don't believe. I tried to concentrate on managing my effort, and I did that quite well. I wasn't a young rider; I was experienced.'

Pelier was a typical *équipier*, or domestique. A team man who, if he ever had individual goals, had learned that if he wanted a professional career he had to forget them. His career had been shaped by such hard lessons. In his first year, 1985, he was riding the Tour de France; they were in the Alps, on the 269km stretch between Morzine and Lans-en-Vercors, and he felt strong. So, in a moment of impulse, he attacked. 'There were eight cols, and I attacked on the second one. What I didn't know was that the leaders had decided to neutralise the race until the seventh climb.'

Pelier jumped away when he saw the Colombian, Luis
Herrera, sprint for points for the King of the Mountains competition. He didn't realise Herrera was not attacking: that
he only wanted the points on offer at the top of the climb.
Herrera sat up, but Pelier carried on. And Bernard Hinault,
in the yellow jersey, set off after him. 'Hinault caught me on
the descent, and grabbed my jersey. He said, "What are you
doing?" I said, "Don't touch me!" He was angry and he told
me, "You will never win a race!"

'We had an argument, but then I understood. He was the
patron, but afterwards it was exaggerated into a big story by
the journalists, who saw Hinault go away on the descent to
catch the little idiot who attacked.'

Three years later, as Pelier rode alone towards Futuroscope,
Hinault set off in pursuit of him once again. When he caught
him, he shouted – again. But Hinault was in a car this time,
working for the Tour organisation in retirement, and his yells
were of encouragement. He and Pelier had become friends
at the 1986 world championships in Colorado, which Pelier
rode for the French team, in support of Hinault. Now, as
Pelier battled into the wind, Hinault repeatedly pulled alongside, winding down the window to speak to him. 'He really
supported me,' Pelier says, 'keeping me up to date with the
time gaps, giving me constant encouragement. I think he was
happy to see me have a go.'

Hinault knew this was a rare, perhaps unique, opportunity for a rider who had endured mainly misfortune in
his career. A year after their run-in at the Tour, Pelier made
the headlines again, and once more for the wrong reasons. At
the finish of stage seventeen of the 1986 Tour, at the summit
of the Col de Granon, he collapsed. It had been a particularly
tough and high climb; indeed, the Granon is one of the highest roads in Europe, ascending to 2,413 metres, and steep
too. But Pelier didn't just collapse, he lost consciousness. An
oxygen mask was strapped to his face as he was loaded into a

helicopter and taken to hospital. Then he slipped into a seven-hour coma. He plays this down, dismissing it as simply the consequence of a 'massive *fringale'* – hunger knock. 'I was hypoglycaemic. I had to stay in hospital overnight. I recovered quickly but not quick enough. You can't have a day off at the Tour ...'

Pelier's career refused to run smoothly. Unusually for a French rider, he opted to join a Spanish team, BH, for the 1989 season. 'I wanted an atmosphere that was warm and welcoming and I found that in Spain,' he says. 'I was lucky when I turned professional to ride for two years for Jean de Gribaldy.' De Gribaldy, known as 'The Viscount', died, aged sixty-five, in a road accident on 2 January 1987. Pelier joined Cyrille Guimard's Système U team the same year. 'The Viscount is someone I think about often, even today. De Gribaldy loved cycling and loved his riders. And I needed that kind of atmosphere. With Guimard, I found a different atmosphere, one that didn't work for me.

'In 1988, I didn't have a good season and it was difficult to find a team,' Pelier says. 'The Spanish put their trust in me and there was another Frenchman, Philippe Bouvatier, who encouraged me to join BH. The Spanish teams were full of *grimpeurs* [climbers], so they were always on the lookout for riders who could do everything, especially *baroudeurs* [fighters].'

His decision to cross the border was vindicated when, in April, Pelier crashed and fractured his sacrum, the large pelvic bone. It was another serious setback and yet it served to emphasise Mínguez's qualities as a manager and his faith in Pelier. 'I spent all of April, twenty-five days, lying in a plaster. The day of the accident, I thought my season was finished and I cried like a baby in the hospital in Pamplona. I was in a team that had recruited me specifically for the Tour de France. But my directeur sportif, Mínguez, he told me, as I lay in my hospital bed, to focus on getting better and that I could still be there at the Tour.'

'If there is one rider I want to see at the Tour de France, it's you,' Mínguez told him. 'For me,' says Pelier, 'that was huge. Your morale is really fragile when you do sport at this level.

'You have doubts, of course. After coming out of the plaster and being able to move again, I spent the whole month of May doing rehabilitation. In June, I returned to racing. It was very, very difficult. But I knew Mínguez trusted me, and that helped a lot. It was only fifteen days before the start of the Tour that I began to get on track, to feel that I could reach my previous level.'

*   *   *

Still, on the road to Futuroscope, Pelier battled the wind and tried to remain focused on the task, crouched over his bike, grinding his way for kilometre after kilometre after kilometre, through largely featureless, flat countryside.

Then it began raining. The roads became greasy and wet, which helped Pelier – there was a big crash in the peloton, and they became cautious. With thirty-eight kilometres to go, Pelier led by eleven minutes. It was a big advantage – there was a full four kilometres between him and the peloton but it was tumbling from the maximum of twenty-five minutes. Pelier's mind was a jumble of positive and negative thoughts, competing with each other: 'I tell myself that I'm going to win, then I hear the gap is falling quickly and I think, it's fucked, I'm going to be caught.'

As the gap began to fall, the sprinters' teams could smell blood. Greg LeMond was in the yellow jersey and his team, ADR, had been first to take up the chase, reckoning that even a journeyman like Pelier shouldn't be allowed so much time. Panasonic, the Dutch team, whose sprinter was Jean-Paul van Poppel, then got involved. 'When the peloton started chasing I was consistently losing time, my lead was really falling,' Pelier says. 'But I had been trying to manage my effort.

And when they started chasing, I accelerated. I knew I had to spare myself as much as possible, especially in that wind. I was economical with my effort all the time.

'But the advantage you have, it's the peloton who decide it. At 100km from the finish, it was feasible for them to catch me. A rider on his own can lose ten minutes in ten kilometres.'

The wind picked up. Pelier's face was a picture of agony. 'If Pelier does hit the wall, they'll wipe him up very quickly indeed,' said the TV commentator. He turned and hit cross-winds: treacherous in the peloton, but offering some relief to the lone rider. Then it was back into the teeth of the head-wind, as torrential rain began to fall, spattering the lens of the TV camera. Through this distorted picture, the viewer could make out Pelier's grim expression, which spoke of the torture of labouring for four and a half hours into the wind. 'Pelier looks to be dying ten deaths,' said the commentator.

With 10km to go, his lead had collapsed to five and a half minutes. Now there was a thunderstorm. 'It gave me an advantage,' Pelier says. 'For one rider, it's easier in those conditions; in the peloton it's messy and becomes disorgan-ised. It helped me. But at ten kilometres to go, I was still very worried. I knew they could still catch me.'

Inside the final three kilometres Pelier had entered the pleasure and business park that is Futuroscope. The roads were like a motor-racing circuit: wide and exposed to the full force of the wind. Pelier, as he had been for so much of his ride, was hunched over his bike, getting as low as possible, his upper body rocking as he forced a huge gear round. Earlier he had tried to keep the gears low, spinning his legs, saving his muscles. Now it was all about grunt rather than finesse. He got out of the saddle, searching for more power. Despite the greyness and rain, he kept his sunglasses on, and wore a white headband. A few bedraggled spectators stood at the side of the road, but only the hardy had bothered to come out and brave such atrocious conditions. Still Pelier could not be sure that he would hang on. 'It was only when I was two kilometres from the finish that I knew I was going to win. I knew then that it was impossible for them to catch me.'

Inside the final kilometre, with barriers lining the road, the crowd didn't thicken until the final 500 metres. The road rose to the finish and Pelier lifted himself once more out of the saddle. The clock ticked past six hours, 57 minutes. He had spent four and a half hours alone.

Behind Pelier as he approached the line, the official car, containing Hinault, flashed its headlights twice as though in celebration. And then, finally, Pelier sat up, at last able to straighten his back, and wearily lifted his arms. The peloton arrived a minute and a half later: they had been closing all the time.

Beyond the line, Pelier was intercepted by an army of Tour workers clad in Coca-Cola outfits, and behind them the photographers and reporters muscled in as the winner slumped over his handlebars, absolutely exhausted. 'It was a bit suicidal,' he managed to tell reporters, 'because of the headwind. I think nobody behind me believed I could make it to the finish. They all thought they would see me again before the end of the stage.'

Then Pelier looked up, and stretched to see over the crowd. Word had reached him that his parents were there. But he refused to believe it until he saw them with his own eyes, and the TV cameras captured the moment when his face crumpled and tears began streaming down his cheeks. He raced towards them and as he neared his father, reached out, saying, 'Mon père, mon père!'

It altered the narrative of the stage; surely, thought reporters, Pelier had been spurred on by the knowledge that his parents, Pierre and Janine, were at the finish. But Pelier had no idea. 'No, absolutely not,' he says now. 'It was a total surprise. I didn't know they had decided to come. To see them at the finish was a big surprise.

'My dad had had the opportunity to see me at some races in my career, but my mum could never make it because she always cared for my brother, and stayed with him. But my brother was in a specialist centre for the holiday, and it fell during the Tour de France. My parents found themselves with a few days free and alone. It was the first time in six years my mum came to see me in a race. It was very emotional, very special.'

It was evident to all the world when he appeared on the podium and Pelier, jaw quivering and tears still streaming, accepted his prize, and his place in history, with the second longest solo breakaway in Tour history.[2]

*   *   *

'I was married, I had four children, and I was thinking of my future.' Pelier is talking about his retirement, just over a year after Futuroscope, when he was still only twenty-eight. 'I had an offer to join LeMond at Z, but in 1990 I had another accident. I fractured my knee in the Tour of Spain. I had to stop for a month and during that period I decided to retire. Having two serious accidents in two years influenced my decision. The career of a sportsman hangs by a thread. A rider is like a Kleenex. Once it's been used, you throw it away.'

He was offered a job with the Regional Council of Franche-Comté, helping professional sportspeople manage the transition to 'civilian' life. 'They wanted a sportsman to run this and they gave me a budget to put in place a programme that allowed top sportspeople to retrain and find a job after their career.'

---

2   Two years later, another Frenchman, Thierry Marie, managed an even longer solo breakaway, staying clear for 234km to win stage six in Le Havre. The record, 253km, still belongs to Albert Bourlon, who died a month short of his 97th birthday in October 2013.

Pelier's own transition did not run smoothly for long. His wife, whom he described as 'an extraordinary woman', passed away. And after three years running a programme for ex-athletes, Pelier left to set up his own business, a bike shop. It didn't work out, and now with five children to look after he struggled with financial problems. These days, he works part-time for the municipal council in the tiny village of Chaux-la-Lotière in Franche-Comté, western France. In this role, Pelier is a handyman who might be cleaning the streets, or clearing rubbish. It is not what he dreamed of, he has said, adding: 'If it is not rewarding, it is not dishonorable.'

But that is not all. Pelier has something else. Art. He is a sculptor, producing in his workshop magnificent wooden objects, from figurative representations of animals to swirling abstract creations. Some of the abstract objects are large but delicate looking; one could represent an athlete, perhaps a cyclist, head tilted back, arms in the air. 'Even as a rider, I was passionate about art,' Pelier says. 'But I really started in the last ten years and I progressed quite fast. I have a feeling for it, and I now have a job that allows me to do it.'

When the 2012 Tour visited Belfort, close to Pelier's home, the 1989 stage winner paid a visit. He had something for Bernard Hinault: a wooden sculpture, almost like a giant hand, with five prongs, one to represent each of Hinault's Tour wins.

As for his previous life: 'I follow cycling from afar, and the Tour always makes me excited, but I don't feel the need to go to races.' The only memento in his wood-carving workshop, where he spends so much time and where he says he feels happiest, is a framed picture of his first mentor, The Viscount, Jean de Gribaldy. 'I have my life now,' Pelier says, 'and I give myself one hundred per cent to that. Cycling is behind me.'

Classement

1 Joël Pelier, France, BH, 6 hours, 57 minutes, 45 secs
2 Eddy Schurer, Holland, TVM, at 1 minute, 34 secs
3 Eric Vanderaerden, Belgium, Panasonic, at 1 minute, 36 secs
4 Adrie van der Poel, Holland, Domex, same time
5 Rudy Dhaenens, Belgium, PDM, s.t.
6 Eddy Planckaert, Belgium, ADR, s.t.

L-R: THOR HUSHOVD, MARK CAVENDISH, GERALD CIOLEK

Chapter 5

THE BOY WITH FIRE IN HIS EYES

24 July 2009. Stage Nineteen: Bourgoin-Jallieu to Aubenas 178km. Undulating

On 20 July, at his hotel in the Swiss Alps, on the second rest day of the 2009 Tour, Mark Cavendish was approached by a rival team manager, Bjarne Riis.

A controversial figure who had admitted to doping when he won the Tour in 1996, Riis was now running the Saxo Bank squad, and one of his riders, Andy Schleck, was still in contention to win the 2009 Tour. As a manager, Riis had earned a reputation as one of the sport's thinkers and innovators, whose teams were tactically astute and exceptionally well organised. Partly this reputation might have been due to his demeanour: Riis, a Dane, was cold and inscrutable, his aloof manner suggesting he was in possession of a secret code.

But today, Riis had something else on his mind when he walked over to Cavendish's table as he ate dinner.

'Have you looked at the profile for stage nineteen, the finish in Aubenas?' Riis asked.

'Yeah,' said Cavendish. 'Kind of. Looks like a massive climb at the end.'

'You can get over it. We trained around there. The first half – the first three or four ks – are hard, but if you can get over that, you can settle into it. The last 10km are steady.'

'Really?'

'You can go for that one.'

The riders were coming out of the Alps, heading west: the stage was a bridge to the final mountain of the Tour, on the penultimate day: Mont Ventoux. But the stage Riis was talking Cavendish into – stage nineteen, from Bourgoin-Jallieu, in the Rhône-Alpes, into the Ardèche valley, then on to the town of Aubenas – was anything but flat. It was mountainous; the etymological root of the town's name, 'Alb-', means 'height'. Aubenas sits on a hill overlooking the valley.

It was the kind of stage that Cavendish, the best sprinter of his or perhaps any other generation, would have studied and then probably dismissed. Cavendish and Riis had this in common, if nothing else: both were assiduous in their preparation. Every evening, while some riders were playing computer games or phoning home, Cavendish would study the official road book: the bible of the Tour, detailing every village, every hill, every bend in the road, along with brief tourist-style descriptions of the start and finish towns ('Aubenas,' read the entry for stage nineteen, 'perched on a rocky spur overlooking the Ardèche Valley, with a population of 12,000, benefits from the temperament, the accent and the radiant smile of the south. In the summer, the sunlight illuminates the treasures of the town, captivating the senses of those who visit the city of the Montlaurs ...').

When Cavendish looked at the profile for the stage to Aubenas, it did not look promising. A lumpy first 50km included two category-four climbs, and four peaks in total: up, down, up, down, up, down, up. These so-called 'transitional' stages can be the hardest of all. There would be too many riders who would fancy their chances. And it would be their last one, with Ventoux reserved for the overall contenders, and the Champs-Élysées, on the final day, reserved for the sprinters: for Cavendish.

It was the final week; everyone was tired. Nerves were frayed, tempers were short. The day before the stage to Aubenas was a time trial around Lake Annecy, over 40.5km, which Cavendish wanted to treat as another 'rest' day. Only, it didn't quite work out like that. When he heard his time, at half-distance, he realised there was a danger he could finish outside the time limit and be eliminated. He had to ride the second half almost flat out. And he had wasted some seconds – and expended needless nervous energy – when he rode past some British fans on the hill. 'Cavendish, get up off your arse!' yelled one. Cavendish briefly stopped pedalling, glared at the spectator, and yelled back his own insult.

It was typical Cavendish. But in the end he comfortably made the time limit in the time trial: 126th, five and a half minutes down on Alberto Contador.

He had already won four stages at the 2009 Tour, the same as in 2008, when he didn't finish, pulling out with a week to go. Now he was going to finish, at least. But for Cavendish, 'at least' was never enough. Still only twenty-four, this feisty, edgy young man from the Isle of Man already had the air and attitude of someone who knew he was capable of something special. He was cocky; he carried himself with the swagger of a boxer rather than a cyclist.

He wasn't big-headed, he said after explaining that he was the fastest sprinter in the world. It was just a fact. How could telling the truth be construed as arrogance? Never mind that he was speaking in June 2008, before he had won any stages of the Tour. He had a point, and it wasn't long before he hammered it home. When he sprinted to those four stage wins in 2008, it was an arresting sight. He was unlike any other sprinter. He was Usain Bolt in reverse. Just as the giant Bolt broke the mould among track sprinters, so did Cavendish, a diminutive five foot nine in a field of six-plus monsters. Low-slung, weight forward, elbows bent to about seventy degrees, nose almost touching his handlebars, he resembled a cycle-borne missile. Perhaps only Djamolidine Abdoujaparov, the 'Tashkent Terror' of the 1990s, looked so fast. Alongside Cavendish and the equally diminutive Abdoujaparov, other sprinters were bigger, more powerful, and punched a larger hole in the air. Unlike the crash-prone Abdoujaparov, Cavendish could ride his bike in a straight line. In fact, his bike-handling skills were extraordinary, honed by riding on the steep, sloping boards of the velodrome in fast, chaotic madison races.

Cavendish was a bundle of contradictions. Hot-headed yet analytical. Supremely self-confident and yet, at times, cripplingly self-conscious. Highly sensitive – he would burst into tears and declare his love for his team-mates – and at times coarse and aggressive. Just ask those British fans in Annecy. Blessed with intelligence, but sometimes unable – to his own frustration – to express himself as he would like.

He worried about his Scouse-sounding Isle of Man accent; about how people would judge him. 'Although I talk like an idiot, I'm not really a fool, like,' he tells me. Then there was the question of his athletic ability: were his gifts of the body or mind? As a teenager, Cavendish famously 'failed' the lab test designed by the British Cycling Academy to weed out those who didn't have the physiology to make it as a professional; he was given a reprieve, and went on to become not just a decent rider, but one of the greatest. Whatever his physical gifts, one thing was certain: his desire. Cavendish didn't seem to want success; he needed it. And he had decided, long ago, that he would have it.

There was something else. His ability to analyse what happened in the frenetic closing kilometres and metres of a stage of the Tour de France was uncanny, even a little spooky. It was as though Cavendish had been watching the action unfold not from ground level, but from the air; as if he had access to the TV camera in the helicopter hovering overhead.

Call it spatial awareness, or peripheral vision; whatever it was, Cavendish seemed able, invariably, not only to be in the right place, but to know what was happening around and behind him: where riders or teams were moving up fast, or slowing down, or switching; and adjusting his position accordingly to emerge from the mêlée and throw his arms in the air in victory. (The peloton might look organised and fluid, even serene at times. It's not. And in the final kilometres, it's chaos. A neo-pro, Joe Dombrowski, sums it up best: 'People don't realise how argy-bargy it is. When you watch it on TV, it looks like everybody just nicely rides together and occasionally there's a crash. But it's a constant fight for position.')

Road racing was memorably described by the American journalist Owen Mulholland as 'chess at 150 heartbeats a minute'. In the bunch sprints, it is chess at 200 heartbeats a minute. Coincidentally, chess is something Cavendish plays. But speed chess. 'Ten seconds a move. You can't think, you just have to move.'

The 2008 Tour offered a glimpse of Cavendish's other weapon, besides his lightning speed, his bike-handling and analytical and positioning skills. His team, Columbia-High Road, formed a lead-out the likes of which the sport had seldom seen. It was a team of strong riders but built around their young sprinter. Few teams are so assured in their focus. Their confidence in him could be seen in the way they rode. The cockiness, the swagger: it seemed that his team bought into this, and fed off it, reflecting their leader's confidence, and reinforcing it.

*   *   *

I meet Cavendish in the deserted coastal town of Calpe in southern Spain, in the bar of an out-of-season hotel. It's early January. It is a pretty bleak setting. And Cavendish is cagey and monosyllabic when asked about recent controversies

– there are always recent controversies with Cavendish – and immediate plans. But ask him to discuss his best ever stage win in the Tour de France and he is tranformed. He sits upright. His eyes – framed by long, cow-like eyelashes – widen and sparkle. He uses his hands to speak. And he recites what happened as though he was reading from the road book, recalling every corner, every hill, every pothole.

But first, he has to settle on which stage win is his 'greatest'. He thinks aloud. There are some contenders. Stage eighteen in 2012, from Blagnac to Brive-la-Gaillarde, three days from Paris, is one. 'It was a fucking hard day. Block headwind, 230k, and it wasn't flat, it was heavy roads.' It was doubly – or triply, or quadruply – hard because he felt he was going against the orders of his team, Team Sky, who led the race with Bradley Wiggins. The team meeting that morning had been confused: Sean Yates, the director, told them to take it easy, at which point Cavendish, who had been led to believe they would set it up for him, raised his hand: 'What about me?'

Wiggins piped up: 'I'm in favour of riding for Cav,' and the plan was changed. But Cavendish did not have the support of old; he was feeding off scraps. In the end, in the final kilometres into Brive, it was Wiggins and Edvald Boasson Hagen who helped him, but Cavendish still had an awful lot to do: there were riders up the road in a break, strong riders, and going into the final kilometre it seemed that they would hang on.

'At 750 metres to go, I did this calculation,' says Cavendish. 'I used Edvald to slingshot to the break; I did it in a split second. I knew, if I go now … I timed it perfectly. I didn't sprint; I got my speed up; into the slipstream; slingshot off. Then [Luca] Paolini was there; I slingshotted off him; then there were three more. Then I started sprinting. I was sprinting for a good while, 350 metres, but I had that much energy to spare, because, contrary to popular belief, sprinters aren't lazy until 200 metres [to go]. The amount of muscle damage you do in a bunch sprint is … You can't recover from that muscle damage, you know. I hadn't done much sprinting that Tour. I had fire in my eyes. I saw it and I just went.'

He has fire in his eyes now, as he relives it. His heart might be racing, as it was when he caught and passed the Spaniard, Luis León Sánchez, in the finishing straight in Brive. He settles back in his chair. He lifts a hand to his mouth. His brow furrows: not an unfamiliar sight. It's difficult to tell if he is still thinking or if he is allowing himself to become pissed off, again, as he reflects on his 2012 Tour with Team Sky, when he was made to feel like a bit-part player: a luxury in a team built around Wiggins.

Then he leans forward again and the furrow vanishes: 'Nah. That wasn't the best one. I would say Aubenas.

'Yeah, Aubenas.'

*   *   *

'I wouldn't even have gone for it, if Bjarne hadn't come over and said that,' Cavendish says.

Even after his conversation with Riis, he didn't feel confident when he went back to the road book and studied the profile for stage nineteen. Yet he also concluded that he might never have such a good chance of winning such a tough stage. He was in the midst of his greatest season. He won thirteen times before the Tour even started, including his first 'Monument', the Milan–San Remo classic, in late March. That, too, had included two tough climbs towards the end, the Cipressa and Poggio. Then he had won three stages of the Tour of Italy. When it came to the Tour, he won stages two, three, ten and eleven.

Stage three to La Grande-Motte had, in some ways, been the most impressive. It was a different kind of Cavendish win. In the Camargue, where the huge plains south of Arles stretch to the Mediterranean, his team had a plan. This desert-flat but marshy expanse, where white horses gallop through the long reeds, is notorious for the strong wind that blows off the sea. When it comes from the side, as it usually does, it wreaks havoc, causing the peloton to split into echelons – especially if a team is driving at the front.

Cavendish's team had two people, sprint coach Erik Zabel and team owner Bob Stapleton, riding the course ahead of the race. From the Camargue they reported that when the road turned sharply, with 31km to go, they would suddenly be hit by a crosswind. Just before that turn, Cavendish and his team-mates massed at the front; then they rode hard, in formation, as they came out of the bend. With the wind coming from the left, they hugged the right gutter: the other riders, each one scrabbling for shelter behind the rider in front, stretched in a line behind them, and snapped. Twenty-nine riders raced clear, including six of Cavendish's team-mates. The sprint victory in the hideous, garish Mediterranean resort was a formality.

Two weeks later, after the Pyrenees and the Alps, and stage nineteen presents Cavendish with a chance – a slim chance – of a fifth win. But he knows that the climb at the end, the 787-metre Col d'Escrinet, is a potentially insurmountable obstacle. The Cipressa and Poggio were pimples in comparison: the Escrinet was 14km long, averaging a gradient of 4.1 per cent, but, as Riis warned, much steeper at the bottom.

The stage gets off to a tough start: the 2.6km Côte de Culin after 6.5km, the first of two category-four ranked climbs. An obvious platform for an early break. Several riders attack, and a group of ten goes clear up the climb, with two more riders joining over the top. Five more try to get across, including perennial contender Cadel Evans, but when the dust settles, just 16km into the stage, the group is eleven-strong. Nine more bridge the gap over the following fifteen, rolling kilometres. The break includes some big hitters: Evans, David Millar, David Arroyo, Luis León Sánchez, Carlos Barredo. And Kim Kirchen.

Kim Kirchen's presence is strange. Sitting in the peloton, Cavendish wonders why Kirchen, his team-mate, has joined the break. Cavendish had said in the morning, in front of everybody in the team meeting in the bus, that he fancied this stage, and thought he could win it. 'But I need you guys,' he told them. 'I need you to help me just like you helped me over the Cipressa and Poggio.'

Most had written off Cavendish. In the Astana team bus, as a Eurosport on-board camera crew will reveal, that team's directeur sportif, Johan Bruyneel, was apparently telling his riders: 'Cavendish will be dropped on the Escrinet.'

Cavendish recalls: 'We went over these two climbs early in the stage, cat. 4s. On the first one, the peloton split. There were Bouygues Telecom [the French team of Thomas Voeckler] on the front and it was all over the place. Little groups of three riders, all over the shop. There was another climb after that first one.' La Côte de la forêt de Chambaran, 40km into the stage. 'And it settled down on the descent, at least in the peloton. But the break had gone. And we had Kim Kirchen in it. I had said I wanted to go for it, but I don't think Kim believed me. That's why he went in the break. It meant we couldn't chase.'

The gap, as they went over the second climb, was still only 40 seconds. The peloton had yet to decide whether to allow the break a 'pass' for the day. But as Cavendish says, the pressure went off on the descent; the gap went up to one minute thirty. Though the front group was big, six teams had failed to place any men in it. One of the teams that had missed out was Rabobank, who had Oscar Freire, their Spanish sprinter who was more than a sprinter. He was a better all-rounder than Cavendish; he specialised in sprints that followed tough little climbs. With the gap creeping towards three minutes, and 100km still to race, Rabobank went to the front and began chasing. This was a sign, too, that they didn't expect Cavendish to survive that last climb.

'When the break went and the bunch settled down, I thought we were going to be in for quite an easy day,' Cavendish says.

'Then we hit the crosswinds.' Rabobank, a Dutch team, are past masters of riding in crosswinds; they anticipate them. 'Freire fancied it,' says Cavendish, 'so he got his team to ride, and when they did, it was one line. Crosswinds, crosswinds. A couple of guys ended up being eliminated because of the crosswinds. It was brutal.'

For 60km, the road was undulating, twisty, through Montelier, Beaumont-lès-Valence, Beauvallon and into the Ardèche, the geographically diverse pocket in the south-east of France, famous for its forests and rivers, gorges and plateaux. The type of terrain that doesn't lend itself to straight, flat roads: the kind of place that is beautiful to look at, punishing to ride in.

Cavendish did as little as possible as Rabobank, with help from Milram, working for their sprinter, Gerald Ciolek, led the chase. So Milram didn't think Cavendish would survive the final climb, either.

Up front, the size of the break was proving unwieldy. It is difficult to get twenty riders to co-operate, or to continue to co-operate once the lead starts to fall; and with 65km to go, it dipped below two minutes. Then it began to break up; Millar, Popovych, Arrieta, Gutierrez and Duque go clear. They work well, building a 45-second lead; the bunch is just under two minutes behind them. But the peloton piles it on, racing towards an intermediate sprint in Saint-Julien-en-Saint-Alban with 37km remaining, at the foot of the Escrinet.

The break is swept up, but the five leaders hang on, just. Still Rabobank lead into the base of the climb. Then they are swamped by Cervélo, working for Thor Hushovd. The panic at the front is because so many are trying to be there for the steep early part of the climb: the all-round sprinters like Freire and Hushovd, who both fancy that they can hold on and profit when the inevitable happens and Cavendish is dropped; and the overall contenders, who cannot risk any surprise attacks, or being caught among the bodies further down the peloton. So Astana are near the front – Contador, Lance Armstrong;

and Andy and Fränk Schleck are marking them; and Bradley Wiggins is there, guarding his fourth place overall.

The helicopter shots show the town of Aubenas – perched on a rocky outcrop, as the brochure described, surrounded by verdant slopes. The village looks cramped, old, the roofs of the buildings forming a terracotta patchwork. The cameras switch to an alternative angle on the race, at the rear of the peloton, the business end; it shows riders being spat out the back, including a few Rabobanks, their work done.

The bunch snakes up the climb. Fabian Cancellara is another big name dropped. Wiggins moves up the outside. Armstrong is lurking there, ominous. Off the back go his team-mate, Popovych, then Stuart O'Grady, then the King of the Mountains, Franco Pellizotti. Where's Cavendish?

'Bernie Eisel got me up to second in the bunch coming into the climb,' says Cavendish. 'I just sat there and counted; counted down the kilometres. It was Tony Martin at the front; he sat in front of me and rode me up. The first three and a half, four kilometres, I was riding as though that was the summit there. I remembered what Riis had told me: that if I could get past the first 4k I could hang on up the rest of the climb. And we came to this town, and I could hear on the radio there were guys getting dropped. I heard that [Heinrich] Haussler [another strong sprinter, second to Cavendish at Milan–San Remo] was dropped.

'I just kept my rhythm. But I stayed in the top fifteen up there. I could see Rabobank go to the front, with [Denis] Menchov up there, and I remember just feeling comfortable. Then it kicked up again, the last couple of ks. And that did hurt.'

At this point, Laurent Lefèvre attacks, and he's joined by the world champion, Alessandro Ballan. With the increase in pace behind them, Cavendish drops to fourteenth wheel, still with Martin in front, shepherding him. He has his hands on his brake hoods, perched on the nose of his saddle, and he is frowning. But additional support arrives in the shape of his Belgian team-mate, Maxime Monfort. He sits behind Martin; Cavendish sits behind both as riders pass him and he slides down the peloton. 'I went halfway down the peloton. Luis León Sánchez attacked over the top, and he was getting behind the [TV and photographers'] motorbikes. The motorbikes that year, they were notorious for coming close to the peloton; they came really close to breaks and that.' And riders could profit: tucking in behind them, getting shelter from the wind: even a brief moment would help.

Ballan and Lefèvre persevere – they have thirteen seconds' advantage going over the top – but Cavendish is still there. 'I recovered in about 300 metres of the descent, and went straight back to the front. I can descend better than the others, and the peloton was small.'

Monfort, George Hincapie and Tony Martin now mass at the front, Cavendish behind them. They reel in Sánchez, while Ballan and Lefèvre hang on. They tear down the descent. Cavendish takes one last drink before, with 2.2km remaining, and a little uphill kick, they catch the last two escapees.

'It was wet on the descent,' says Cavendish. 'It had been a dry day, but it was wet – that was strange. I didn't understand that. We could see the two guys up the road, behind the motorbikes – again. Maxime was riding. Tony was riding. And Milram were riding for Ciolek.

'And we caught them with a couple of ks to go. George was still there for me, and he went first. Then Tony.' Cavendish screws up his face as he recalls the effort made by Martin. 'Tony did, uphill, about a 1,600m lead out. And it *was* uphill; he was slowing down, slowing down, but hanging on at the front. I knew it was a kind of uphill finish; but it still looked like a sprint. You could see the finish. It was coming. I just whacked it in my 14[-tooth sprocket: a relatively low gear for a sprint]. Because Tony was slowing, slowing, slowing. So it was your acceleration that was the most important part of the sprint.'

There was a sharp right just before the slight uphill. The

burly figure of Hushovd lurked behind Cavendish. They go into a tight roundabout; Freire misjudges it and goes straight across the grass in the middle, but doesn't fall. He bunny-hops down the other side and ends up back where he was: eighth in line. At the kite, with a kilometre to go, Martin leads, Cavendish is second, Hushovd third.

Over a bridge, high above a river, and it's clear that Hushovd fancies it. He glances around; he knows there's a climb coming; he can out-power Cavendish on this kind of finish. Watching Martin is painful: he swerves from one side of the road to the other, and, with 500 metres remaining, gets out of the saddle: one last effort.

Cavendish flicks his head to the left, glancing over his shoulder, as Martin fades away and Ciolek starts to sprint. Hushovd begins his effort at exactly the same moment as Cavendish. 'I'm in the 14,' says Cavendish, 'sitting there, waiting for Tony to swing over; I leave it, leave it, leave it, then I go.' He nods, like a football manager mimicking a header by one of his players.

Cavendish's eyes blaze as he replays the sprint. 'And because I'm in a smaller gear than the others, who are in the 11, I get that gap. It was slow. But I got the gap. Nobody could get near me.'

Now he sits back, satisfied. More than that: vindicated. In Aubenas, he crossed the line a full length clear, five fingers held up, one for each stage win. And in Paris, two days later, he would make it six.

Classement

1 Mark Cavendish, Great Britain, Team Columbia-HTC, 3 hours, 50 minutes, 35 secs
2 Thor Hushovd, Norway, Cervélo, same time
3 Gerald Ciolek, Germany, Milram, s.t.
4 Greg Van Avermaet, Belgium, Silence-Lotto, s.t.
5 Óscar Freire, Spain, Rabobank, s.t.
6 Jérôme Pineau, France, Quick-Step, s.t.

L–R: Frankie Andreu, Lance Armstrong, Alvaro Mejía

Chapter 6

FOR FABIO

21 July 1995. Stage Eighteen: Montpon-Ménestérol to Limoges 166.5 km. Flat

The memory is as vivid as the stain that could be seen darkening the road. It was a patch of damp, a small puddle emanating from the stricken rider's head, expanding on the asphalt as riders sprinted past, rubber-necking at 70kph to catch a glimpse of the figure on the road. He was lying on his side, knees curled to his chest in the foetal position.

The riders streaming past included a twenty-three-year-old American, Lance Armstrong. 'I had been behind, it was on the descent of the Portet d'Aspet, and we were in single file. It wasn't as if you were bunched up, and one side saw, one side didn't. Everyone saw him. I was one of those guys. And, yeah ... I knew it was Fabio.'

Less than three years earlier, Armstrong had ridden the Olympic road race in Barcelona. It was his final race as an amateur; he turned professional the following week and rode the Clásica San Sebastián, finishing last. But in Barcelona he had been expected to shine; he had been expected to win, not least by himself.

Instead a twenty-one-year-old Italian, Fabio Casartelli, rode a masterful race. Casartelli escaped with two other riders, Erik Dekker of Holland and Dainis Ozols of Latvia, as the rest of the field watched the big favourites – Armstrong and Casartelli's Italian team-mate, Davide Rebellin. Casartelli, in a washed-out, faded version of the famous *Azzurri* jersey, judged the uphill finish perfectly, putting his bike in a big gear and jumping hard at 200 metres. He won easily; behind him, Dekker and Ozols were celebrating their silver and bronze medals before they crossed the line. Thirty seconds behind them, a young German, Erik Zabel, won the bunch sprint for fourth. Armstrong was a disappointed 14th.

Casartelli turned professional with Ariostea the next year and joined Armstrong's Motorola team in 1995. He was twenty-four. It was the year he was selected for the Tour de France. 'I didn't know Fabio that well,' Armstrong says now. 'It was his first year on the team. We had raced together as amateurs. But ... and I don't want this to sound the wrong way ... but he didn't act like all the other Italians. He was less serious; he whined a lot less; he was more fun loving. A lot of the other Italian guys, I always considered them to be whiners. Fabio was more jovial. He had a free spirit; he laughed at a bunch of shit that those guys wouldn't have laughed at.'

It was stage fifteen of the Tour de France, the toughest day, the 'Queen stage'. They were 34km in; 172km remained, including much tougher climbs: the Col de Menté, Col de Peyresourde, Col d'Aspin, Col du Tourmalet, before a summit finish at Cauterets. It was sunny and hot in the Pyrenees. It was 11.48am.

Until 18 July 1995, the Col de Portet d'Aspet, in the central Pyrenees, was just another climb that featured regularly on the Tour itinerary. What happened on the descent changed that. The TV cameras showed the aftermath of a crash: bikes on the road, a rider, Dante Rezze, lying in the ravine having gone over the edge. He was the lucky one. On the road, curled up like a cat, was Fabio Casartelli. The dark stain on the tar-mac was blood. Just behind his head were square, concrete posts, only a few inches high: just enough to stop a vehicle ploughing over the edge. Casartelli, bare-headed like almost all of his peers, had collided with one. More accurately, his head had slammed into it.

A helicopter arrived, a stretcher was produced: brilliant white sheets in the blinding sunshine. Casartelli was taken to hospital in Tarbes. He suffered three cardiac arrests in the air.

Up ahead, still riding, was Casartelli's team-mate, Arm-strong. He was in the *gruppetto*, the last group that forms on tough days in the mountains. 'We finally got to the bottom of the Portet d'Aspet,' Armstrong recalls. 'The thing that sticks out for me the most on that day was that when we got to the bottom I went to the back. I was looking around, waiting for him to come back up, and Erik Breukink was at the back too. And Breukink looked at me and said, "Don't wait. He's not coming back."

'Breukink was an older guy. I was a young kid. But he saw the severity. He saw something I didn't see. But he meant that he wasn't coming back into the race. Nothing more than that.'

At 2.39pm, the Tour director, Jean-Marie Leblanc, announced over race radio that Casartelli had died. 'I arrived ten seconds after the fall,' said Dr Gerard Porte, the Tour's chief doctor. 'I could tell it was a serious injury. Casartelli had wounds that were bleeding badly. We did everything in the best conditions and as fast as we could. But he had very serious wounds, and when there's such heavy bleeding you know it was a very powerful impact.'

Armstrong heard the news before the stage was finished. 'One of the motorcycles, a press motorcycle I think, came up … It was a hard stage. I was in one of the dropped groups. And the motorcycle came up and told us. I almost didn't believe it.'

Ahead, Richard Virenque climbed through exuberant crowds to the stage win at the ski resort in Cauterets, chased by the always-aggressive Claudio Chiappucci. Virenque crossed the line smiling, arms in the air. On the podium, he celebrated by spraying champagne.

*   *   *

It was as though it took the Tour de France twenty-four hours to process what had happened. A rider had died. Virenque always denied that he knew before the podium ceremony; he said the information was held from him. It seemed that only the stragglers, like Armstrong, riding in the *gruppetto*, learned of the tragedy before the stage finished. It seems hard to believe. The Tour organisers appeared reluctant to let the death of a rider get in the way of proceedings or interrupt the show; a strange, but perhaps revealing, response.

It fell to the riders to respond appropriately. Some, like Bjarne Riis, apparently just wanted to put the incident behind them and to move on as soon as possible. So did Marco Pantani: he thought the peloton should pay its respects two days later, on the day of the funeral. If they paid their respects on stage sixteen, from Tarbes to Pau, they lost their final day in the mountains: Pantani's last chance of a stage win, Riis's last opportunity to move further up general classification.

The majority ruled: stage sixteen resembled a funeral cortège. There was a precedent: the day after Tom Simpson's death on Mont Ventoux in 1967, the Tour proceeded slowly and sombrely to Sète. Barry Hoban, Simpson's team-mate, rode off near the end to win the stage, an uncontested victory, but a result that stood. Twenty-eight years later, the stage was neutralised. It took them eight hours to cover the 149km from Tarbes to Pau, and at the finish the six Motorola riders clipped off the front. A gap was allowed to open back to the peloton and they crossed the line together, eyes hidden behind dark glasses. Some wore helmets, but not everyone. The Tour doctor maintained a helmet would not have saved Casartelli, but opinion was divided. It was sixteen years before a similar scene was replayed in a Grand Tour, at the Giro d'Italia, the day after the death of Wouter Weylandt, also after a crash on a descent. By now helmets were mandatory. Weylandt was wearing a helmet.

Casartelli had a young wife, Annalisa, and a two-month-old baby boy, Marco. It was his widow who, on the night of his death, persuaded the Motorola team not to pull out: to stay in the race. Armstrong says he wanted to withdraw.

At the finish in Pau, the Motorola team manager, Jim Ochowicz, said of Casartelli: 'He was a super kid, somebody you were proud to be associated with. The [team is] taking it hard, which is to be expected. We think Fabio is there behind us; he wants to keep us going, to keep in the race, so the boys have decided to continue on in his memory.' Casartelli's bike remained on the roof of the team car, a black ribbon tied to the frame.

At the start of the next day's stage, stage seventeen to Bordeaux, the day of the funeral, another of the Motorola riders, Frankie Andreu, spoke of the previous day's tribute: 'The first 10, 15km of the race everyone was broken up, crying. The whole day was in honour of Fabio. The hard part is, it's going to be super hard getting to Paris, doing that lap with that missing slot. It's not a fun Tour any more. You're not so much looking forward to finishing. You're not so much looking forward to getting to Paris. You want to get away from it now.'

'Maybe I'm the only one who thinks so,' said Bjarne Riis, 'but I think it was a mistake what we did yesterday. It was too long. It was a very hard day. To ride eight hours and think all day of this poor guy. I think we shouldn't have started or just ridden 100km, or just done the stage as normal. I think it's best for everybody to leave it behind as quick as possible.'

And Armstrong: 'I can't sit here and say I was his best friend. But what I knew I really liked. And he was going to be part of this programme. He was our friend, our team-mate, our brother. He was just a great guy. Yesterday was certainly the toughest of my career.'

Armstrong was speaking to ESPN, who broadcast the Tour in the US. The commentator, in a heavy American accent, then told us, presciently, that Armstrong's was 'a young career that may improve, in part, because of hardship'.

*   *   *

Lance Armstrong was a young, talented, brash Texan, who ruffled feathers as soon as he entered professional cycling. He didn't, like so many non-Europeans, adapt to the European ways; didn't even try. He brought his own ways, his own attitude. But after his unpromising professional début at the Clásica San Sebastián in 1992, his performances improved dramatically, and almost immediately. In 1993, in Oslo, he won the world road race championship. On the finishing straight, where he arrived alone on a murky, wet day, he pumped the air, as part of an extravagant celebratory ritual, and yelled, letting everyone know that he, Lance Armstrong, had arrived.

Armstrong was the 'second American'. Greg LeMond had been the trailblazer a decade earlier, and they had this much in common: they were non-conformists. When LeMond won one of his first European races he, too, celebrated in a distinctly American way, screaming 'Yeeee-haaaa!', cowboy style, as he crossed the line. But where LeMond made himself popular with his charm and humility, Armstrong's trademark was arrogance and abrasiveness – or you could call it attitude. Some loved it: loved the fact that, in such a tough sport, with deep working-class roots, with a rigid hierarchy, where the majority were humble workers rather than stars, Armstrong was different.

Initially, it seemed that Armstrong's vision of his place in the cycling pantheon would prove to be at odds with his abilities. As a rider, he appeared limited. He didn't have the build to be a Tour contender; for a road cyclist he was bulky, with muscular arms and broad shoulders from his swimming training as a triathlete. When he first met him, LeMond told him he looked like a footballer. 'I was trying to be friendly, but apparently he was devastated,' said LeMond.

His body might have held Armstrong back. His mind accepted no limits. What Armstrong did have was a will to win and a dread of losing; if ever a competitor would do what it took to win, or avoid defeat, it was Armstrong. And he was certainly strong for such a young man. It has become fashionable to dismiss the young Armstrong as a rider of mediocre talent, but this ignores his world title at twenty-two – the second youngest ever world champion after Merckx – and his stage victory in his début Tour, a couple of months before Oslo, when he won in Verdun from a small group. The following year, he showed a glimpse of something else: he was second in the hilly classic, Liège–Bastogne–Liège. He was also second in the race in which he'd finished last on his professional début, San Sebastián, which was also hilly. Perhaps he wasn't so limited after all.

But the sport was in a period of transformation. If any cycling historian was to identify the very worst year for a young rider to turn professional, it might be 1993. Since the early 1990s, the use of EPO, the blood booster, had spread like a contagion. It was banned, but there was no test. In many eyes, that meant there was no reason not to use it.

It transformed the sport. It transformed riders. With EPO, big, bulky and strong cyclists could transfer their power on flat roads to climbs, soaring up them like mountain goats. The riders who used to dominate in this terrain – the slight, bird-like climbers – had their natural advantage eroded, though with EPO pumping through their own veins they could also be transformed. Eighty-kilogramme powerhouses became climbers; featherweight climbers became time triallists. Everything was topsy-turvy. Some performances beggared belief. At the 1994 Flèche Wallonne, a hilly classic in the Ardennes, three riders from one team, Gewiss-Ballan, simply rode away from the field to occupy all three steps of the podium. Afterwards, the team's doctor, Michele Ferrari, with what might be considered refreshing candour, said: 'If I were a rider, I would use the products which elude doping controls if they helped to improve my performances and allowed me to compete with others.' Was he talking about EPO? He told *L'Equipe*: 'EPO is not dangerous. Only excessive consumption of EPO is dangerous, as the excessive consumption of orange juice is dangerous.'

Ferrari's comments prompted a furore. He was forced to step down as the Gewiss doctor. But he didn't disappear, working with more riders than ever, but becoming more careful with his public comments, making hardly any at all.

In the first major classic of the 1995 season, Milan–San Remo, Armstrong was way off the pace. He was 73rd. Seventeen years later, George Hincapie, a young teammate on Motorola at the time, said that he and Armstrong had a conversation on the way home. Armstrong was 'very upset', said Hincapie. 'As we drove home Lance said, in substance, that, "This is bull. People are using stuff," and "We are getting killed." ... He said, in substance, that he did not want to get crushed any more, and something needed to be done. I understood that he meant the team needed to get on EPO.'

When did you first start doping, Armstrong was asked by Oprah Winfrey in his famous confessional interview in 2013. 'I suppose earlier in my career there was cortisone and then the EPO generation began,' he replied. 'When?' she asked. 'For me?' said Armstrong, 'The mid-nineties.'

Armstrong says that in his early years the doping was 'low-octane'. 'High-octane' was EPO. 'We made the switch in 1995,' he confirms: the year he began working with Ferrari.

*   *   *

Stage eighteen of the 1995 Tour, 166.5km from Montpon-Ménestérol to Limoges, was one that Armstrong would probably have targeted regardless of the loss of his team-mate, Casartelli. But he felt an imperative to make his continued presence in the race count for something; otherwise, what was the point in being there at all?

It was a classic late transitional stage, largely flat, and it came the day before the final time trial. 'It was logical for me,' Armstrong says. 'It was late in the race, the GC had been set, and that's how those stages go on the Tour; they're good for breakaways. You had to know that there was going to be a breakaway, so I kept my eyes open for the right move.'

It was hot, 38 degrees C, and the racing was intense. The previous day had been a sprinters' stage to Bordeaux, won by the young German, Erik Zabel. Today was the last chance for the opportunists. Armstrong was 39th on general classification, almost an hour and a half behind Indurain, who was set to win his fifth and final Tour. That didn't make it easy to get in the break, because so many others wanted to be in it.

It wasn't until halfway through the stage, at 80km, that the move was finally established. Attacks had been going off the front all day, but they were always brought back. When the group went, it was large, with twelve riders, and some interesting names, among them Max Sciandri, Rolf Järmann, Laurent Dufaux and Massimiliano Lelli. Also in the break were riders with whom Armstrong would in future be closely associated: Johan Bruyneel and Viatcheslav Ekimov. Armstrong has almost forgotten they were there: 'I only knew them as guys in the peloton at that time. I didn't know them like I know them now.'

It was the size of the group, says Armstrong, that enabled it to go clear – the fact so many teams were represented. 'There were twenty teams in the race, almost all of them wanted to be in the move, so it had to be the right circumstances, the right mix of teams, where it sticks. But I was pretty dead set on being in that group.'

Wearing number 111 (the '1' at the end denoting team leader) and a white cotton team cap (judging from the exposed heads, Casartelli's death did not shift attitudes to helmets), Armstrong always seemed to be near the front of the group. It was a criticism that had been levelled at him; that he was too eager, too enthusiastic, not smart or shrewd enough. He was frequently out of the saddle, too, stamping aggressively on the pedals, while others sat, legs turning smoothly, looking relatively relaxed.

Armstrong's over-eagerness and tactical naivety had perhaps cost him a stage already in the 1995 Tour. Stage thirteen, from Mende to Revel, had seen him escape with the Ukrainian Serguei Outschakov, but he was surprisingly outsprinted by him at the finish. Afterwards, face concealed by the peak of a baseball cap, he seemed to be eaten up by disappointment and regret: 'I'm surprised. I mean, they said he was fast, but ... I didn't think he was that fast.'

How did it feel to go so close to a first victory since '93 – it seemed like a long time. Armstrong glanced up: 'Terrible. It's terrible.' He laughed and shook his head. 'I mean, I really feel bad. I can't tell you how bad I feel.'

Five days later, on the road to Limoges, Armstrong was second over the top of a small climb. There were 26km left. Andrea Ferrigato led. Armstrong shadowed him but looked restless and kept glancing round. Then, without warning, he jumped hard up the inside, sneaking past Ferrigato on the right, a move nobody would have expected so far from the finish. 'That part of the world is not mountainous, and it's not flat,' says Armstrong. 'You have these big rollers. We came to the top of a big roller and I got a gap. I thought, well, shit, I'll just turn on the pedals here and see what happens. When I turned around I had quite a gap and at that point we'd started going downhill and I gave it everything I had.'

It seemed a strange move to make so far out; to try and out-ride such a large group over 26km seemed like suicide. Armstrong disagrees. 'I actually thought going like that from the bigger group would be better because there was so much dissension in a group like that. It's hard to get those groups organised, so if you can get a gap and get away then nobody's going to work together; they're going to bicker: "You do this, you do that." And next thing you know, you're gone and they don't catch you.

'It's one thing if you do those moves that are sort of … TV attacks and you don't have anything to back it up,' Armstrong continues. 'But for whatever reason I felt … perhaps it was the circumstances leading up to it, but I felt sooo good. It was as if I had not ridden any stages before that.'

Before long, Armstrong had 12 seconds. Behind, there was no co-operation. Dufaux had a go at bridging the gap, jumping after Armstrong, but he was chased down and the impetus was lost again. There were two riders from the MG-Technogym team, Sciandri and Järmann, and most looked to them to do something. But they were in a bind, too. What could they do?

Still, it was remarkable that a lone rider was gaining time on the group. Armstrong was flying. He said later that he felt as though there were four feet on the pedals, his and Casartelli's. His gap increased to 40 seconds. He removed his hat. He wore a black armband; it covered his left sleeve. What was evident was his commitment. Watching Armstrong in full flight wasn't pretty: he shifted around on the saddle, punching the pedals, teeth gritted and nostrils flaring as he threw his bike around corners and dodged the straw bales on the road in to Limoges.

Was he thinking of Casartelli? 'Oh, of course, of course,' Armstrong says now. 'Yeah, and I wasn't alone. I think everyone in the race was thinking about that. But, y'know, I was not going to get caught. My most vivid memory is Hennie Kuiper, who was the director in the car; he kept coming up and giving me my time splits. Back then we didn't have radios. So he kept coming up beside me and giving me the times. He was kind of an annoying guy anyway, but finally I told him: "Hennie, don't come up here again. They're not going to catch me."'

The lead hovered around 45 to 55 seconds, even as two chasers, Maarten den Bakker and Andrea Tafi, set off in pursuit. Anything under a minute was a fragile advantage, especially as the final two kilometres were up a drag. The win only seemed safe as Armstrong entered the final kilometre.

The white cap was off by now. Armstrong looked around, sat up, shook his head. He stuck his fingers behind his sunglasses to rub his eyes, then ran his hand through his cropped dark hair. He zipped up his Motorola jersey. He looked round. He sat up again. This wasn't showboating like we'd seen in Oslo; his expression was serious and sombre, his jaw clenched. He pointed with one finger, then two, towards the sky, head tilted up, towards the heavens, or heaven.

'I'm not religious,' he says, 'but I know that Fabio was, and I know his family is, and I know that his country is very religious, so it was more on their behalf than mine. I don't necessarily believe … but certainly his mother and father, his community and country, they do believe he is in heaven.'

Beyond the finish line, Armstrong, with his sunglasses removed to reveal red, bloodshot eyes, said: 'I won a stage, which is nice. Certainly I wanted to win a stage. I was close to one the other day but came up short. Then we had the tragedy and I didn't think … phew … it was going to happen. Because

I was … too devastated; everybody was too devastated and my mind was in another place. But just, it all came together today.

'Certainly Fabio was motivating me today. I thought about him every second.'

He had ridden as though he was possessed, suggested the interviewer. 'No, I *was* possessed,' stated Armstrong. 'Certainly.'

He continued: 'It was super, because all day the people on the side of the road never let me forget, not that I was going to forget, but the people were very supportive and there wasn't a minute that went past when I didn't hear, "For Fabio".'

Classement

1 Lance Armstrong, USA, Motorola, 3 hours, 47 minutes, 53 secs
2 Andrea Ferrigato, Italy, ZG Mobili, at 33 secs
3 Viatcheslav Ekimov, Russia, Novell, at 44 secs
4 Jean-Cyril Robin, France, Festina, same time
5 Maarten Den Bakker, Holland, TVM, at 48 secs
6 Andrea Tafi, Italy, Mapei-CLAS, same time

L–R: Frans Maassen, Marc Sergeant, Jean-Claude Colotti

Chapter 7

DUTCH COLD WAR

**22 July 1992. Stage Seventeen:
La Bourboule to Montluçon
189km. Flat**

It wasn't initially clear what was happening. It was late in the 1992 Tour, only four days from Paris, and a typical transitional stage in central France. After a frantic first hour, when numerous riders tried to get into the break that inevitably forms on stages such as this one, three riders were rewarded with their freedom.

The trio was over fifteen minutes clear of the peloton; now there were only 35km remaining, it was certain that one of them was going to win.

Then one of the three, having spoken to his team car (or been spoken to by his director, sitting in his team car), stopped working. He moved to the back. When he moved forward to do his turn on the front, he soft-pedalled. The speed dropped dramatically.

It was way too early for cat-and-mouse tactics. What was he doing? For almost ten kilometres one of the other riders tried to coax him to carry on working, to pull his weight at the front. Then this second rider spoke to his team director.

And then he stopped working, too. The two non-workers shrugged, looked at each other, spoke to each other, and shrugged again. When they did go to the front, they eased up, soft-pedalled. The impetus was lost; the momentum went out of the break. And the third man, Jean-Claude Colotti, was confused.

The two non-workers were Marc Sergeant of Panasonic and Frans Maassen of Buckler. Both rode for Dutch teams, with directors Peter Post at Panasonic and Jan Raas at Buckler, who had once been allies – the bespectacled Raas had been a mainstay of Post's all-conquering TI-Raleigh team in the 1970s – but were now bitter enemies.

One rider who knew both well, riding for Post and alongside Raas, puts it bluntly. 'They hated each other,' says Leo van Vliet.

It was their enmity that provided the context to one of the strangest Tour de France stages; one described as 'diabolical' and 'grotesque' by French TV commentators. What happened was weird; the instructions Post and Raas gave their riders were perverse and self-defeating, and brought shame – as well as a severe reprimand from the Tour organisers – upon them and their teams.

But what happened later that evening, in a forest close to their hotels, was perhaps even stranger.

Twenty years later, I meet Sergeant, now the director of the Lotto-Belisol team, at their winter training base in the south of Spain. We talk about his team's plans for the upcoming season, and then I say that I'd like to ask him about stage seventeen of the 1992 Tour.

'The stage with Colotti?' he asks.

'That's the one.'

'Ha ha ha.'

*   *   *

There was certainly history when it came to Peter Post and Jan Raas. The rivalry between the pair seemed to begin in 1983, when Raas left Post's TI-Raleigh team to ride for another Dutch squad, Kwantum. But its roots were deeper, despite the fact that for the previous decade Raas had been an integral unit in one of the greatest teams ever built, one that seemed to mimic, on two wheels, the 'total football' of the 1970s Dutch national team.

It was an approach that would prove Post as a visionary. Rather than the old model, which saw hierarchical teams comprising one leader and a collection of domestiques devoted to his service, Post's TI-Raleigh team – which became Panasonic in 1983 – was more democratic, meritocratic and fluid. Post's riders were encouraged to be aggressive, to attack, to bend the race to their will; and then to support whichever rider happened to be in the best position or shape to win. The idea of a single designated leader was anathema to Post.

'Post was famous for building a team,' says Sergeant. 'His only interest was in winning the race. His attitude was, "I don't care who wins, but it has to be one of us." That philosophy was nice for me; it was nice to know that was possible. It was not like the time before, when somebody like Merckx was the absolute leader, or the Italian teams, who still said, we have Saronni, or we have Moser, and if other guys won it wasn't important.'

From the outside, Post's men, in distinctive red, black and yellow as TI-Raleigh, then blue and white as Panasonic, did resemble the Dutch football squad: they were slick, efficient and successful. But the Dutch team, as well as being famous for beautiful, fluid football, has always been notorious for internal strife, too. Post walked a fine line, desiring that his riders felt emboldened to attack and express themselves, while also keeping them on a tight leash. He was part artistic director, part sergeant major.

Although his team rode with attacking flair, it *was* hierarchical in one sense. Post was the boss. Tall and imposing, he was a strict disciplinarian; a stern, serious, old-school director who, in his day, had been a great rider. In the 1960s, he was a dominant force on the track in the winter six-day races, but in 1964 he also became the first Dutch rider to win Paris–Roubaix, winning at a record speed (45.129kph) that stands to this day.

When he retired in 1972, Post became manager at TI-Raleigh. Three years later, he signed Jan Raas, who went on to win ten stages of the Tour de France, and a bounty of classics – Milan–San Remo (though in 1977, when he spent a year on another team), Paris–Brussels, Paris–Tours, Ghent–Wevelgem, Paris–Roubaix and, on five occasions, the biggest one-day race in Holland, the Amstel Gold Race.

Even while Raas was excelling for Post and TI-Raleigh, the pair were often at loggerheads. The comparison with the Dutch football team is apt, says Leo van Vliet. 'The problem was that Post was a team boss, but Raas was a boss too. Raas was a special guy, he had real confidence – continuous confidence. He and Post were guys who could do business together, but they were never friends.

'It was a problem, because you cannot have two captains of the ship. It was a constant struggle. Post pushed people hard, too hard. Even if you won seven stages of the Tour, he was not satisfied. Raas was the same – maybe even harder.

'It was like a football team, like Ajax in the early 1970s. They win the European Cup in 1971, '72 and '73, then everyone wants to go his own way.' Like the national football team, enormously talented but hugely individualistic? 'Exactly.'

At the end of the 1983 season, Raas and Post went their separate ways. 'It had to finish,' Van Vliet says. 'They couldn't go on together.' Van Vliet left too, joining the Kwantum team, where Raas raced one more full season before taking over as director. If relations had been bad between Raas and Post before, they were about to deteriorate further.

With Post compared by some of his riders to an army major, or headmaster, Raas, it became clear, was cut from the same cloth. Or, as Van Vliet says, 'Worse.' 'I think they were both winners,' says Frans Maassen. Maassen spent his entire career with Raas, riding for the Superconfex team, which succeeded Kwantum in 1987, before morphing into Buckler, WordPerfect and then Novell. They were all the same team in different incarnations: all run by Raas. In 1996, Raas introduced yet another new sponsor, Rabobank, who remained in the sport until 2012. These days, the team carries on as Belkin – and Maassen (full name: Franciscus Albertus Antonius Johannes Maassen) is still there, working as a sports director, while Raas stopped working for the team in 2003.

Of Post and Raas, Maassen continues: 'They were winners who could not stand the other winning. And they were stubborn.'

Contrary to his image, Post did not have a bad temper, claims Sergeant – as long as you were immaculately turned out in team uniform: team-issue tracksuit off the bike, racing clothing on it. And as long as you were on time. Raas was exactly the same. 'He was very correct, he was very strict,' says Hilaire van der Schueren, who worked for Raas as a director. 'If he said one o'clock, you had to be there at one o'clock. Not a second later.'

Of Post, Sergeant says, 'He could yell, but not often.' (Though another former Post rider, Robert Millar, once said that Post 'used to wear my ears out'.) Sergeant continues: 'It was more like, he could get into your head; he could go into your brain and try and find a weak spot. Some guys couldn't handle that; they couldn't bear it.' He would undermine them, says Sergeant, believing it would motivate them – bring out the fighter. 'But it didn't work with some guys. It did not work with me, because he did it to me in 1990.

'In that Tour de France, we had three sprinters – Jean-Paul van Poppel, Eddy Planckaert, Olaf Ludwig – and we had Steven

Rooks for general classification. I had to work for the sprinters, and that meant helping Rooks; I had to work every day. Then I read an interview with Post in the paper, after a week or so. It said that Post was a bit disappointed that I was not getting in the break. I read that and thought, what the hell? I worked my balls off every day and I have to be in the break?

'I went to his room, knocked on his door, and said, "I hear you're not so happy with my performance." He said, "Who said that?" I said, "It's in the paper." He said, "I didn't say that. It must be a mistake. I'm very happy with your performances."

'From then on, I didn't have any negative stuff with Post. If you confronted him, showed some character, he respected you.'

*   *   *

On 30 May 1991, the west Flanders coastal town of Knokke-Heist was host to a 200km kermesse that was more than a mere kermesse, due to its timing (just before the Tour) and the quality of the field. All the major teams were there: ONCE, Z, Carrera, Motorola, Panasonic and Buckler.

With 30km to go, a two-man break was well clear and set fair to contest the finish. They had an advantage of seven minutes: all they had to do was to carry on working together, taking turns at the front before attacking each other in the final stages, or letting the sprint decide it. The riders were Frans Maassen of Buckler and Marc Sergeant of Panasonic. With 15km to go, their lead had dropped to ten minutes – still more than enough. Behind, the peloton had all but given up.

Yet, inexplicably, the lead began to tumble. With 5km remaining, it was down to two minutes. And still they were slowing down, and showing no urgency at all. The win beckoned – for one of them. Yet side by side they rode, neither really riding. They were coasting, soft-pedalling, neither willing to expend an ounce of effort. The peloton smelled blood.

They could see them on the long, straight concrete roads. And 2km later, with 3km left, they went flying past them.

What made this lack of cooperation so strange was that Sergeant and Maassen got on; they were friends. Yet each seemed more desperate not to lose to the other than to win for himself. Why?

                    *   *   *

What happened on the road to Knokke-Heist was a premonition. Same riders, same scenario, except for the presence of a third man, Jean-Claude Colotti, a French journeyman sprinter who would never come close to winning a stage of the Tour de France – apart from today.

'We were struggling and battling for an hour to be in the break, and finally we managed to get away,' Sergeant says. Five went clear. But there was a problem: included in this quintet were Miguel Indurain, in the yellow jersey, and Claudio Chiappucci, who was second overall. This pair were engaged in a petty battle: Indurain on his way to winning his second Tour, Chiappucci indulging in a bit of crowd pleasing, always attacking, even though he had no chance of overhauling the Spaniard, not with a long time trial to come two days later.

Chiappucci attacked, as always, and Indurain chased, as he had to. For once, too, Indurain was aggressive, launching his own counter-attack, perhaps to teach Chiappucci a lesson. In this frenzy of activity, Colotti, Maassen and Sergeant also went clear. But they cursed the presence of the two big guns. With Indurain and Chiappucci there, there was no chance the move would be allowed to go. 'We were not interested in the GC [general classification],' says Sergeant, 'only the stage win.' He spoke to Indurain and Chiappucci: 'Come on guys, you're not interested in the stage.'

'Right, OK,' said Indurain, and he and Chiappucci sat up and dropped back to the peloton. 'We were like, whoo, they're gone,' Sergeant says. 'And that was it. An easy day for us.' Working together, they soon established a big lead.

There was pressure, particularly on the two Dutch teams, Buckler and Panasonic. They had had a poor Tour: not a stage win between them and only one rider apiece in the top twenty. The Italians were resurgent – and there was the unstoppable force that was Indurain. Dutch cycling, so dominant in the 1970s and '80s, was beginning to struggle. To make it worse, there were stage wins for Dutch riders and teams, but not the teams of the pre-eminent personalities – Post and Raas.

It would not do.

With Indurain and Chiappucci back in the peloton, 'We took one minute, five minutes, ten minutes,' says Sergeant. 'The three of us were working,' says Maassen. 'Marc and me were on different teams, and the teams were big rivals, but we were sort of friends.'

'But we were also enemies.'

The rules of the breakaway dictated that, while the lead was being built, they were allies. In the end, there would be a stage to be fought over. But for now, a pact: the war would wait until the closing stages, perhaps even the final 200 metres. Colotti could be a problem. He was a good track rider, a decent sprinter, but he was also the weak link in the trio: he didn't have the palmarès of Maassen, who had won lots of big races, including the Amstel Gold Race and the first stage of the Tour in 1990, or Sergeant, a Tour stage winner in 1987, and a strong *rouleur*. Maassen was a *finisseur* – he had claimed many of his wins by clipping off the front towards the end. Maassen was Dutch, Sergeant Belgian, and they were typical products of the Low Countries. Each was strong; each knew how to win races.

The pact lasted until 45km to go. 'Then, all of a sudden, the team car came up to me,' recalls Sergeant. 'And Theo de Rooy [Post's assistant director] said: "You have to stop working."

'We have almost fifteen minutes,' said Sergeant. 'Why?'

'You can win the stage,' de Rooy told him. 'But Maassen can also win the stage. That's why.'

'You're kidding me.'

'Maassen winning would be a disaster for us,' said de Rooy. 'If you don't win, and he does, that's a disaster.'

Initially, Sergeant paid little heed. 'For the first 10km after that, I didn't listen. I kept on working. Then Theo came up again in the car, shouting: "Do I have to hit you or something? You can't do this! We are paying you!" And so I had to stop.'

He stopped taking his turn at the front, leaving it to Maassen and Colotti. When he did go through, he virtually stopped pedalling. They call it 'glass cranking' – riding as though your cranks are made of glass; as though you are scared of applying pressure, in case you break them.

Maassen knew what was going on. He spoke to Sergeant, cajoled him gently at first. He rode alongside him, gesturing with his hand for Sergeant to follow Colotti's wheel. Sergeant stared at his handlebar stem, trying not to catch Maassen's eye. He was only following orders.

'Maassen was angry,' says Sergeant. 'He said, "Come on! You have to work!"'

Then Maassen's team car, with Raas's assistant Hilaire van der Schueren at the wheel, pulled alongside him. 'You cannot pull any more,' Maassen was told. Maassen shook his head; he was disgusted. He didn't listen.

'I didn't agree,' says Maassen. 'I went against the orders. I kept riding. I tried to convince Sergeant to keep working. But it was a really dangerous situation for me. I was afraid that if I kept working he would attack me. And I could not hold them both, Colotti and Sergeant. So in the end I had to stop. It was too risky.'

'And of course Colotti felt there was something going on.'

Sergeant recalls: 'Colotti was smart, and he thought, if those two are fighting, I'm going.'

Riding along a narrow lane, Colotti dropped back, then sprinted hard, overtaking the other two on the left. There was no reaction. Maassen was on the front, but neither he nor Sergeant moved an inch. Maassen turned around, and gestured once again, even more forlornly this time, at Sergeant, holding out his hand, pleading with him. Sergeant remained glued to Maassen's back wheel, still staring at his handlebar stem.

Colotti, the weak link but a decent sprinter, attacked with 35km remaining. A long way to ride alone and, in normal circumstances, a suicide move. Not today. 'Behind him,' recalls Sergeant, whose countenance is dour at the best of times, and who now shakes his head in renewed resignation, 'we were doing 10kph.'

*   *   *

When Colotti arrived alone in Montluçon, he celebrated as though he had won the world championship. For the entire length of the finishing straight, he indulged in an elaborate routine, punching both fists in the air, using both hands to whoop up the crowd, kissing his fingers, waving at the crowds and, at one point, sticking both arms up and thrusting his groin forward. This was a gesture that, ironically in the circumstances, was deemed inappropriate and earned him a caution from the Tour organisers.

Sergeant and Maassen appeared three minutes later. Their ride to the finish had been preposterous: as though they were contesting a slow race. But in Montluçon they fought for second place on the stage as though *they* were racing for the world title, and it was suitably close. Maassen edged it. Then the trouble began, even before the peloton arrived almost sixteen minutes later (two other riders tried to bridge the gap but finished five minutes behind Maassen and Sergeant). 'Immediately after the stage, a well-known

Dutch commentator wants to speak to us both,' says Sergeant. 'Colotti has won the stage but nobody is interested in that story.

'"What have you got against Frans?" he asked me. "Nothing," I said. He asked Frans, "What have you got against Marc?" "Nothing."

'"Then why are you not fighting to win a stage?"

'We both said: "Because of the team."'

The Tour organisation was livid, sending official warnings to Post and Raas, stating that their 'unsporting behaviour' gave the race 'a deplorable image'. Maassen was also angry, and said so to reporters. 'I am asking Raas to stop it,' he said. 'I have lost 25 races because of this nonsense. I have won a few, too, but I want to race at a sporting level.'

There had been other, less obvious examples of the two teams riding to prevent the other winning, even if it meant losing themselves. As early as the 1984 Tour, Raas admitted: 'We could have won several stages but the Panasonics were so quick to stop us that all they succeeded in doing was handing the victory over to a Belgian or a Frenchman on another team. And we did the same thing to them.'

But seven years later, it was so blatant, and became such an international talking point, that it brought things to a head. 'There was always a cold war between the two teams,' Sergeant says. 'It affected us in lots of races. But this exposure, at the Tour, was too much. Nobody could understand it. Everybody asked: "What is happening there? They can win the stage and they don't want to?"

'It was a big story. I know Post and Raas had some angry phone calls from the sponsors. And I got a lot of criticism. Most people didn't understand the context. In Belgium and Holland they knew about it; they knew it was war between those guys; they understood. But people in France and the rest of the world, they couldn't understand. I remember we had a time trial two days afterwards. I was yelled at the whole

way. Frans had the same problem. But we couldn't do anything about it. It was really embarrassing.'

Who would have won had they carried on working, and
stayed clear with Colotti? 'I felt strong,' says Sergeant. 'I
was good. But I have to admit, it was a gamble. Fifty-fifty,
and Colotti was the fastest sprinter. So of course, Frans and
I should have worked together to beat the French guy. But
there was no chance of that happening!'

A Buckler–Panasonic combine would certainly have been
odd. But perhaps not as odd as what happened later that
night. Maassen mentions 'a meeting between Post and Raas
in the woods', adding: 'But you'll have to ask Hilaire van der
Schueren about that.'

Van der Schueren, now a veteran director and one-time
right-hand man to Raas, confirms it. 'The Tour was angry,
very angry. We received a reprimand. So there was a meeting,
that night. In the woods. In the middle of the woods, between
the teams' hotels. In the middle of France.

'There was no light,' Van der Schueren continues. 'It was
at one o'clock. It was Peter Post, Jan Raas, Walter Planckaert
and me. And at 1.45 it was finished and everything was okay.'

Van der Schueren shrugs, as though this meeting in the
woods was perfectly natural. He is coy on what exactly was
said, as if he has taken a vow of secrecy. But he recalls: 'Peter
said, "Jan, it's nice to meet you. What happened today, we
shouldn't do that again."

'It was a civil meeting,' he adds. 'There was no anger. And
there was peace after that.'

Permanent peace? 'For a few days, huh?' Van der Schueren
laughs. 'Then it was back to normal.'

*   *   *

Peter Post retired when he lost his sponsor at the end of the
1994 season, though he returned to the sport briefly in 2005

as an adviser to, of all teams, Rabobank. It was the team that had been formed and run, for close to two decades, by Jan Raas. But in 2003 Raas was ousted by the Dutch bank; a decision that, according to those I spoke to, has left him bitter, and accounts for his total disappearance from the sport, and his ongoing refusal to speak to anyone connected with it.

Post died in January 2011, aged seventy-seven. He, too, had vanished from professional cycling in his later years. I had occasion to phone him in 2007, seeking an interview for my book, *In Search of Robert Millar,* who rode for Post. Post's wife took the call, I introduced myself, and she said she would get her husband. 'Hello?' said a gruff voice. 'Hello,' I replied. 'I'm a British journalist and ...' which was as far as I got before the phone was slammed down. I didn't call back.

As for Raas, neither Maassen nor Van der Schueren know why he has severed his ties so completely, though both think it has something to do with his treatment by Rabobank, and the tumultuous times the sport has seen in recent years. 'I hear a little bit from Raas,' says Maassen. 'He wants to stay quiet and be left alone by cycling. But he follows it; he knows everything. Sometimes I get a little SMS, but it's rare.'

Nobody knows for sure why he stays away – or if they do, they don't say. 'He's a strange character,' Van Vliet says. Maassen says: 'I have a feeling, but I don't want to talk about it. But it's a pity. Soon we will have a reunion, for the Tour de France squad from 25 years ago. We invited him, but he won't come.'

Classement

1 Jean-Claude Colotti, France, Z, 4 hours, 34 minutes, 55 secs
2 Frans Maassen, Holland, Buckler, at 3 minutes, 31 secs
3 Marc Sergeant, Belgium, Panasonic, same time
4 Philippe Louviot, France, ONCE, at 8 minutes, 34 secs
5 Guy Nulens, Belgium, Panasonic, s.t.
6 Søren Lilholt, Denmark, Tulip, at 15 minutes, 43 secs

 EDDY MERCKX LEADS LUIS OCAÑA

Chapter 8

TRILOGY

1971:

**8 July. Stage Eleven: Grenoble to Orcières-Merlette
134km. High mountains**

**10 July. Stage Twelve: Orcières-Merlette to Marseille
251km. Flat**

**12 July. Stage Fourteen: Revel to Luchon
214.5km. Mountains**

To speak of stage eleven or twelve of the 1971 Tour de France in isolation would be like talking about only one half of a great football match. To then ignore stage fourteen would be like not mentioning extra time in a World Cup final.

One of the two protagonists is Eddy Merckx, 'The Cannibal', the greatest of all time. He gobbled up races, devoured opponents, yet the curious thing is that he did not win any of these three stages, and, naturally, excludes them from his list of personal favourites. It didn't stop Jacques Goddet, the Tour director, describing one of these *losing* performances as the most 'moving' of Merckx's career, while Merckx's own team-mate, Rini Wagtmans, described the second as 'the greatest stage in Tour de France history'.

I meet Eddy Merckx in Doha, where he can be found most Februarys, in his role as ambassador at the Tour of Qatar. In the mornings, he rides his bike with the Belgian friends who work on the race in a variety of roles – clearly being a friend of Big Eddy has its advantages. In the afternoons, after returning and clack-clacking across the hotel's polished marble floors in cleated cycling shoes and lycra that struggles to contain his fuller figure, Merckx heads back into the desert to supervise the stage finishes. In the evenings, he dines and wines in one of the expensive rooftop restaurants. And throughout, Merckx wears an impassive expression, revealing nothing.

Merckx is not merely a retired cyclist. He is his sport's GOAT: Greatest Of All Time. In cycling terms, he is Ali, Pelé and Jordan rolled into one. Yet the Merckx mystique is difficult to measure. Perhaps it is his ubiquity, which is due to his regular presence at the major races, or the impassivity that is his trademark. He often looks bored. His face – doe eyes, eyebrows like dark caterpillars, high cheekbones, down-turned lips – appears to convey deep sadness, or boredom; or vacancy, as the journalist Odélie Grand observed when she interviewed him for *L'Aurore* in the 1970s. Grand noted that most of her male interviewees betrayed some sense that she was a woman, even some interest, 'But in front of Eddy Merckx … nothing! His gaze gets lost somewhere over your shoulder and erases you from the picture. It's a blackout. You no longer exist. He replies with a yes or a no, but he's thousands of kilometres away, on his own inaccessible planet.' (Never mind failing to acknowledge the fact she was a woman, there is almost the sense that Merckx didn't even register that Grand was a *person*.)

The paradox, of course, is that Merckx's impassivity is so at odds with his engagement with – or immersion in – his sport. Merckx's behaviour – his attention to every detail relating to body and bike, his semi-permanent state of high anxiety, his crises of confidence, his failure to ever be satisfied, his need to win every race he rode – was obsessive-compulsive before the term became fashionable.

You cannot appreciate Merckx, and what he did, by sitting and talking to him in the opulent lobby of the five-star Ritz-Carlton hotel in Qatar, or from watching the bloated figure clack-clacking across the marble floors; you must go back to the lean, sculpted and sideburned cyclist of the late 1960s and early 1970s, who came upon the scene like a hurricane, a tornado, and was capable of deeds so extraordinary that the language of the sport seemed inadequate in describing them.

The trouble with Merckx is that there are so many deeds to choose from. The pick for many is 1969 and his Tour de France début, specifically the stage that tackled the 'Circle of Death' in the Pyrenees – Col de Peyresourde, Col d'Aspin, Col du Tourmalet and Col d'Aubisque. Merckx attacked over the top of the Tourmalet, then rode alone for 140km to win in Mourenx. That performance prompted the Tour director, Jacques Goddet, to coin a new word: *Merckxissimo*; and indeed, when I ask Merckx to select his greatest ever performance, this is his initial choice. 'Sixty-nine, Luchon to Mourenx?' Merckx suggests. 'I think also '68 to Tre Cime di Lavaredo [stage twelve of the Giro d'Italia, on his way to his first Grand Tour victory]. And Paris–Roubaix in 1970.' Merckx chuckles. 'There are a lot.'

There are.

But in 1971 there appeared to be a chink in Merckx's armour. He is adamant, in fact, that he was never the same rider after a crash in the velodrome at Blois, in which his motor-cycle pacer died, at the end of 1969: 'Absolutely. Absolutely. After '69 I was no longer the same, for sure.' (It didn't stop him winning four more Tours, four more Giri d'Italia, one Vuelta a España, four Milan–San Remos, two Paris–Roubaixs, four Liège–Bastogne–Lièges, one Tour of Flanders, two Tours of Lombardy. And lots more.)

Even if his strength was diminished, the Cannibal's appetite was not. During the 1970 Tour, Goddet despaired of

Merckx's domination, telling a *L'Equipe* editorial meeting, 'Gentlemen, this is a catastrophe!' It was the year he won seven stages plus the prologue and arrived in Paris with a lead of over twelve minutes on Joop Zoetemelk. A year later, on the eve of the 1971 race, the front page of *Paris Match* asked: 'Merckx – Is he going to kill the Tour de France?'

Merckx arrived at the start in Mulhouse on 26 June having tinkered with his winning formula, skipping the Giro d'Italia for the first time in five years. He had started the year with a bang, winning the Tour of Sardinia, Paris–Nice and, for the fourth of an eventual seven times, Milan–San Remo. Then came wins at Het Volk and the Tour of Belgium. The list would be extraordinary, yet for Merckx it was routine; business as usual. Which was surely why, in Paris–Roubaix, when he punctured five times, his rivals seemed so eager to capitalise on his misfortune, racing clear instead of waiting. Normal etiquette would see sympathy extended to a rider who suffers bad luck, but because Merckx was not normal, normal rules did not apply.

On the eve of the Tour, he won the Dauphiné, but not without some difficulty. He struggled in the Alps where, as William Fotheringham writes in his biography, *Half Man, Half Bike*, he was experimenting with a new, raised pedal, to compensate for the fact that one of his legs was shorter than the other. Such tinkering could often bring trouble: in the next decade, Bernard Hinault would suffer knee pain after adjusting his saddle height. And so it was with Merckx, a persistent tinkerer (a symptom, no doubt, of his constant fretting), who experienced problems with his knee at his next stage race, Midi Libre. But equally ominously, the Spaniard Luis Ocaña pushed him hard at the Dauphiné, placing second.

Now Merckx tells me: 'I was not good at the 1971 Tour. I was not in good condition. I didn't do the Giro, I did the Dauphiné and Midi Libre and had some problems with my knee. I came to the Tour, and my condition at the beginning

was not good. On the first climbs, I was suffering a little bit …
For me the best preparation for the Tour was always the Giro,
because the climbs are harder. I was always better in the Tour
when I had done the Giro.'

Ocaña smelled blood and thought he could take advantage. He might have been in a minority of one: on the eve
of the Tour, a newspaper cartoon showed Ocaña in the
role of matador facing a much larger, more aggressive and
determined-looking bull – a bull with Merckx's face – rear-
ing up and over the cowering matador. In the cartoon, as in
some pictures, it was actually quite difficult to tell Ocaña and
Merckx apart: both were dark, with strong jaws, and promi-
nent cheekbones with long sideburns. Not that they were
identical: Merckx was taller, and Ocaña had the more expres-
sive face; his eyes could sparkle or appear downcast and
haunted. They had something else in common: mental fragil-
ity. But it manifested in different ways, and was of a darker
hue in Ocaña's case. As his old team-mate Johny Schleck told
Daniel Friebe, for his Merckx biography *Cannibal*, Ocaña's
skin was 'so thin you could practically see through it'. He was
'sensitive to everything, even success'.

Ocaña, born in Spain but raised in France from the age of
six, was second to Merckx at the Dauphiné but made life difficult for him on the climbs. The winner of his own national
tour, the Vuelta a España, in 1970, he was eight days older
than Merxkx but a later developer; and by 1971 he felt he was
gaining on his rival. 'They all surrender to Merckx, but I'm
going to stand up to him,' he said. Earlier in 1971, he bought
an Alsatian and called it Merckx. 'Obey, Merckx!' he would
tell the dog. 'I'm your master, your boss.'

The prologue to the 1971 Tour was unusual: a team time
trial that Merckx's Molteni team won comfortably. The next
day included no fewer than three road stages: 1a, 1b and 1c
(of 59.5, 90 and 74km respectively). The day after that, to
Strasbourg, saw fifteen riders go clear 100km from the finish,

a move that included most of the favourites, including Merckx and Ocaña. They finished nine minutes ahead of the peloton. And in the velodrome in Strasbourg, who else but Merckx won the stage. Once again he was in yellow.

Attention turned to stage eight, to the extinct volcano of Puy de Dôme in the Massif Central. It was where Raymond Poulidor and Jacques Anquetil famously duelled in 1964, grazing shoulders as neither gave an inch. A viciously steep climb of just 14km, it last featured on the route of the Tour in 1988 and these days cannot return – the road is too narrow and the Tour is too big. But in 1971, with Merckx still in yellow, he appeared to be struggling as they began the climb. The scent of blood filled Ocaña's nostrils. He jumped away. Merckx was left behind.

Emerging through the mist at the summit, Ocaña won the stage, with Zoetemelk second at eight seconds and Joaquim Agostinho of Portugal third. The hysterical French TV commentary conveys just how strange it is for a hilltop stage to finish with no sign of Merckx. The mist adds to the mood of tension and suspense: where is he? 'Can he keep yellow?' yells the commentator as the tall figure of Merckx appears through the gloom, his big shoulders rocking with the effort of damage limitation. 'He's sprinting!' Merckx heaves his body across the line in fourth place, 15 seconds down.

Although Merckx kept yellow, the talk was now all of Ocaña, who, when the road went up, appeared stronger – there was no getting away from that. 'Before '71 he had great qualities,' says Merckx of the Spaniard, 'but he never did anything amazing until then and the Puy de Dôme; it was incredible, that attack.' According to Zoetemelk, Ocaña 'was riding like a mad man. I'll never forget it.'

Next, it was on to Grenoble, the finish of stage ten. Merckx punctured on the descent of the Col du Cucheron, with 32km remaining. Again etiquette was ignored: Ocaña attacked 'like a bullet out of a gun'. Merckx, having waited for a spare wheel, fought hard to try and close the gap on the next climb, the Col de Porte, but paid for his efforts and came into Grenoble almost a minute and a half down on Ocaña and the Spaniard's three companions. Joop Zoetemelk was the new overall leader.

The obituary-writers now smelled blood, too. 'Has the Merckx era begun slipping away to its conclusion?' wrote Jacques Goddet in *L'Equipe*. 'The least we can say is that it has entered a new period. The glorious bird has lost a little plumage ... he is no longer in a class of his own.'

Then came Orcières-Merlette. Stage eleven. The Côte de Laffrey was early: not one of the bigger-name Alpine climbs (though the first ever included on the route of the Tour), yet capable of inflicting serious damage; a steep ramp up a sheer cliff. There were 120km remaining of a relatively short stage when they started to climb, but Ocaña's team manager, Maurice de Muer, had a plan: 'We set the whole team to work, and the race was hard from the off because we had seen the day before that Merckx wasn't in his best form.'

Ocaña, so determined to 'stand up' to Merckx, also had the advice of Jacques Anquetil, the first five-time Tour winner, echoing in his head. 'Go,' Anquetil had told him in Grenoble the previous evening, 'on the Côte de Laffrey.'

It was Agostinho who was the first attacker; Ocaña, Van Impe and Zoetemelk followed. Merckx had suffered a sleepless night – as well as his usual anxieties, he was now suffering stomach pain, too – and did not react. A gap opened. The Laffrey 'only' climbed to 910 metres, but by the top Merckx was already two minutes adrift. Was Goddet's prophecy correct?

The twenty-six-year-old Ocaña sensed his time was now. One by one, he dropped his companions until on the Noyer climb, with 60km still to go, he was on his own. This was the way Ocaña rode: he wasn't explosive, but as strong as an ox; he dropped riders not by attacking but by steadily ratcheting up the speed, like a torturer tightening thumbscrews. The roads were poor, the heat was stifling, but soon Ocaña had three minutes and 45 seconds on Van Impe, four minutes on Agostinho and Zoetemelk, five and a half on Merckx and the other nine riders in his group.

At the foot of the final climb to the ski station at Orcières-Merlette, with 20km left, Ocaña's lead had increased further: over five minutes on Van Impe; an enormous nine minutes on Merckx. Yet Merckx was relentless in his pursuit; he never gave up. Nor did he receive any help.

While Ocaña was on the rampage, Merckx fought all the way up to the ski station at Orcières-Merlette where, typically, he led in his small group. 'Even when he is beaten, he still has his pride,' said the French commentator. He won the sprint, but he had lost eight minutes – *eight minutes* – to Ocaña, who was now in yellow.

The Tour was over, was the opinion. Ocaña seemed the only one unconvinced, telling reporters: 'The Tour is not finished. It would be if Merckx were not in it, but a rider like him is capable of anything.'

'Today Ocaña tamed us all,' said Merckx. 'With the lead he has I cannot see, right now, how he can lose, but I'm not quitting, though I can tell you that at one time today I thought of it.'

Merckx was down that night; Wagtmans later recalled him being 'completely depressed, saying silly things, like that he'd never beat Luis Ocaña again. We all tried to gee him up, but he was having none of it.'

'For the first time, I was dictated to by a stronger rider than me,' said Merckx that evening. 'Now I think it's all over. Ocaña has been dominating for three days ... I don't know what's wrong, but I'm incapable of attacking.'

There was one word for Ocaña's performance: 'Merckx-issimo'. But such a performance from a rider other than Merckx was new and unprecedented. The Tour was about to enter uncharted territory. The question was, how would Merckx respond?

*   *   *

In the lobby of the Ritz-Carlton in Qatar, Merckx's phone rings. He stares at it, as though unsure whether to answer, then answers and talks in Flemish. His facial expression remains fixed, frozen, inscrutable: sad or bored? After four minutes, he finishes the call without saying goodbye. He resumes our conversation, without apologising for the interruption. Then again, he is Eddy Merckx.

What does he recall, now, of the day everyone agreed he had lost the 1971 Tour, to Ocaña? 'Well, first, I had bad luck the day before to Grenoble with the puncture, and I remember Ocaña attacking. There were other riders in the break, but nobody would help me. If it happened today, the sports director would say, "Wait – there are some riders at seconds [behind]," but at that time, well, anyway …

'The day after, on the Côte de Laffrey, Ocaña was super that day. *Super.* When I arrived at Orcières, I thought the Tour was over, for sure.' What had it been like, chasing for mile upon mile without any help from anyone, and with the gap increasing to almost ten minutes? Merckx shrugs. 'It was normal that no one helped me. When someone dominates the sport like I was dominating cycling … I wouldn't expect gifts from anyone else, because I didn't offer any gifts. It was payback. But then we had the rest day and I went training with my team. And I said, "Maybe we can try tomorrow?" We started at the top of the mountain. Ocaña was not so good on the descents …'

In *Cannibal*, Friebe's biography of Merckx, a curious incident is related. It is from immediately prior to the stage. Raymond Riotte of the Sonolor team had been up early that morning, and 'as he made his way through the grotty bowels of the Club du Soleil, Riotte noticed a strange whirring noise coming from an adjacent room. He followed it to a doorway, poked his head around the corner and rubbed his eyes. It looked like … no, it was Merckx, churning away on the rollers.'

Riotte said: 'Eddy, Eddy, what are you doing?'

'Oh, you know, my legs didn't feel great so I was just trying to loosen up.'

'But have you seen the length of the stage?' Riotte asked. 'We've got 250 kilometres to do, in this heat …'

Was Merckx warming up? Was he up to something? He denies the story now. 'No. No, no, no. You don't warm up for a descent. We had trained on the rest day, but on the morning of the stage? No.'

*   *   *

The stage from Orcières to Marseille was 251km. After the descent from the ski station where they had been camped on the rest day, it was more or less a flat run to the Mediterranean. The kind of stage that would ordinarily be quite uneventful.

Stage starts at the Tour follow a typical routine: the flag drops and the riders roll out. Some will be left behind, but there's no need to panic, no sense of urgency. At some point the attacks will start. And then the race will be on. But nobody attacks from the gun, before some riders have even got their feet in the pedals.

In Orcières, on top of the mountain, something was up. As they lined up for the start, Merckx and his Molteni men nudged their way to the front. And there they stood, as though lining up for a Formula One Grand Prix, at the front of the grid. 'We planned to start at the front,' Merckx explains now. 'Ocaña was at the back of the bunch, speaking with journalists because he was in the yellow jersey.'

Matter-of-factly, while passing his mobile phone from one hand to the other, and with his expression unchanged, Merckx adds: 'And at the start, we attacked.'

Johny Schleck had spotted Merckx and his team gathering at the front and had an inkling that something was afoot: 'I said, "Luis, look out. *Le Grand* [another nickname for Merckx that needs no explanation] is on the front line." Luis just said, "Come on, he's not going to attack on the descent."'

But attack on the descent is exactly what he and his Molteni team did. As Wagtmans told Friebe: 'BOOM! Off I went. Like an atomic bomb.' Wagtmans led the line while Merckx and two more Moltenis, Joseph Huysmans and Julien Stevens, did their best to follow. Eight other riders joined them, including a team-mate of Ocaña's, Désiré Letort. A sense of panic gripped the peloton. There was chaos, not least, as Barry Hoban told Friebe, because 'Everyone had had new tyres glued on the previous day, and they hadn't bedded down yet.' Tyres were rolling off rims. 'People were falling off all over the place.'

By the foot of the descent, with the lead group whittled down to ten, the gap was a minute. Merckx and team-mates hammered away at the front, while Ocaña and allies (not all of them from his own team) chased. It was relentless. Under the pressure, the peloton splintered into five groups. After 20km, the gap was creeping up. It was 1:20. Then 20km later, another 20 seconds had been added. But at 80km, it had come inside a minute: 55 seconds. In the main peloton, as more bodies joined the chase, one of Merckx's team-mates, Joseph Bruyère, punctured. The other Moltenis were ordered to wait for him: an error. They never got back on. It meant they couldn't make a nuisance of themselves in trying to disrupt the chase. Then Ocaña punctured, and the gap momentarily expanded to two minutes. By the top of a small climb, the Padequette, at 147km, it was back down to 1:20.

For 240km and five hours, it didn't let up. Nobody blinked. The speed didn't drop below 50kph. And the gap hovered around a minute. Merckx began at one point to lose heart, but his director, Lomme Driessens, encouraged and cajoled.

There was a greater prize at stake; greater, perhaps, than any time to be gained on Ocaña on this particular day.

At the front of the peloton, Ocaña's Bic team received help from the Spanish Werner squad and Cyrille Guimard's Mercier men. Guimard was an old adversary of Merckx who would later claim that by chasing he was protecting his own interests – an argument Merckx found about as credible as the tooth fairy. Once again, there was an unholy alliance against *Le Grand*. Payback.

Merckx and his fellow eight fugitives raced into Marseille almost an hour ahead of the fastest predicted schedule. This had unfortunate consequences. Streets that should have been lined with thousands of fans were all but empty; TV crews were still setting up; barriers were still being erected; most seriously of all, the mayor of the city, Gaston Deferre, was still lunching with his VIP guests. They missed the finish completely.

Merckx launched himself at the line but he had to go the long way around Huysmans. An Italian rider, Luciano Armani, nabbed the stage win by centimetres from the lunging Merckx. Two minutes and twelve seconds later, the peloton arrived. Ocaña was angry, complaining that Wagtmans attacked before the flag had even been dropped. That might have been a first: a false-start in a road race. The Marseille mayor, Deferre, was even angrier: 'The Tour de France will never set foot in this city again, as long as I live,' he said. He was as good as his word. Deferre died in 1986; the Tour finally returned three years later.

But Merckx wasn't exactly happy, either. 'Too much for too little,' was his mantra. He was interviewed on the podium, the interviewer telling him he had done 'something incredible today'.

'If there had been more of us, we would have made a real break,' said Merckx. 'Not many were riding hard.'

Ocaña was riding hard as well, he was told. 'Yes, it was very hard today,' shrugged Merckx.

Was Merckx satisfied? 'No, we pushed a lot for not much.'

'You don't want Ocaña to win the Tour easily,' the inter-viewer teased. 'The Tour de France finishes in Paris,' Merckx replied. 'Obviously Ocaña has a strong advantage on me ... It's still very difficult. But you should never give up.'

At this stage, the jury was out on whether Merckx's great escape had been a success. What everybody could agree on – everybody except Ocaña – was that it had been thrilling. 'Cold realists could consider whether the gain was worth the effort,' said the report in *Cycling Weekly*, 'but that was not the attitude of those privileged to follow a Tour stage that will go down in history – the day when Eddy Merckx took flight over the long hot road to the sea, taking eight more men with him, to finish over an hour up on the fastest schedule in a record average speed of 45.351kph (28.26mph).'

Raphaël Géminiani, one of the great figures of French cycling, a leading rider of the 1950s who then became a top manager, agreed: 'It was sublime. I rate this effort better than Ocaña's on the Merlette.'

But Merckx was down, in a figurative and literal sense – the gap to Ocaña remained a yawning chasm of seven min-utes, 34 seconds. Wagtmans sought to reassure him, telling him that although the time reclaimed seemed insignificant, the psychological damage done to Ocaña was anything but. Physically, too, the 240km pursuit match must have drained Ocaña; it was always tougher to chase than be chased. Wagtmans studied Ocaña on the podium and concluded that he was a shadow of the swashbuckling rider who had won at Orcières-Merlette forty-eight hours earlier. 'All the colour had drained from his face,' he recalled. 'He had lost too much power that day. When Merckx came down off the podium, I stopped him and said, "Eddy, Ocaña has no future in this Tour de France. Trust me."'

Had it been worth it? 'Maybe not,' reflected Merckx. But in a way that wasn't the point; to debate it endlessly was to

misunderstand the cyclist known as the Cannibal. 'All I know
is that I will attack to my limit,' he said, 'even if it means I
finish the Tour in twentieth place.'

*   *   *

'That day, I think the Tour changed,' says Merckx now of
Marseille. The balance began to tilt, but would have tilted
more, he believes, had it not been for his team-mate Bruyère's
puncture, and the sacrifice of other team-mates to a forlorn
chase. 'If they had stayed together in the group, with Ocaña,
I think we could have taken fifteen minutes.'

Does he remember arriving early in Marseille, and the odd
experience of racing through empty streets? 'Ha ha ha! Yes.
We were on the rivet all day, absolutely. Absolutely.' He seems
infused, for the first time, with a nostalgic glow. And yet he
says the stage is not among his most memorable. 'Not especially, because I did not win the stage, and the Tour was not
finished. And we didn't take that much time ...'

But did he feel Ocaña was beatable? Merckx turns serious,
solemn even. 'Yes, yes. Yes. Yes. After that there were only
two riders [in contention]. After that stage, I believed again I
could win the Tour.'

He won the next day's time trial in Albi but only edged
eleven seconds closer; then they were in the Pyrenees, for the
214km fourteenth stage to Luchon: Act Three, the final part
of the trilogy.

At the start in Revel, Merckx told a team-mate: 'I'm going
to batter Ocaña until one of us breaks, him or me.' The bat-
tering began as they climbed the Col de Portet d'Aspet, but
Ocaña wouldn't give an inch. Then, on the Col de Menté,
as Merckx would later write in his book, *Carnets de Route*, 'I
notice that Ocaña's progress isn't as smooth as it was and,
above all, that he hasn't been able to eat. Could he be on the
brink of collapse?'

As they climb the Col de Menté, Merckx has a few more digs, and Ocaña responds as, among the peaks of the mountains, dark clouds begin to gather. Again Merckx goes and again he is shadowed by the yellow jersey. 'Luis, calm down!' urges his team-mate, Schleck. Then, with a clap of thunder echoing in the valley, the storm breaks. The heavens darken and open as they crest the summit. Gloom descends; visibility is reduced to about five metres. Merckx, his woollen jersey plastered to his skin, seems oblivious and unconcerned, leading Van Impe, Ocaña and a select group of favourites down. He slightly misjudges a left-hand hairpin but remains upright. Where Merckx goes, so does his shadow; but Ocaña, following Van Impe, who is following Merckx, does not have Merckx's composure. He careers into the bend: too fast, out of control; his upper body locked rigid, his hands pulling hard on the brakes, which in the rain don't work. He runs out of road and crashes against the verge. Quickly he picks himself up, but Zoetemelk and Agostinho have the same problem, entering the corner too fast. Zoetemelk skids and hits Ocaña, then Agostinho slams into him. He is floored a second time.

Ocaña lay on the wet road, his yellow jersey covered in mud, screaming in pain. 'I thought I was dying,' he wrote in his autobiography. 'It was as if my chest was smashed in, but my mental state was simply atrocious.'

His Tour was over. He was taken by helicopter to Saint-Gaudens, but there is an enduring mystery about just how serious Ocaña's injuries were. Though he lost consciousness in the helicopter, the diagnosis at the hospital was that he was suffering from 'thoracic contusions and a pronounced state of shock'. He was discharged the next day.

Ocaña's wife, Josiane, would later claim to have had a 'bad feeling' the morning of the fourteenth stage to Luchon. It is tempting, though, to trace Ocaña's downfall back to the stage to Marseille, when Merckx didn't gain much time, but did sow seeds of doubt in the sensitive Ocaña's mind. By attacking on

that stage, then relentlessly on the Portet d'Aspet and Col de
Menté, he confirmed that he would not give up. It was why
Ocaña felt he couldn't let him out of his sight; why he felt
he had to follow him even as the sky blackened and the rain
fell. Perhaps it wasn't the crash and subsequent collision that
'broke' Ocaña, but Merckx. The agony and trauma, as he lay
in that wet ditch on the descent of the Col de Menté, seemed
both physical and psychological.

In Luchon, where the stage finished with a win for Fuente,
Merckx became the new overall leader. He refused to wear
the yellow jersey the next day: a symbolic gesture of sympathy for his fallen rival, but for one day only. He put it on
the next day and kept it to Paris where he won by almost ten
minutes from Zoetemelk. Merckx won two more Tours, in
1972 and '74, then retired quite young, at thirty-two, when
his form had dipped and decline seemed irreversible. 'I was
nineteen when I turned professional,' he tells me. 'Mentally it
becomes hard. Look at the top riders, the number ones, they
all stop quite young.

'But I ride a lot now,' he adds. 'I like riding my bike. I ride
when I can, when it's nice weather. Not every day, but 6,000,
7,000 kilometres a year.'

Merckx has described Ocaña as his bête noire, but the
Spaniard had his own demons and they weren't slayed by
his victory in the 1973 Tour – which, tellingly, was the one
year Merckx stayed away. In retirement, Ocaña suffered
with failed business ventures and ill health. In 1994 he
was diagnosed with hepatitis, liver cirrhosis and cancer, and
given a few weeks to live by his doctor. In early May he
met the L'Equipe cycling writer, Philippe Brunel. He was in
a reflective, nostalgic mood, telling him: 'Nowhere else in
life have I got back the feelings I used to have as a cyclist. If
someone told me now that I could ride the Tour de France
and die the second I crossed the finish line, I'd sign without
a moment's hesitation.'

'They all surrender,' Ocaña had said of Merckx, 'but I'm going to stand up to him.' It might be crass to compare his subsequent actions with his avowed refusal to be dictated to by his old nemesis. But a couple of weeks after speaking to Brunel, on 19 May 1994, Ocaña took matters in his own hands. At the age of forty-eight, at his home in Gers, southwest France, he put a gun to his head and shot himself.

Classement

Stage Eleven: Thursday 8 July, Grenoble to Orcières-Merlette, 134km

1 Luis Ocaña, Spain, Bic, 4 hours, 2 minutes, 49 secs
2 Lucien van Impe, Belgium, Sonolor, at 5 minutes, 52 secs
3 Eddy Merckx, Belgium, Molteni, at 8 minutes, 42 secs
4 Joop Zoetemelk, Holland, Mars-Flandria, same time
5 Gösta Pettersson, Sweden, Ferretti, s.t.
6 Bernard Thévenet, France, Peugeot, s.t.

Stage Twelve: Saturday, 10 July, Orcières-Merlette to Marseille, 251km

1 Luciano Armani, Italy, Scic, 5 hours, 25 minuens, 28 secs
2 Eddy Merckx, same time
3 Lucien Aimar, France, Sonolor, s.t.
4 Jos van der Vleuten, Holland, Gazelle, s.t.
5 Enrico Paolini, Italy, Scic, s.t.
6 Désiré Letort, France, Bic, s.t.

Stage Fourteen: Monday, 12 July, Revel to Luchon, 214.5km

1 José-Manuel Fuente, Spain, Kas, 6 hours, 11 minutes, 54 secs
2 Eddy Merckx, at 6 minutes, 21 secs
3 Lucien van Impe, same time
4 Vicente López-Carril, Spain, Kas, s.t.
5 Lucien Aimar, s.t.
6 Joop Zoetemelk, s.t.

L-R: Luis Herrera, Bernard Hinault, Laurent Fignon

Chapter 9

GUERRILLA WARFARE

16 July 1984. Stage Seventeen:
Grenoble to l'Alpe d'Huez
151km. Mountains

A contrast in styles. The spindly legs of the small climber, Luis Herrera, spinning fluidly. The lumbering and painful grinding of the Badger, Bernard Hinault, forcing a huge gear, shoulders rolling.

Herrera floats out of the saddle and eases clear. Hinault lifts himself heavily and accelerates back up to him. Then he passes Herrera. But it's a façade. The Badger is bluffing. It has been the story of Hinault's day, of his Tour. If he's going to go down, he will go down fighting. Herrera, who looks like a child on an adult's bike, pulls effortlessly clear again and Hinault, still snarling, has no response. Daylight opens between them.

Herrara, the little bird, is set free. Now he is flying up l'Alpe d'Huez, while Hinault labours, and a little lower down the mountain, Laurent Fignon, in the *tricolore* of French champion, sets off in pursuit …

Let's freeze the picture there.

Herrera was an amateur, riding for the Colombian national team. For a twenty-three-year-old débutant, he arrived at the start of the 1984 Tour with quite a reputation. Big things were expected. There was even talk of him winning. He had won a major stage race in his own country, the Clásico RCN, three times. All twenty-three editions of the Clásico had been won by Colombians, but in the early 1980s it opened its doors to European teams and some of the stars had gone prior to the 1984 Tour de France – including the '83 Tour winner, Fignon.

Fignon talks about his visit to Colombia in his book, *We Were Young and Carefree*. 'An astonishing experience,' he writes. He and the other Europeans were there primarily because it was at altitude, over 2,000m. It was thought to be good preparation for the upcoming Tour. Fignon was struck by the vast crowds, by the remarkable mountains, the equally remarkable climbing ability of the Colombian riders – and the cocaine. He later admitted he dabbled on the final night. But in the race itself, the Tour champion was nowhere. Fignon finished 43rd in the Clásico, humbled by Herrera.

The question was, could the Colombians demonstrate their talent overseas, in Europe? At the Dauphiné Libéré, a month before the 1984 Tour, Hinault was beaten by another Colombian, Martin Ramírez, despite some dubious tactics that spoke of the disdain in which the Colombians were held – or, perhaps, the threat these *ingénues* posed. Ramírez defended his overall lead by positioning himself on Hinault's wheel, and later claimed to Matt Rendell for his book, *Kings of the Mountains*, that Hinault 'responded by braking hard to make me fall, while his team bombarded me with elbows and fists'.

'No one knew who we were,' Ramírez continued. 'Cochise [Martin Emilio 'Cochise' Rodríguez, the first Colombian to ride the Tour de France in 1975] had raced in Europe, but that had been long before. So it was clear that they saw us and called us "little Indians", "savages". We showed up all of a sudden, and managed to beat them in a big stage race on the eve of the Tour de France … Well, that just wasn't something they wanted. So the reception was not very good.'

*   *   *

What was not appreciated or even widely known in Europe was how developed Colombia's cycling culture was. It had prospered quite apart from the European circuit, separated by a chasm even wider than the Atlantic. The Colombian scene had its roots in the early 1950s when a national tour, the Vuelta a Colombia, started, followed a decade later by the Clásico RCN. Like the Tour de France, the Vuelta was founded by a newspaper, Colombia's biggest daily, *El Tiempo*.

Almost immediately, both races attracted enormous crowds and dominated the national conversation. According to Klaus Bellon, the Colombian journalist, they unlocked something, revealing that 'the entire mountainous South American country was delirious with passion for cycling'. That passion simmered for almost four decades before finally boiling over and spilling into Europe.

If nobody in Europe knew about the popularity of the sport in Colombia, the ignorance was reciprocated: few in Colombia knew about the great European riders and races. 'My first Tour de France was in 1972,' Hector Urrego, another Colombian journalist and broadcaster, tells me. 'I worked for *Mundo Ciclistico*, a monthly cycling magazine in Colombia. My impression at the Tour de France was, this is the best, the biggest event in the world.'

Well, of course it was. It was the Tour de France. But in the pre-mass media, pre-Internet age, they did not realise this in Colombia, where the Vuelta a Colombia or Clásico RCN were the biggest bike races. Biggest in South America? The world? Who knew?

Major stars had raced in Colombia, including Fausto Coppi; but he, like Fignon three decades later, struggled in the mountains and altitude of Colombia. Any debate about who was better, the Europeans or Colombians, remained tantalisingly unresolved.

Urrego returned to the Tour de France as a journalist in 1975, '77 and '78. He was besotted by it, and dreamed of a Colombian team one day competing. To that end, on his way home from the Moscow Olympics in 1980, he stopped off in Paris, calling in at the offices of *L'Equipe*, where the Tour organisation was based. He asked about the possibility of a Colombian team riding the Tour de l'Avenir, the 'Tour of the future', for young riders and amateurs, and was told 'yes', Venezuela had just pulled out. But an answer was required in twenty-four hours. The race started in a few weeks.

With incredible haste, sponsorship was secured and a team put together. A Colombian rider, Alfonso Flórez, then won overall, beating the Olympic champion, Sergey Sukhoruchenkov of the Soviet Union. The Eastern Bloc riders were, like the Colombians, amateurs. And for similar reasons. The Colombian Cycling Federation resisted professionalism mainly because they were so focused on the Olympic Games, which were still restricted to amateurs. The first Colombian professional, Giovanni Jiménez, faced significant opposition from his Federation when he raced in Europe in the 1960s.

Three years after the Colombians' success at the Tour de l'Avenir, the door to the Tour de France opened when amateur teams were invited. 'For all Colombian people it was very new, but not for me,' recalls Urrego of that first Tour. 'I was interested and curious to know the level of our riders compared to the big riders in Europe – Fignon, Millar, LeMond, Hinault – at the best race in Europe.'

Before the 1983 Tour, there was another pressing question: how would it be received back home? 'There was enormous interest!' says Urrego. 'On the radio there were four to six hours of transmissions a day. And so the people in Colombia discover the Tour, the great champions, France – and they see the Colombian cyclists fight against the best climbers in the world ...'

Cycling in Colombia, Urrego stresses, is 'the most important sport – the most popular is soccer'. The distinction is important. 'It's not about titles, medals, victories and legends,' he says. 'We have sixty years of cycling history, and that is important, but the bike in Colombia is also a vehicle to work, to study, for transport, for health. The bike means a lot. And the Colombian races, they help us know the country and the people.'

In their début in 1983, they rode respectably, impressively at times, with Patrocinio Jiménez coming close to a stage win when he escaped in the Pyrenees with Robert Millar, who attacked on the final climb, then plunged into Luchon to take the win. Jiménez was fourth, but took over the King of the Mountains jersey and held it for five days. He was eventually second in that competition and 17th overall, with his teammate Edgar Corredor one place above him. Five out of the ten Colombians made it to Paris, where they finished tenth in the teams' classification. In the mountains they had ridden well, more than holding their own; but in the time trials, over the cobbles, and on the long, flat stages, they struggled.

At home, millions tuned in. There were twenty-three Colombian journalists on the race, including three radio stations, with Radio Caracol purchasing the live rights. Consequently, they broadcast every minute of every stage – a first for anyone. But as Matt Rendell recorded, 'the rivalry between [the radio stations] was so intense that it soon erupted into violence'. Radio Caracol, annoyed that the other two stations were basing their broadcasts on theirs, 'began broadcasting fictional attacks' to try and catch them out.

There were other stories, including those of Urrego's station, RCN, broadcasting from payphones, feeding an endless supply of coins into the meter as they relayed the day's action, interrupting the broadcast only to hold a cassette recorder to the mouthpiece to play pre-recorded adverts during commercial breaks. Urrego confirms this story, recalling that 'one of our primary jobs during that first Tour de France was to find a bank, and get as many coins as physically possible'. But he clarifies some points about the dispute between RCN and Caracol: 'Before the 1983 Tour, the president of the Colombian cycling federation had a problem with RCN and they arranged for the rights of the Tour to go to Caracol. But I had a good friend at the Tour de France, Xavier Louy, the vice-director, and I took a plane to Paris, spoke to him, explained the situation: that RCN were out of the Tour. So he did a deal with Félix Lévitan, to authorise RCN to also transmit the Tour de France.

'So,' Urrego continues, 'there are two Colombian radio stations transmitting the Tour de France from 1983 to 1986. Yes, there are tensions and fights. RCN had been broadcasting cycling for sixty years, Caracol just came on the scene. But eventually, RCN won. Today, we are the only radio station to broadcast cycling in Colombia.'

Even when it was shown on TV, radio was the preferred medium. Urrego's broadcasts were (and still are) essential listening. This had much to do, as Klaus Bellon says, with 'the tone and delivery of the radio broadcasters'. Other broadcasters reported with amusement, awe and bemusement the broadcasts of their Colombian colleagues: they filled the many hours of air time with breathless, non-stop, highly charged and emotional commentary, 'sometimes breaking down into unintelligible fits of crying due to the excitement of a Colombian's performance'.

Urrego says: 'The surveys told us that from 1983 to 1988 fifteen million people listened each day to the Tour de France and Tour of Spain. The same as in Colombia for the Vuelta a Colombia and Clásico RCN.'

Fifteen million people: one in three Colombians.

*   *   *

'The Colombians had come to Europe with dreams of becoming conquistadores, subduing the natives with their firepower and potent magic. It hadn't happened that way.'

So wrote Sam Abt, the American journalist, as the high mountains of the 1984 Tour de France, the second to feature a Colombian team, loomed. The Colombian presence had increased: again there were ten in the national team, with another five on European teams. The press corps had swelled to forty. They had been through the Pyrenees, but still their much-vaunted climbing ability hadn't shone as brightly as many expected it to. Why was that? Luis Herrera, the twenty-three-year-old star of the team, had a theory. The climbs were not long enough.

Not long enough? It was pointed out to Herrera that some of the passes in the Alps and Pyrenees were 20, even 30 kilometres, climbing to over 2,000 metres. Herrera didn't scoff – that wouldn't have been in his nature. Instead, he quietly pointed out that the Alto de Letras, the longest climb in Colombia, was 83km long, 3,195m high.

Luis 'Lucho' Herrera was the archetypal Colombian cyclist. From a humble background, he was known as 'El Jardinerito de Fusagasugá' (the little gardener of Fusagasugá, his home village). 'I met Lucho for the first time in 1981,' says Urrego, 'in the Vuelta de la Juventud [an under-23 stage race]. He was fourth and the best climber. A year before he had been 97th. Sure, I thought Lucho would be a great rider. Then he raced in the Clásico RCN and won the most important stage, which finished at La Línea, a mountain 3,550 metres high. He was racing against the best Colombian riders of the day and some others. I thought, he will be the best climber in the world.

'Lucho is a special person,' Urrego continues. 'He's very quiet, not much words in a conversation, he smiles not much, he's serious, but he has a great personality.'

It wasn't the mountains that did for Herrera and the Colombians in the first half of the 1984 Tour, however. It was the flat stages. 'They warned me,' said Herrera a week into the race, 'but I didn't believe the Tour could be so difficult. The last fifty kilometres of each stage are raced at a terribly fast pace. It's impossible to compare the Tour with our usual races. Here in Europe, it's ten times tougher.'

It wasn't just the speed of the flat stages. They also suffered prejudice and harassment, similar to that Ramírez experienced a month earlier at the Dauphiné. The Colombians were small, hardly suited to the argy-bargy at the sharp end of the peloton. They were lightweight *grimpeurs*, not powerful *rouleurs*. They tended to ride at the back, which inevitably meant they were caught up in more crashes. But they were lampooned for their bike-handling skills, blamed for the crashes, and criticised for riding their own race, for appearing oblivious to the complicated (sometimes dirty) politics of the peloton.

In this system, a favour done for a rival team one day could be repaid on another. But the Colombians didn't get involved. Hinault called them amateurs (which was, at least, accurate), and Peter Post, the fearsome dictator at the helm of the Panasonic team, complained: 'The Colombians refuse to work. They just sit there and let everybody else do the work. From them, nothing.' Plus, added Abt, 'They had no sense of tactics. And they subsisted on coffee, which cost them sleepless nights.'

Speaking to Herrera now is not that easy; he seems to have disappeared from the sport. But talking on the phone from Fusagasugá, where he was born and still lives, about 60km from Bogotá, he recalls his and his fellow Colombians' induction to the Tour and the professional peloton: 'There was the old established European system, and we were new to it. Maybe we just didn't have the abilities that they had on the road. So when there was a crash, we always got the blame, but it simply wasn't true [that it was our fault] for every crash. I mean, before we arrived there were crashes too, so things weren't exactly as they portrayed them.

'I think it's more likely that they were bothered that we made our presence known, and performed well in races,' Herrera continues. 'We kept attacking in all the climbs, and I think maybe that bothered them a bit, you know?'

In his first Tour, after ten days of flat stages and time trials as they travelled from Paris in a semi-clockwise journey around France, Herrera finally had his chance when they reached the Pyrenees. On stage eleven, he chased Robert Millar to the summit of Guzet-Neige, failing to catch the Scotsman, but finishing second, 41 seconds down. Stage fifteen, into Grenoble, over 241 hilly kilometres, saw more flashes from Herrera whenever the road went up. The Colombian commentators cried and screamed: 'Viva Colombia! Viva Colombia!' Often they could be heard over other nations' broadcasts; a breathless stream of words, delivered at a relentless speed.

There were four days in the Alps. But it was the first, to the summit of l'Alpe d'Huez, that fired the imagination. The twenty-three-year-old Colombian Edgar Corredor had finished third the previous year, but it was new to Herrera, who didn't know the history – that l'Alpe d'Huez was the scene of the Tour's first ever summit finish in 1952; that the great Fausto Coppi had dominated that stage; that it had since assumed mythical status on account of its twenty-one hairpin bends, the way the road slashed in zigzags up the sheer face of the mountain; that it was a natural amphitheatre, offering spectacular vantage points for the fans who lined the roads, perching and peering over the side to see the riders approach from the valley and the town of Bourg-d'Oisans.

On Monday 17 July 1984 an estimated 300,000 people packed the Alpe. 'Samba rhythms echoed around the ski resort,' reported *Cycling Weekly*, a well-intentioned but misguided reference to the large number of Colombian fans, as Samba is a Brazilian dance. That wasn't as bad as the reports describing the Colombians as Indians.

They were still an unknown quantity. But not for much longer.

*   *   *

Laurent Fignon and Bernard Hinault were the demi-gods of European, and, by extension, world cycling. The duel between them in 1984 was compelling, the greatest French rivalry since Anquetil and Poulidor, but with more of an edge. Hinault had grown up on Fignon's team, Renault, under his directeur sportif, Cyrille Guimard. With Guimard and Renault, he won four Tours de France. But everything changed in 1983. At the Tour of Spain he suffered a knee injury – something that had first bothered him in 1980, after the stage to Lille described in an earlier chapter – and, although he won in Spain, had to withdraw from the Tour. In his absence, twenty-two-year-old Fignon assumed leadership of Renault. And he seized the opportunity. To widespread surprise, he won.

The rise of Fignon and fall of Hinault was sudden, dramatic and simultaneous. In the public imagination, it happened over the three weeks of the 1983 Tour: Fignon would later recall Hinault's glowering, brooding presence at the Renault after-Tour party in Paris. In truth, his mood perhaps owed less to Fignon's win than to the fact that he had fallen out with Guimard. 'It was war,' said Hinault of his relationship with the man who directed him to his first win in 1978, and the other three.

Following the Tour, Hinault went to the bosses at Renault with an ultimatum: Guimard or him. But Fignon's victory, given his age and potential, gave Guimard and Renault the perfect excuse to dump Hinault. Not surprisingly, Guimard (and Fignon) stayed and Hinault, whose career was said to be in jeopardy after an operation on his knee, was left without a team. In the autumn, he hooked up with the colourful businessman, Bernard Tapie, to set up a new squad, La Vie Claire.

Hinault was widely written off, though he was only twenty-eight. The Badger had said almost from the start of his career that he would retire on his thirty-second birthday, in 1986. He had already won four Tours; if he returned to full fitness, he believed he could win three more, beginning in 1984. Thus was the scene set when the riders and teams gathered in Montreuil. 'At the start of the Tour de France the journalists were working themselves into a frenzy,' said Fignon. 'France was cut in two, split between him and me.'

Hinault struck the first blow, winning the prologue time trial. 'It's funny,' he said after accepting the first yellow jersey. 'I feel as if nothing has changed.'

But something had changed. Hinault's old iron rule was more difficult to impose when there was a younger, stronger opponent. What's more – and making the situation worse for Hinault – Fignon's team was so strong they were dubbed 'The New Cannibals' by *L'Equipe*. For Renault, Marc Madiot won stage three; then they won the team time trial, 55 seconds ahead of Hinault and La Vie Claire; then Vincent Barteau took over the yellow jersey after stage five; then Fignon won the long seventh stage time trial in Le Mans; and then Pascal Jules won stage eight. Hinault, who lost 49 seconds to Fignon in the time trial, became desperate. 'I looked on as Hinault got all hot and bothered, racing for time bonus sprints as he began to wage what he thought was a war of attrition, every day, on every kind of terrain,' wrote Fignon in his autobiography. 'It might have worked on a rider who was mentally weaker than me. But I had an answer for everything, and above all, contrary to how he saw it, I never lost my head even if the guerrilla warfare occasionally got a bit tiring, because you had to keep your eyes open all the time.'

He maintained some respect for Hinault's 'audacious character', Fignon added. But Fignon had a major advantage: Guimard. Tactically, Guimard possessed a touch of genius. And Fignon himself was certainly a much stronger and far more confident rider than he had been as a Tour débutant in 1983.

On the eve of the Alpe d'Huez stage, Hinault was a lowly seventh overall, three minutes, forty-four seconds down on Barteau, who was still in yellow. Fignon was second, now two minutes up on Hinault after stage sixteen, another time trial, which Fignon also won. Hinault had previously dominated time trials; defeat stung.

He had a plan on the morning of the seventeenth stage, from Grenoble to l'Alpe d'Huez. The plan was to isolate Fignon. All too aware of the strength of the Renault team, Hinault believed that his only chance of beating Fignon was to get rid of his team-mates and set up a *mano-a-mano* battle on l'Alpe d'Huez.

That explained his tactics as the stage got underway. There were two early climbs, the Col de la Placette, a category-three mountain, then the Côte de Saint-Pierre-de-Chartreuse, a second cat. The riders scrapping for King of the Mountains points contested these, while Hinault waited. After 53 kilometres they reached the Col de Coq, where Patrocinio Jiménez, the Colombian now riding for the Spanish Teka team, attacked. Now Hinault made his first move. Fignon was alert to it and chased him down. But it was, said Fignon later, 'a vicious attack'. A taster.

Next came the Côte de Laffrey, 104km into the stage: the brutal climb that featured in 1971, when Luis Ocaña put Eddy Merckx on the ropes. On the approach, five of Hinault's La Vie Claire team-mates mass at the front: something is up.

As soon as the road starts to steepen, Hinault jumps. Just like Ocaña. Hinault goes once. Twice. Three times. But Fignon is not suffering the kind of off day Merckx had thirteen years earlier. He responds each time. It's an 8km climb, but horribly steep. A quarter of the way up, only fifteen riders remain in the front group. Barteau, in the yellow jersey, has slipped away. Hinault has one team-mate, and so does Fignon: the American riding his first Tour, Greg LeMond.

Hinault digs. And Fignon jumps after him again, while the others cling to his back wheel, gasping, reacting to each acceleration like it's a punch in the stomach. The group is reduced to seven. Herrera is there. But just when they start to settle into a rhythm, *boom!*, Hinault goes again. And again Fignon goes after him, dragging him back. That makes it five attacks from Hinault. It's more like bare-knuckle fighting than cycle racing. Robert Millar, one of those clinging on for dear life, will later write: 'I haven't witnessed savagery at this level before and it seems more like hatred than just plain competition.'

Next, LeMond has a go – it seems to Millar that they're ganging up on Hinault. Right enough, when LeMond is brought back, there's another attack – Fignon this time. The counter-punch. This blow lands. Fignon opens a gap. And it's Herrera who dances up to him. The pair cross the summit together, only for Hinault to chase after them on the descent.

There's a regrouping in the valley. Through the villages of Séchilienne, Gavet, Les Clavaux, Riouperoux and Livet, before Bourg-d'Oisans and the Alpe, the riders take on supplies – Fignon and LeMond collect bidons from Guimard, and Hinault chats to his director, Paul Köchli. 'I'm sure he smiled as he took his bidons,' reported Millar.

Hinault is the ultimate warrior. Pride is the word to describe him. If he feels strong, he attacks. If he feels tired, he attacks, 'so the others don't know I am tired'.

It's a headwind through the valley; the worst conditions for any kind of attack. A truce seems to have been called. It will all be decided on the mountain. Then, *boom!* Hinault attacks. Almost with a sense of weariness, LeMond and Fignon go to the front and bring him back. Guimard drives alongside. Talks to them. It settles again. Then Hinault goes again. This time he's away on his own.

It's suicide, it must be suicide, but, racing through Bourg-d'Oisans, Hinault has a lead approaching a minute. Fignon will later describe his attack as 'unexpected – almost pathetic'. He added: 'I started laughing, I honestly did ... Bernard was just too proud and wanted to do everything gallantly.'

*   *   *

Now is Luis 'Lucho' Herrera's moment. Remember him? Nobody has. Sam Abt, the American journalist on the Tour, said: 'Radio Tour, which links all cars and offers periodic reports on the race, spoke of nobody but Hinault and Fignon for most of the day.'

On the lower slopes of the Alpe, Herrera tested the water, jumping clear. 'I was having a good day,' he says now. 'I felt good. In the moment when I was off the front [with Fignon towards the summit of the Laffrey], I knew I was feeling good. From there on, I had to wait and hope that things would go well for me. But I wasn't sure because the only thing I knew was that Hinault would go hard, and that it would be difficult.

'Then, on l'Alpe d'Huez, I attacked, just to see what would happen ...' It was still very early on the climb. 'Yes, it was. I didn't know the climb, so I guess it was perhaps premature of me to go then. I didn't know how much of it was left.'

Herrera bridged the gap to Hinault, who was visibly tiring. His snarling expression had an air of desperation now, as though he was drowning. He didn't have the smooth cadence of Herrera, perched on his bike that looked too big. They rode together but Herrera could tell immediately that he wouldn't be in Hinault's company for long. The contrast extended to their clothing, too: Hinault wore the ultra-modern Mondrian-influenced colourful patchwork of La Vie Claire, while Herrera's was a more simple jersey, red at the bottom, then royal blue with 'Colombia' in white letters, and an inverted yellow V at the shoulders, for their sponsors, Varta Batteries (Herrera would have been an AAA).

Herrera didn't know Hinault. 'The dialogue I had with him was minimal. We almost never spoke. I had respect for him; he was No.1. There was no tension, no friction – never.'

When Herrera took off, leaving Hinault to his struggle, he knew the threat would come from behind – but not from Hinault. He was finished. It was Fignon he feared. By now the bespectacled, blond-haired Fignon, in the *tricolore* jersey of French champion, had counter-attacked and was motoring up to Hinault. He didn't alter his pace when he caught Hinault, at least not initially. But then he eased up, allowing Hinault to believe that he might catch him again. 'I stayed about thirty metres ahead of the Badger. Guimard wanted to crack him completely.' Or as Abt put it: 'Fignon seemed to believe that if you couldn't kick a man when he was down, when could you kick him?'

Hinault's punishment – like a form of waterboarding on a bike – didn't last. Fignon could only hold back for so long. Then he was off. But perhaps, he wondered later, his games with Hinault – and Guimard's earlier orders not to go too early – had cost him the stage.

Hinault continued to toil up the steep slopes of the Alpe, conceding three minutes. He was caught by Millar, who would later recall: 'I could go past him and give him some shelter, some temporary relief from the misery, but then I remember Laffrey and the valley and how much it hurt … I let him take a bit more wind … I'll have a little rest, thanks.' Millar leaves him too, and again Hinault, reaching into the rear pocket of his jersey for food, has no response. 'He wanted to be on his own anyway,' was Millar's pithy observation.

The main picture on the front page of the next day's *L'Equipe* would capture the key symbolic moment, Fignon riding away from Hinault (perhaps a premonition that this 1984 Tour would be the last time, in three decades and counting, where two Frenchmen would battle for the win). Inside, Jacques Goddet, columnist and Tour director, wrote: 'Hinault carried himself like a combatant born of cycling legend. He took off down the road the way a boxer enters the ring, to strike, to destroy, to try and finish alone – yes, alone, in whatever condition, as long as he is still standing.'

But the other story of the day was told by the *L'Equipe* headline: 'Fignon-Herrera: the Tour rocked.' Up ahead, the little Colombian climber was still alone, still looking comfortable, fluid and relaxed as he pedalled through the 300,000 people, including a few Colombians waving flags. Although Fignon later claimed that his conservatism at the foot of the mountain cost him the stage win, Herrera actually pulled further away close to the summit. 'I knew he was chasing,' says Herrera of Fignon. 'In each of the turns, I would be exiting and I would then see him coming into the turn. I knew that the difference was slim. When we were done with those tough turns, we went into some steep straights that were longer. That's where I was able to get a greater advantage on Fignon. When I got to the top, with almost two kilometres to go, or the last kilometre, I realised I was alone. That's when I finally knew I could win.

'I didn't have to be told where Fignon was – I could see him. And then there was the chalkboard on the motorcycle, which always tells you the time gaps. So based on that, I could tell whether the gap was increasing or not.' And it was increasing.

Herrera wasn't aware of the crowd, he says. 'I was too concentrated on what I was doing.' But he says he was aware of what it meant to his country, and those fifteen million people listening to their radios. 'Yes, I think so. I knew I had a great opportunity to win and I had to take it. The best way for me to do it was to do things properly at that moment, and I did that.' In other words, not to be distracted, to focus on managing his effort on a climb he didn't know. 'It was an incredibly important moment, one full of hope. It was going to be the first Colombian victory at the Tour.'

At the top, after the small, dark-skinned, black-haired Herrera crossed the line with his stick-like arms in the air, 49 seconds ahead of Fignon, he was swamped by the Colombian journalists on the race. Seemingly all forty of them. He had made history: the first Colombian stage win; indeed, the first by a Latin American, and the first by an amateur. The flags waved, and a small but vocal knot of people chanted: 'Colombia, Colombia!'

Back home, the response matched the feverish, rapturous commentary that formed the soundtrack to Herrera's ascent of l'Alpe d'Huez. The stock exchange in Colombia suspended operations for half an hour to allow the whole country to catch the end of the stage.

'The meaning of that victory was above and beyond that of sport,' says Klaus Bellon. 'That's because we Colombians feel we have been so maligned on the world stage, that sport sometimes affords us the ability to settle scores. Actually, it's not about settling scores, but about something that Gabriel García Márquez mentioned during his Nobel Prize acceptance speech, which is to merely make our lives real in the eyes of the world. Such was the lowly way in which we felt we were portrayed, and conversely such was the value of that victory. Márquez said: "Our crucial problem has been a lack of conventional means to render our lives believable. This, my friends, is the crux of our solitude."'

Bellon considered Herrera a 'symbol of Colombia due to his humble background, and so to see him win something that we suddenly understood had great meaning, was astonishing. It's once you realise that, that you start to understand Colombia's infatuation with the fact that these riders were taking simple peasant foods with them to Europe. In reality, this only happened at first, and out of need and ignorance. But we saw it as humble Colombia taking on superpowers with nothing other than our indigenous street-smarts. Doing things our way, and defeating the Europeans at their own game, and on their roads.'

*   *   *

Hinault was proud in defeat, Fignon ungracious in victory. He appeared on French TV's daily post-stage programme, hosted by Jacques Chancel, and was asked what he made of Hinault's final attack, on the approach to l'Alpe d'Huez. 'When I saw him go up the road like that, I had to laugh,' said Fignon. He had taken the yellow jersey but regretted that he hadn't been able to win the stage. The regret would grow as the years went on, as Fignon admits in his book: 'Could I have imagined back then that I would never in my entire life win at l'Alpe d'Huez?'

Meanwhile, at the top of the Alpe, Hinault said, 'Today I've been thrashed, but I won't stop attacking before Paris.' In the end, he finished second but ten minutes behind Fignon: a dominant victory that seemed to confirm Fignon as the new *patron*. But how things change. The 1984 Tour was not the end of Hinault: it was more like the end of Fignon. The defending champion missed the 1985 race through injury, while Hinault won with the help of his new team-mate, LeMond.[3] In 1986, Hinault's final season, he finished second to LeMond. But he won at l'Alpe d'Huez.

Fignon, though still only twenty-three the year he won

---

3 A postscript to the Alpe d'Huez stage in 1984 is that later that same night LeMond was persuaded to join Hinault's team, La Vie Claire. The American was picked up by a woman dressed in black leathers on a motorbike, who took him to a hotel, and led him into a room with Hinault and Bernard Tapie. 'How would you like to earn more money than you've ever dreamed of?' asked Tapie. Hinault wanted LeMond to help him beat Fignon in 1985. So, even after his most humiliating defeat, Hinault was plotting revenge.

his second Tour, never won again, and never recaptured his form of '84, even in finishing a close second in one of the greatest ever Tours, in 1989. He died from cancer in 2011, at the age of fifty.

And Herrera? 'Lucho' says that his win at l'Alpe d'Huez didn't change his life, even if it made him a celebrity in Colombia. 'Opportunities came my way,' he says, 'but I took it all in very carefully.

'My life didn't change, not really. It continued to be as it was. By then, cycling was such a part of my life, and I was so focused, that the only aspect that changed was the fact that I started to get even more satisfaction out of things like training. I became more dedicated.' Three years later, he became the first Colombian to win a Grand Tour when he took overall victory at the 1987 Vuelta a España.

There was always a darker side to Colombian cycling, as Fignon found when he raced there in 1984. There was drugs money in the sport, with the notorious Pablo Escobar, whose vast fortune was built on mountains of cocaine, indirectly involved through his brother, Roberto, in running a team in the 1980s. Another pioneering Colombian rider, Alfonso Flórez, whose Tour de l'Avenir win in 1980 was so significant, was murdered by hired assassins in 1992.

Herrera retired the same year. Eight years later, he was kidnapped. He was at his mother's home in Fusagasugá when he was taken by six masked intruders, thought to be from FARC, the guerrilla organisation. They bundled him into an SUV, drove for hours, marched him up a mountain near La Aguadita, then held him in a remote building. Then he was interrogated about his cycling career – his kidnappers were fans. As Herrera later told Bellon: 'The whole time they asked me endless questions about l'Alpe d'Huez, Lagos de Covadonga, and La Linea, as though this was a perfectly good time to have a pleasant conversation on the matter. Sitting there talking to them only made me more nervous, because they were purposefully trying to intimidate and terrorise me as well.'

The outcry in Colombia at Herrera's kidnapping was swift and loud. It backfired on his captors. Within a day, he was told he was free. In a later TV interview, one of the men behind the plot said: 'I'd like to take this opportunity to apologise to Mr Lucho Herrera for the very uncomfortable position that he was put in as a result of the kidnapping, particularly keeping in mind that he's a great figure of Colombian cycling; one who, instead of being harmed, should be protected.'

Herrera doesn't dwell on his kidnapping, either. Now, he says, 'I dedicate most of my time to business and on weekends I ride my bike.' He's fuller in the figure, with closely cropped dark hair rather than his glossy black mane of the mid-1980s. It's a livestock business that he runs. And he's a father to three boys.

Herrera remains understated, modest and humble; on the other hand Hector Urrego, who commented on his victory at l'Alpe d'Huez, not so much. He can recall it as though it happened yesterday. Talking about it now inspires the same passion and emotions. He slips into the present tense as he recalls Lucho's great victory, as though reliving it:

'In the last three kilometres, Herrera goes solo. Is not possible in the world of cycling, but is true! Herrera goes to the victory with the Colombian flag on his jersey! Millions in Colombia and around the world see the birth of a new champion from Colombia, South America. We're happy! We're the best in this moment!'

Classement

1 Luis Herrera, Colombia, Varta, 4 hours, 39 minutes,
   24 secs
2 Laurent Fignon, France, Renault-Elf, at 49 secs
3 Ángel Arroyo, Spain, Reynolds, at 2 minutes, 27 secs
4 Robert Millar, Great Britain, Peugeot, at 3 minutes, 5 secs
5 Rafaël Antonio Acevedo, Colombia, Varta, at 3 minutes,
   9 secs
6 Greg LeMond, USA, Renault-Elf, at 3 minutes, 30 secs

SHELLEY VERSES AND JEAN-FRANÇOIS BERNARD

Chapter 10

ANARCHY

20 July 1987. Stage Nineteen: Valréas to Villard-de-Lans 185km. Mountains

'There's a photo of me washing his face at the finish,' says Shelley Verses, 'but really I was trying to cover his face, to hide it.'

Verses was soigneur to the Toshiba team, whose leader in 1987, after the retirement of Bernard Hinault and the serious injuries suffered by Greg LeMond in a hunting accident in April, was Jean-François Bernard. 'Jeff' Bernard was twenty-five, he had won a stage in 1986 and was the great hope of French cycling, the man who might fill the void left by Hinault.

Verses was waiting for Bernard at the finish of stage nineteen in Villard-de-Lans. She was the only soigneur from the Toshiba team with an 'A' on her accreditation, the only one allowed at the Arrivée (finish). She was also Bernard's personal soigneur. It was his first day in the yellow jersey.

When Bernard finally appeared, after a dramatic, calamitous day, Verses sprinted to meet him. The photographers followed. She got to him first. 'The photographers crowded around me so hard and so fast; I was short, there was a crush, and I couldn't get the towel around his face. When I saw that he was starting to cry, I got his head down and I scooshed water on his face, so it looked like that was why his face was wet.

'We got away from there as quick as we could,' Verses continues. 'My hotel room was on the first [ground] floor. They always put the soigneurs on the first floor because we had a lot of equipment: massage tables and all. The journalists were banging on my window from the outside. They knew Jeff was on my table. Jeff was still crying. I left him on the table, pulled the bedspread off my bed, and draped it over the curtain rod so they couldn't see through the crack. And every time a tear came out of his eye, I just dabbed it.

'I told him to stay sharp as a knife. "Sharp as a knife, Jeff," that's all I said.'

*   *   *

What happens when a leader of men retires? When a mafia boss is murdered or a dictator dies?

Bernard Hinault retired, as he always said he would, on 14 November 1986, the day of his thirty-second birthday. And with that, the peloton was deprived of its *patron*. 'He was Mussolini, he was Stalin, he was Hitler, he was all of them, rolled into one,' said Verses. 'They had to ask Hinault if they wanted to stop for a piss.'

Hinault's fifth and final Tour victory came in 1985. In his final year, he was second to his team-mate Greg LeMond, but LeMond's win was on Hinault's terms. Hinault attacked relentlessly, seemingly breaking the promise he had made to help LeMond. One interpretation – Hinault's – was that Hinault made his American team-mate work for it. Another – LeMond's – was that the Badger was trying to win his sixth. Hinault said that he was 'stirring the pot', and having fun. 'I never had so much fun as I did in my final Tour.'

Not only was Hinault missing the following year but so, too, was LeMond, the victim of a freak, nearly tragic, accident in the spring. He was shot by his brother-in-law while they were out hunting turkey: his life almost ended, his career curtailed in its prime.

Yet here was the strange thing: while many complained about Hinault when he was around, they missed him when he was gone. Because the control exerted by the rider known as the Badger was also gone. Laurent Fignon, the double winner in 1983 and '84, was riding in 1987, but with his aura diminished, his authority reduced by his years out with injury. Nobody was in charge. There was a vacuum. There was anarchy. In *Hunger*, his autobiography, the Irishman Sean Kelly described the opening week of the 1987 Tour as 'like being back in the amateurs with everybody thinking they had a chance … Fignon was the only former winner in the field but he didn't have the authority of a *patron*. He was yelling to the guys at the front that they should let the lunatics go, but no one was listening.'

During one stage, Kelly told Fignon: 'If Hinault was here, this would be stopped immediately.'

'We're going to kill ourselves if we carry on like this all the way to Paris,' Fignon replied.

Kelly's fellow Irishman Stephen Roche, fresh from winning the Giro d'Italia, acknowledges that, by his absence, Hinault continued to have an influence. 'When you had Hinault, or for that matter Indurain or Armstrong, a lot of people were riding for second place. So not having him there changed the tactics. It was a very open race. We knew before the start there were about ten genuinely capable of winning: Delgado, Kelly, Fignon, Mottet, Bernard, Herrera, Alcala, Hampsten, me. All capable of winning. It made it very strategic. Tactics played a bigger part than normal.'

*   *   *

There is a stage that has come to define the 1987 Tour de France. It was deep into the third week, to the summit of La Plagne, in the Alps, when the race seemed to be slipping away from Roche. It is most famous for Phil Liggett's excited commentary at the mist-shrouded summit. 'Who is that appearing? ... That looks like Roche. It is Stephen Roche!'

But according to the main actors, this is not the stage that decided the race. Indeed, La Plagne and Roche's desperate pursuit of Pedro Delgado into the mist might never have happened – certainly it would not have had the same significance – if, a couple of days earlier, the nineteenth stage to Villard-de-Lans had not happened. And Villard-de-Lans would not have happened without the previous day's stage, a mountain time trial to the summit of Mont Ventoux. It marked the twentieth anniversary of the death of Tom Simpson, who died near the top, having collapsed due to a combination of heat and drugs. It was a 37km test: a rolling 16km to the base of the mountain, then a murderous slog up its 7.6 per cent slopes, climbing to 1,912 metres, the riders alone against the hill and the clock and another challenge of this dome-like climb, which juts out of the Provence plains: the Mistral wind.

If Simpson lying unconscious near the summit was a tragic icon of Ventoux's vicious demands in 1967, the image of Jean-François Bernard came to define its visit in 1987. One of the most stylish riders in the bunch – he sat back in the saddle, appearing to stroke the pedals with his long legs – Bernard was an absolute mess as he approached the summit. He looked as though he had been broken by the mountain. In fairness, most did. There was no way to ride it other than flat out, arriving at the top having, as Roche put it, 'left everything on the road'. Yet with Bernard, such a consummate stylist, the spectacle was most striking.

Strings of spit and snot swung from his mouth and smeared his black shorts. A yellow headband dates the image of him grinding his way up: as 1980s as *Fame*. In his colourful patch-work jersey, his shoulders were hunched, his face fixed in a painful grimace, his dark eyes screwed up, squinting at the road ahead, reduced to small dots. In the saddle, out of the saddle, he laboured his way up; it was ugly to watch yet effective, as he ate into the three minutes that separated him and Roche at the start. No sooner had Roche crossed the line at the top than Bernard appeared in the near distance. He won the time trial in one hour, 19 minutes, 44 seconds; Luis Herrera was second, over a minute and a half back. Delgado was third and Roche fifth. Bernard was in yellow for the first time in his career, with a healthy two-and-a-half-minute buffer on Roche.

This, you felt, was his destiny. All of France felt it. Bernard felt it, talking confidently and bullishly at the summit of Mont Ventoux about defending the yellow jersey over the final week. 'There are still some climbs and one more time trial to come in Dijon,' Bernard said, 'but I've just shown everybody that I'm the strongest guy in the race.'

Dark, handsome and French, he was the heir to Hinault. And yet Jean-François Bernard was not Hinault. That was apparent to Andy Hampsten, who had been a team-mate at La Vie Claire the previous year. Hampsten and Bernard were the same age, but in a French team Hampsten, an American, could feel himself being squeezed out. On the eve of the 1986 Tour, the flamboyant team owner, Bernard Tapie, had prom-ised Bernard a Porsche if he won a stage. 'What about me?' thought Hampsten. Bernard duly won a stage, and claimed his Porsche. Hampsten performed better overall, finishing fourth in Paris, but got nothing. At the end of the season he left for the American team, 7-Eleven. 'I wasn't going to stick around for what I could see was gonna become the Jean-François Bernard show.'

Shelley Verses, the American soigneur, went the other way, from 7-Eleven to Toshiba (formerly La Vie Claire). She felt

protective of Bernard because she could see the pressure on
him and that he would struggle to cope with it. 'At the start of
the Tour in Berlin, Jacques Chirac came to visit,' Verses says.
Chirac was the French prime minister. 'And Tapie, he was
president and owner of Olympique Marseille, the soccer club,
and he helicoptered in. Jeff was set to be the next Hinault, he
was the golden boy of France, and everybody wanted to be
seen with him. When Chirac arrived to have dinner with us,
French TV were there. And there was Tapie, in his beaver coat
with the big fur collar, demanding that the boys were pulled
off the massage table so they could meet Chirac. And that
night he's telling Jean-François, "When you win the Tour I'm
going to get you a ranch."

'Berlin was already very loud, very stressful for the riders,'
Verses continues. 'I had to buy sixty pairs of earplugs because
they couldn't sleep. It was crazy, it was chaotic and stressful.
And the race hadn't even started yet.'

Verses was already feeling protective of Bernard in a way
she never would have been – never would have needed
to be – with Hinault. 'He was stepping into Hinault's shoes,
but he was different,' she says. 'There was this storm around
him and he could be calm at the centre of all that, but at
the same time there was something about him. You could
see from his face, he almost looked depressed. He was
very inside himself. I told him if he was feeling nervous
or anxious that he could knock on my door at any time. If
it was half-midnight, one in the morning, whatever, he'd
come and say, "Shelley, I'm sweating," and I'd get him on
the table, rub his legs and back and he'd fall asleep. I'd wake
him up, "You're OK now, you're centred," and he'd go back
to bed.'

Before the Tour, Toshiba organised two training camps in
Provence, close to Mont Ventoux. The mountain time trial
was where the race would be decided, thought Bernard. His
strategy was to start on his time trial bike and finish on his

lighter road bike. 'He had almost like a GPS in his brain,' Verses says. 'He knew every curve and turn on that road. He knew which side of the car he wanted the mechanic to get out. He rehearsed the bike change. In his head, he had done it so many times.'

Perhaps that was why he spoke with such confidence at the summit, after winning the stage and taking the yellow jersey. Having convinced himself that Ventoux would be decisive, he didn't seem to have thought beyond it. The evening of the Ventoux stage, Roche sat in his room with Eddy Schepers, his domestique. He was stung by his defeat and by the margin of Bernard's victory. But his ears pricked up when he heard the winner's interview. 'We were all watching television after the Ventoux stage and we all saw Bernard,' Roche says. 'We heard him saying, "You saw how strong I was; how far ahead I was of everyone … And since there's one more time trial to come, I'm going to win this Tour."

'We all saw that. And I think all the favourites said to themselves, "Who does this guy think he is? Has he read the road book? Does he realise there are still seven days to go?"'

Roche had also been interviewed at the top of Ventoux. After such a humiliating defeat, some of his usual ebullience had gone; his eyes had lost their sparkle. 'The time trial Jeff rode, I thought he had a chance to win,' Roche said. 'What surprised me was the time he put into the second person. I thought the first five would be within a minute.'

Would he attack him in the mountains to come? Roche looked thoughtful. 'I think I'll wait and see how he is in the mountains. There are three hard stages to come, on Tuesday, Wednesday and Thursday. If I see he's weak on one of those days, I'll have to go for it. But Bernard is going very, very well.'

Did he still believe he could win? 'I think it's not lost.'

Interesting that, in looking ahead to what he thought would be the decisive days, Roche didn't mention Monday's

– the next day's – undulating nineteenth stage in the Isère, to Villard-de-Lans.

*   *   *

On the morning of the stage, Roche was approached by Charly Mottet, who had been in yellow until deposed by Bernard. He was a team-mate of Laurent Fignon at Système U, the team managed by one of the sport's great strategists, Cyrille Guimard. Guimard had fallen out with Hinault and viewed his former team, Toshiba, as bitter rivals. According to the American journalist Owen Mulholland, Mottet presented Roche with a plan. It owed something to Mottet's local knowledge, because he was from the area. But it had the imprint of Guimard.

'Today the feed station is in a tiny town, Léoncel,' Mottet told Roche. 'The road comes down off one hill, squeezes across a narrow bridge in the village, and starts climbing immediately. We all are taking extra food from the start so we can skip the feed and attack out of the town. If Jeff is just a little way back, he'll be held up by the riders slowing for the *musettes* [food bags]. Who knows, but it's worth a try.'

After studying the road book the previous evening, Roche knew it would be a challenging day. Certainly a difficult first day in yellow for Bernard. 'We'd all made a big effort,' says Roche, 'but Bernard, had he left a lot on the road? The bike change made a difference, but for him to put so much time into us, he must have buried himself.'

Even before his conversation with Mottet, Roche identified the feeding station as a dangerous point on the course; a place to stay alert and close to the front. Attacks in the feed zone – where for several hundred metres the soigneurs stand at the roadside, handing out *musettes* – were a breach of etiquette, but hardly unheard of, especially in the absence of a *patron* like Hinault. 'I didn't know the roads well but Eddy

Schepers was my right-hand man and very good at reading
the map. Davide Cassani [another Carrera team-mate] was
very good, too,' Roche says. 'Looking at the map, you see
that the feeding station is on a very narrow road. You see
the arrows, which mean it's a steep climb. You think, that's
a stupid place to put a feeding station, but if there's a bit of
panic in the bunch it could be a place to force a selection.
You never know ...'

Roche plays down the pre-stage conversation with Mottet.
'All the leaders had the same reaction, they made the same
deduction. That's why when we hit the feeding station all
the top riders were bunched at the front. All the leaders had
their right-hand men beside them. And if the opportunity
was there, they were going to ride their eyeballs out.'

There was a climb before Léoncel, the Col de Tourniol.
It was long but not especially steep and, on narrow, windy
roads, it stretched the peloton without threatening to cause a
major split. Then, just before the summit, Bernard punctured.
It could hardly have happened at a worse point, so close to
the top and before a fast descent. Bernard dropped down the
line, stopped, took the wheel of a team-mate, Jean-Claude
Leclercq, and chased back. He rejoined the peloton; but with
the riders snaking quickly down the descent, regaining his
place at the front was impossible.

After the descent came Léoncel and the feed zone. And as
Roche and Mottet foresaw, it became a bottleneck. Those at
the front got through, those behind bunched up and slowed
to a crawl. Bernard was still threading his way through
the peloton when he suffered an additional misfortune: he
unshipped his chain and had to stop again. Meanwhile, at
the head of the line of riders, Roche, Mottet and eleven others
took flight. The attack was launched by Mottet's team-mate,
Martial Gayant. Others were quick to follow.

Roche says he was unaware that Bernard had punctured and was stuck behind. 'We didn't have radios in those

days.' But he adds: 'Those of us at the front immediately saw that he wasn't with us. He was the only top guy who missed the move.'

Bernard was isolated, with team-mates such as Leclercq behind and three others several minutes ahead. Steve Bauer, Dominique Garde and Heinz Imboden, all Toshiba team-mates, were up the road in the break that had formed earlier in the stage. This now looked like a mistake by the French team. Roche believes Bernard's men 'overdid it. Every time there was an attack, a Toshiba rider was in it.'

Before the Col de Tourniol, Roche even joked with Bernard: 'Jeff, you'll soon have more riders up the road than you do back here.'

'Don't worry,' Bernard replied. 'I'll be OK.'

As well as Roche and Mottet, the front group included Delgado, Luis Herrera, Marino Lejarreta and Fignon. 'You might say, well how come all those top riders found themselves in the front?' Roche says. 'I say, imagine all these top riders at the front and riding together, with no hesitation, fully committed; not thinking or worrying about the next climb, just rolling through.' There was full commitment and co-operation, in other words. They were united in their determination to eliminate the man they had identified – and who had identified himself – as the favourite. Bernard's words from the previous evening were haunting him now.

Roche confirms as much: 'Everyone was riding on the front. Generally you might get a rider who knows he's going to get dropped on the final climb and doesn't come through, or some who are bluffing a bit, saving themselves for later. But on that day, the amazing thing was, everybody was riding, *everybody*. I think it was because they were all so eager to show Bernard that the Tour wasn't over.'

Panicking, Bernard's directeur sportif, Paul Köchli, raced up to the break to instruct the three Toshiba riders to sit up, wait, and help Bernard with the chase. There were 50

kilometres to go and Bauer, when he was reunited with
Bernard, did a lot of work. Bernard, too, did long turns at the
front. He was able to maintain the gap at around a minute
but, against the combined might of the thirteen men, as they
raced through the Vercors forest and another climb, the Col
de Lachau, it was hopeless.

Hampsten was one of the riders stranded in the second
group with Bernard. 'I'd had a terrible day the day before and
wasn't sure about my condition. I was right there at the front
in the feed zone, but I couldn't go with the break. I remember going through the feed, looking up and seeing Roche and
Mottet attack, and thinking, if that goes, the race is done.
I ended up in a tiny chase group with Jean-François. He asked
me to help. I told him: "If I'd been strong, I'd have been with
the break!" Jean-François was pretty disappointed. He was
trying hard to get people to help him. But those were bumpy,
lumpy roads. I remember thinking, this would be a good road
to be away on ...'

It was the biggest test of Bernard's qualities as a leader.
Mont Ventoux had been a test of physical ability. But in some
ways that was the easy part. 'I remember seeing Jean-François
act like a leader, and be very charismatic at the dinner table,'
Hampsten says. 'But I'd say he was a long way from [being] a
leader on the road.

'He had been studying Hinault, and the French press were
all saying he would be his successor. But he never showed
himself tactically or psychologically to be very strong. He was
a nice guy, but very nervous.'

Up ahead, on the Côte de Chalimont, another long, draggy
climb that they tackled before dropping into Villard-de-Lans,
Roche and Delgado broke away from the leading group. Roche
had a well-deserved reputation as a shrewd, calculating rider. He needed all his bluffing skills now as Delgado, a strong
climber, attacked and he followed him. 'I was cooked,' Roche
says. Like everyone, he had been riding hard for the last hour.

'There's a very good photo of me and Delgado climbing side by side [on the Côte de Chalimont], me level with his bottom bracket as if we were welded together.

'I was stuffed. But if I'd sat behind him, on his wheel, he'd have seen me struggling. Because I was level with his bottom bracket, and seemed to be pushing on, he thought I was comfortable. But I was cooked.'

Delgado tried some small attacks but Roche stayed with him. In Villard-de-Lans, Delgado won the stage. Bernard, who cut an increasingly forlorn and desperate figure as he led the chase group, was over four minutes down when he crossed the line and rode tearfully into the arms of his soigneur, Shelley Verses.

While Bernard dropped to fourth overall, Roche took yellow. Delgado claimed the overall lead the next day, only for Roche to win it back the day before Paris in the time trial that Bernard had been banking on – and which he did win. There had been three days in the Alps after stage nineteen and they saw a thrilling duel play out between Delgado and Roche. Yet as Roche says, 'Villard-de-Lans was the crucial day. That was the day I won the Tour.'

In Paris, Bernard was third overall behind Roche and Delgado. Roche's victory in this most open and anarchic of Tours owed much to his outstanding form in the year he also won the Giro and world title, but also something to his tactical awareness and cunning. He has some sympathy for the man who stood below him on the podium: 'Bernard was OK. I liked the guy. He has a great mind for cycling now.

'But I think he didn't learn from his lesson. Even today he says, "If I hadn't punctured or dropped my chain, I would have won the Tour, because I won the final time trial." What he forgets is that on the climbs, on all the other stages after Villard-de-Lans, he was dropped. He got back on again, but why? Because he wasn't a threat. If he had been we'd have kept going. If he'd been in yellow, he wouldn't have got back

on. He won't acknowledge that. He still believes he would
have won in 1987.'

*   *   *

Although he was only twenty-five in 1987, third was as close
as Bernard ever came to winning the Tour. Nor would he
ever wear the yellow jersey after that one stage to Villard-
de-Lans. The following year, he crashed in a badly lit tunnel
during the Giro d'Italia and injured his back. The year after
he developed fibrosis in his knee and was out for months.
The next year, a saddle sore forced him out of the Tour de
France. The year after that, 1991, he joined Banesto, the
Spanish team with two leaders, the fading Delgado and
emerging Miguel Indurain. Bernard was under no illusions:
the one-time great white hope of French cycling was going
to work for two Spaniards. By 1993, having settled into the
role of super-domestique for Indurain, he told *L'Equipe*: 'I'll
never be a leader. I can't be someone that you can count on
one hundred per cent, and if you ask that of me I lose half
my power.'

Shelley Verses wonders if he ever got over the disappointment of losing his yellow jersey on the road to Villard-de-Lans.
It wasn't just the loss of the lead and his dream of winning
the Tour, but the circumstances: the sense he had been the
victim of an ambush. He could never acquire a Hinault-
like aura after that. 'A part of him didn't recover from what
happened at Villard-de-Lans,' Verses says, 'a part of him
dimmed. I've never seen it done to anyone else, that kinda
ganging up. The pressure on him was so intense. The country
couldn't handle the gap of losing Hinault. They needed it to
be Jeff. It couldn't be Fignon. And they put so much on this
quiet, gifted guy.'

These days, Bernard works as an analyst for French TV
and at the Tour de France cuts a relaxed figure, usually in

youthful garb of black T-shirt, jeans and trainers, with a ciga-rette between his fingers. If he looks back with any regret on his career, it doesn't show. 'I was left alone too quickly,' he told me when I spoke to him at the 2010 Tour. He was reflective and rueful rather than bitter. 'I wanted to become the new Hinault and if he had kept going another year with me then, I don't know, maybe … I had the potential, the motor, but I needed more. There are other things than physical potential. Cycling is like that: there are ten champions with the physical capacity, who are at the same level, with the same legs, but what makes the difference is the head.

'I was left on my own a bit too quickly. Like a bird in a nest, if you try to fly too early, you fall.'

Classement

1 Pedro Delgado, Spain, PDM, 4 hours, 53 minutes, 34 secs
2 Stephen Roche, Ireland, Carrera, at 3 secs
3 Marino Lajaretta, Spain, Caja Rural, at 31 secs
4 Anselmo Fuerte, Spain, BH, same time
5 Charly Mottet, France, Système U, s.t.
6 Luis Herrera, Colombia, Café de Colombia, at 1 minute,
   6 secs

CLAUDIO CHIAPPUCCI

Chapter 11

THE DEVIL

18 July 1992. Stage Thirteen: Saint-Gervais to Sestriere 254.5km. High mountains

Casa Chiappucci is a three-storey building on the edge of a small village in northern Italy, near Lake Como. Three storeys, three buzzers, all labelled 'Chiappucci'. But it would appear that Claudio, the dazzling little climber of the 1990s, is not at home. A man appears on the balcony of the first floor, introducing himself as Claudio's older brother. He says he doesn't know where Claudio is. He adds that he never knows where Claudio is.

'You can wait,' he says. 'He'll be back soon.'

Ten minutes later, the electronic gate clicks and whirrs and begins to slide open. Instantly recognisable, the cyclist once known as 'El Diablo' (the devil) appears behind the wheel of an SUV with a twenty-something girl in the passenger seat. He is fifty but looks and dresses about thirty years younger: distressed jeans, tight black shirt, chunky white watch and sunglasses perched on his head, acting as a hairband for his glossy black mane.

'Ciao, ciao, ciao,' a smiling Claudio leads us into the building then bounds up three flights of stairs. At the top, we are greeted by Mama Chiappucci, a small, hunched woman in her late seventies wrapped in an apron. She offers a warm welcome, and shows us into the living room, or shrine. Everywhere you look there are trophies, trinkets and photographs of Claudio riding and winning races, as well as one of him meeting the Pope. There is no escape: on the sofa, the cushions are adorned with his image. Which is ironic, because Claudio himself has disappeared again.

When he reappears, he explains that he has been checking on his new girlfriend, who is in his apartment, on the ground floor. 'She's twenty-five, from Lille.' Chiappucci picks up one of the cushions: the picture on this one shows the happy couple. 'When you feel like this with someone' – he pats his chest – 'the age doesn't matter.'

Sitting down on his own face (on another cushion), Chiappucci explains that he's just back from riding a Gran Fondo held in honour of ... himself. 'I finished fifth. I'm still riding well. The rest were amateurs, but it was a good level. I'm fifty, so to finish with guys who are twenty or twenty-five years old ...'

But we're not here to talk about that. We're here to talk about Sestriere in 1992 and one of the most extraordinary, almost unbelievable, performances in Tour history.

*   *   *

Chiappucci turned professional in 1985 and for five years seemed destined to be a journeyman. It took him four years to win his first race. Then in 1990 he featured in a bizarre breakaway on day one of the Tour de France: bizarre because it gained ten minutes. The yellow jersey passed between three of the four riders who had been in the break, but Chiappucci was, to everyone's surprise, the last to wear it and the most reluctant to give it up. For three weeks Greg LeMond chipped away at his lead but Chiappucci, at the relatively late age of twenty-seven, was a man transformed, who, even while in yellow, attacked LeMond in the mountains. It took LeMond until one day before Paris, and a time trial, to finally wrest the yellow jersey from the little Italian's shoulders. LeMond regarded Chiappucci as a pest, dubbing him 'Cappuccino'.

But for Chiappucci, who finished second, it was only the start. The 1990 Tour made him a star, a celebrity. He was busy that winter: 'Anybody who invited me, I showed up' – to schools, dinners, old folks' homes, orphanages.

The following year, he won Milan–San Remo after a long, lone breakaway, then he finished second in the Giro and third in the Tour, where he was crowned King of the Mountains. Against the steady, stoic, unflashy Miguel Indurain, Chiappucci was everything the Spaniard was not: unpredictable, aggressive, exciting; he was El Diablo, who so fully embraced his nickname that he rode time trials with a cartoon devil on his helmet. He acquired the name in South America. 'I raced there at the start of my career and I'd always attack. They started calling me El Diablo because of it. For them, it was strange to see a European racing that way. When I returned home, I told the story, that they called me the devil, and the name started to stick. Even today, it's incredible, I get people calling me Diablo instead of Claudio.'

He doesn't exactly discourage that. There are devils – sketches and figurines – everywhere in Casa Chiappucci – even a devil-shaped telephone. You wonder if there was a knowingness in his embrace of the 'diablo' moniker, given what we now know about this era of cycling, and especially Italian cycling. But, no. Chiappucci simply liked being the protagonist. He saw himself as a benign and popular devil; a showman and source of mischief. 'I thought that it was better to have personality and style than a long palmarès. I wanted to be different.

'I had tactics,' Chiappucci continues, 'but not the same tactics as everyone else. The majority think there is only one tactic. Who said it has to be that way? You can race a million different ways. I knew my rivals' tactics, and I'd go and destroy their plans. They think the race could only be raced in one way, like today when everyone just rides to the last climb and the race is made there.' Chiappucci's approach was popular with the fans but also necessary against a steamroller of an opponent like Indurain. When taking on the Spaniard, it was clear that a more imaginative approach was needed.

Approaching the 1992 Tour, there was one stage that stood out for Chiappucci: Saint-Gervais to Sestriere. It was brutally mountainous and, at 254km, hideously long. It was a stage that would reward the strong and the brave. It also visited Italy, ending with a summit finish at Sestriere, a climb synonymous with an Italian cyclist whose name was shorthand for panache: Fausto Coppi. Coppi won at Sestriere in 1952; now the Tour was preparing to visit on the fortieth anniversary.

There was a Chiappucci–Coppi family connection. 'My dad and Coppi were in the war together in Africa and my dad would speak with me about that,' Claudio says. Arduino was his father: he and Coppi were prisoners of war in Ethiopia. 'But,' Claudio adds, 'I was closer to [Gino] Bartali.' Bartali was Coppi's frequently bitter rival in the 1940s and '50s. 'Bartali was still alive in my time, and he was Tuscan, like my family.'

In a PoW camp, Chiappucci's father gave up some of his food allowance for Coppi, to help the *Campionissimo* stay fit and healthy (though Coppi looked painfully thin, even in prime fitness). But that was the extent of their relationship, says Claudio. 'My dad and Coppi never saw each other after the war.' Arduino talked about Coppi to young Claudio, though. And his first racing bike, bought by his father when he was fourteen, was a Bianchi, as ridden by Coppi. Sadly, Arduino died in 1985, just as his son was turning professional. He never saw Claudio's metamorphosis into *Campione*, if not *Campionissimo*.

After finishing second in the 1992 Giro (again to Indurain), Chiappucci began to prepare for the Tour. And in particular for Sestriere. 'I've always studied stages in advance,' he says. 'Many things can change: the weather, your rivals, a crash, a mechanical, a team attacking. However, beforehand, I try to have an idea of what I want to do. That stage to Sestriere, I prepared for months in advance. I wanted to do something, I wanted to confirm what I had done at the Tour in 1990 and 1991. That would be a confirmation, a Tour de France stage in Italy. I wanted to win that stage.'

After the Giro, in the company of two Carrera domestiques, Mario Chiesa and Fabio Roscioli, as well as his 'favourite' directeur sportif, Sandro Quintarelli, Chiappucci went to ride the route. The recce has become commonplace, but it wasn't in 1992 (not least because the riders raced so much; Chiappucci points out that in 1991 he raced 143 days, more than any other rider). Indurain also attempted to recce the stage to Sestriere, but was denied by snow blocking the third of the five climbs on the route, the Col d'Iseran.

Chiappucci and his team-mates' ride was a reconnaissance mission with a difference. The stage was so long that they decided to do it over two days, staying overnight in Megève, the small and exclusive ski town close to Mont Blanc and the Italian border. Riding the stage over the two days, Chiappucci was flying; he reckoned he had never felt so strong. 'In training, I was doing more *gregario* [domestique] work for Chiesa and Roscioli than they were for me,' he recalls. 'They weren't able to stay with me.'

*   *   *

The day, 18 July 1992, dawned clear and sunny, especially at the summit of the ski station at Sestriere. 'A tranquil haven under a piercing blue sky with air that could bring back the dead,' wrote the doyen of Italian journalists, Gianni Mura, in *La Repubblica*. 'This is Sestriere.'

This stage, with its five climbs, was a 'Death March', according to some. Unusually, it was also, almost two weeks into the Tour, the first major mountain stage. In honour of the Maastricht Treaty, this was a Tour of the European Community: it started in San Sebastián, Spain, then all but missed out the Pyrenees before visiting Belgium, Holland, Luxembourg, Germany, and now Italy. It had witnessed some extraordinary stages, not least Indurain bludgeoning the field in the 65km stage nine time trial, where he won by three minutes, a margin so enormous that it teetered on the edge of improbability. There were other notable days: Gilles Delion, always an outsider (who a few years later would make a premature exit from the sport after complaining that the use of EPO was rampant), winning a thrilling stage seven into Valkenburg; Laurent Fignon, humiliated by Indurain in the Luxembourg time trial, raging against the dying of the light with a solo victory in Mulhouse.

Chiappucci, who finished five minutes behind Indurain in Luxembourg, was determined to prove that the 1992 Tour was not the Indurain show. But what could he do? Beat him to Paris? Perhaps not. Indurain seemed unbeatable. Make life difficult? Light some fires? He had nothing to lose.

Sestriere was the day. Chiappucci and the other climbers had waited so long for the high mountains that they were itching to go. But Claudio, in particular, had big plans. Not that you would have guessed from his horseplay in Saint-Gervais, when he travelled to the sign-on stage on the back of a team-mate's bike. He explains that such stunts, which were always part of his act, could be misleading. 'I was very tense ahead of the stage,' Chiappucci insists. 'I was concentrated, more than for any of the other stages, because I was prepared, I held it dear to me. I was heading into Italy and I knew there'd be so many fans waiting. I was worried about messing up.'

Chiappucci was interviewed by French TV as he was getting ready, perched on the bonnet of a team car, fastening the velcro straps on his shoes. 'Today, I want to do something good,' he tells them. 'I feel great.'

He is asked if he will attack from the start. He shrugs. 'I hope the race will be hard.'

Is he scared, or worried the race will be fast? 'I prefer a fast race. For me it's easier when there aren't many left.'

The stage began to climb immediately, with the category-two Col des Saisies. After 14km, Chiappucci attacked. At the top, he sprinted for King of the Mountains points – he was already in the polka-dot jersey. The impression was that Claudio was restless and impatient. Soon he was accelerating again, this time at the foot of the category-one Cormet de Roselend, 50km into the stage. Nine riders went with him, including a young Frenchman, Richard Virenque, and the veteran Irishman, Sean Kelly. They had two minutes at the summit, with Sean Yates, the peloton's most fearless descender, joining on the way down. But the climbing was relentless. Soon they hit the third climb, the Col d'Iseran, 37km long, soaring to more than 2,770 metres: the highest pass in the Alps.

Chiappucci tackled the Iseran as though the finish was at the summit: hands on top of the bars, face contorted with the effort, legs churning. Only Virenque could stay with him. Then he was gone, too. After repeated efforts to close a gap that kept opening, Virenque's head dropped; then he was gone. Chiappucci was oblivious: on he climbed, past huge snowdrifts, to the icy summit. By the top, Virenque was two minutes down. Further back, Indurain was in the main group, whittled down to just thirty-five riders, and three minutes, 45 seconds in arrears. There was carnage, with one of the big losers LeMond, who had been dropped and was almost

20 minutes down at the summit. Now Chiappucci was on his own; there were still over 100km left of the stage.

He couldn't maintain this, could he? It was so improbable, or impossible, that journalists in the press room crowded around the television monitors, urging him on. 'It was a brave act, to the point of insanity,' wrote Mura later. 'But it's nice to be so crazy, and to hell with the calculations and tactics! After all, is it or is it not El Diablo? So who better than him?'

Chiappucci says now that his attack was an 'accident'. 'I found myself ahead on the second climb. At first, I didn't realise it. Those behind didn't realise that I was up front, and those up front didn't realise right away that I was there with them. In that time, the advantage grew as we were starting the Roselend.

'Virenque was there, but didn't want to work because [his RMO team-mate] Pascal Lino was in yellow. At first everyone wanted to work, but then nobody. So I had to lift the pace to form a smaller group to see who could help. Also, I heard that Banesto [Indurain's team] and Bugno's team [Gatorade] were working. The fact that Bugno and his men were working upset me a bit ...' Bugno, the world champion, was a fellow Italian. 'I had to lift the pace on the climbs to see what happened,' Chiappucci continues. 'Behind, they kept pulling, but it was getting strung out. Virenque was the last on my wheel. Before the Iseran, I asked him if he wanted to help. I told him Lino was going to lose the yellow jersey that day anyway. He said, "No, no, I can't, Lino is still in yellow." So I lifted the pace.' And he got rid of Virenque. 'I preferred to be on my own.'

It meant losing some of the advantages of being in a group, mainly the shelter from sitting on others' wheels. But there were advantages, says Chiappucci. 'When you're in a group, you can't think about how to manage the effort because you have to battle and attack with the others. It was better to be alone to manage myself the way I wanted to, not to suffer or be forced to follow the others' attacks.

'On the descent of the Iseran, I gained more time. I wanted to see how they reacted behind, if I'd pull out the GC favourites, but nothing happened. So I continued on my way to Cenisio [Mont Cenis]; and on that climb the advantage stayed at three to four minutes. But still I kept thinking they would come.'

For Chiappucci, 'this was not how I imagined it' – riding at or near the front for over 200km, having been on the attack from 14km. 'I remembered the road, what I had done in training, but it was not the same, it was another story. That day in training, I was going well because I saw my team-mates couldn't stay with me. But here ...' Here he was alone, riding on feel, unsure whether he would pay for his efforts on the final climb. He knew enough from the recce to realise that a major test lay ahead: not the climb to Sestriere but in the Susa Valley, before the mountain, where the road climbed deceptively, and the wind swirled mercilessly.

In the valley, 'I managed my effort by not going above myself, by watching my heart rate.' It is a little surprising to learn that this instinctive, impetuous rider did not do everything on instinct and 'feel'; that he was an early adopter of heart rate monitors, a Polar model with chest strap and handlebar-mounted computer. 'I had one of the first Polars and I watched my heart rate in the valley. When I saw it going too high, I eased up. I never went at my maximum. It seems strange, but I always went at my maximum on the descents, where it was easier for me and where I could gain more on my rivals.'

His heart rate in the valley, says Chiappucci, was below the red line: '160, 170 – 180 maximum. I always had a low heart rate, never up to 200. In the valley, if it started to rise, I backed off.'

Quintarelli offered a slightly different version of events afterwards, saying that Chiappucci had repeatedly asked him for reassurance. 'The times! The times!' Chiappucci implored.

'You're killing him!' Quintarelli told him. 'You're slaughtering Indurain!'

Like a lion waking from a long sleep, and feeling pangs of hunger, Indurain was beginning to stir. When he forced the pace, the chasing group reduced to four: Bugno, Andy Hampsten, Franco Vona, as well as Indurain himself. Up ahead, Chiappucci was suffering. 'I thought in the Valle di Susa that they'd come up to me. I gained time on the descents but in the valleys that [time] was important, because I thought, on the straight roads, they'd be able to see me and come and get me. But they weren't gaining on me, though at one point I had only a minute. That was hard, that was a crisis moment for me. I was thinking, what are they doing? Are they going to come and get me or what?'

From the following car, Quintarelli was 'telling me to hold tight, not to give up. But I was cracking, practically in tears. It was very hot, I couldn't eat any more, just drink. I got rid of my helmet, it was so hot. I was afraid that on Sestriere I'd fall apart, after all I had done ... The closer I got, the more tense I became.

'I thought, if they catch me on the climb, it's going to be bad.'

                    *   *   *

Half of Italy had made a pilgrimage to Sestriere, or so it seemed. The *tifosi*, keen to celebrate the exploits of Chiappucci and Bugno as they had once rejoiced in those of Coppi and Bartali, were packed so deep towards the top that the road disappeared. Assuming he made it that far, it would be Claudio's greatest challenge: threading his way through.

It was almost a shrine to Italian cycling, Sestriere having first featured in the Giro d'Italia in 1911. It was introduced after the Tour de France visited the Pyrenees the previous year; if the French could climb 2,000-metre mountains, so could the Italians. There were three ways up the mountain, two from the west, one from the east. The Tour had only approached from the west, Coppi climbing from Montgenèvre in '52. Forty years later, Chiappucci would approach from Oulx, but the two routes – the Coppi route and the Chiappucci route – merge in Cesana Torinese. Then the road curls up in hairpins, rising out of the valley, into the rarefied mountain air, surrounded by 3,000-metre peaks. Monte Fraiteve stands to one side, Monte Sises to the other. On it goes for 11km, climbing to 2,033 metres.

The crowd, hundreds of thousands strong, mainly Italians, are waiting for Chiappucci and for their world champion and world No.1, Bugno. They know Claudio has been out in front for 200km, that he has embarked on a crazy adventure, a move that defies logic and commonsense, but, with transistor radios pressed to ears, they follow his progress through the valley, scarcely believing that he is holding off a group led by the great Indurain. It's a David vs Goliath encounter, with the added tension for the *tifosi* of David being Italian. The heat is stifling and the atmosphere on the mountain frenzied. They know Chiappucci's lead has tumbled in the valley, falling from five minutes to barely one.

Chiappucci began climbing and 'at the start I saw the 10km to go sign, and thought: this is going to be my hardest 10k ever. At that point, I just didn't know how I'd manage the climb, how I'd face it. I tried to stay calm. I lost some time in the first part. But I knew there was a slight false flat in the first part of the climb.'

Working his way up, Chiappucci is accompanied by one, sometimes two, sometimes three bare-topped *tifosi*, running alongside, pouring water on his head, offering a brief push then skipping out of the way of the following motorbikes. Behind, Indurain and Bugno steadily advance, eating into his lead. In contrast, Chiappucci is punchy, his body rocking with the effort of pushing the pedals. He is stocky, too: 'He always had very heavy muscles,' as Stephen Roche says of Chiappucci. 'He was built like the trunk of a tree.'

Indurain and Bugno are rejoined by Hampsten and Vona, who instantly attacks. Bugno slides off the back. So steady is the world champion, his upper body rock solid, that it is hard to tell how tired Bugno is. But he is cooked. Hampsten is next. Now Indurain is alone, tapping out his infernal rhythm – always in the saddle. He grimaces slightly beneath his cap and behind his sunglasses, while up ahead Chiappucci's sweat-dampened black hair frames his impish face. He is also grimacing, but while Indurain seems impassive (wearing 'a look of unemotional determination', in Sam Abt's description), it appears as though Chiappucci is grinning from ear to ear.

And riding not through the crowds, but *into* them. He bounces off them, like a dodgem car, weaving left and right. It means Chiappucci is part of the crowd, too. There's an electric connection between them: you can see it. They respond in a way they don't to Indurain. They are cool towards him and hostile towards the struggling Bugno, who is booed and whistled.

Then, just ahead of Chiappucci, the flotilla of motorbikes – TV, press photographers, police, officials – becomes clogged up. They can't get through the crowds. Horns are blasted, engines revved, but it's no good. 'I was nearly at a standstill,' Chiappucci recalls. In front of him, a cacophany of noise and the stench of toxic exhaust fumes; a maelstrom that mocks Mura's poetic description of Sestriere as a tranquil haven.

There is nowhere for him to go other than to try and squeeze past the motorbikes, overtaking the convoy that was supposed to clear the way. With a bit of quick thinking and improvisation this is what Chiappucci does, sitting up, shouting and waving his arm to clear the road. Then he presses on. 'On the one hand, it bugged me,' Chiappucci says of the moment he almost came to a stop. 'But on the other, it gave me a lot of motivation and strength. At that moment, I regained energy. If the road was empty, I would've just cracked, but instead I took on their energy. I felt they wanted something, and they contributed a lot. I think they understood my undertaking.'

Chiappucci continues his monologue, his mythologising of his great exploit: 'This was an escape in the Tour where my rivals didn't give me any favours. I wasn't let loose like an unknown domestique' – like 1990, in other words. 'They knew who I was and that they couldn't give me space because it'd be difficult to catch me. They thought that I wouldn't be able to make it. They thought that I'd crack.

'But,' Chiappucci adds, 'my legs and the fans were my salvation.'

With 5km to the summit, before he escaped his cocoon and overtook the motorbikes, Chiappucci led by one minute, 25 seconds. Behind, Indurain was revving his engine. Now he would surely haul him back. Everybody thought so. Chiappucci had been riding like this – hard, recklessly, but without fear – for 200km and more than seven hours. With 3km to go, his lead over Indurain was 57 seconds. That was well within Indurain's range.

Chiappucci knew Indurain was closing. 'I thought, oh boy, here he comes. In those last 2km, I risked losing everything that'd I'd done in the 250km before. I touched bottom. I probably wasn't feeling anything, just the fans that were all over me; the whole time, a loud roar, but it gave me a lot of encouragement. I thought, no, Indurain can't come and get me.' He had no way of knowing exactly how close Indurain was. 'We didn't have ear-pieces then, so it was *ciclismo naturale*, based on instincts. My DS was yelling that I was losing time. But I couldn't hear what he was saying. I thought he said the gap came down to 30 seconds …'

One big effort and Indurain would gobble Chiappucci up. Then the impossible: the strain began to tell on Indurain. His shoulders gently rocked, the suppleness went from his legs, the grimace became a frown. He was caught and passed by Vona. Now, as Chiappucci headed into the relative tranquillity of the final 500 metres, where barriers kept the fans at bay, his lead began to increase again. 'I thought, if Indurain caught me, I was faster, maybe I could out-sprint him? Then he cracked! And I took more time.'

In the final metres, Chiappucci raised one arm, though the effort looked as though it might cause him to topple over. Then, just before the line, he managed to lift both arms before wobbling across the line, where his mother was waiting. As he was mobbed by reporters, Renata Chiappucci screamed: 'Let him through, let him through, he's my son!'

Somehow she found him, or Chiappucci found her. She cradled his head in her arms. It was Renata, not Claudio, who gave the first interview: 'I was sure that they wouldn't catch him. Everyone kept telling me: "Stay calm, *signora*, stay calm! This is how Coppi won forty years ago."

'Now I'm calm,' she added, 'now I'm calm.'

Chiappucci lifted his head and addressed her: 'Mamma, off you go and rest now.'

*   *   *

When he could speak, Chiappucci told reporters: 'When I heard that Indurain had dropped Bugno and was chasing me – him, Miguel, chasing me – I felt twice the size, like three Chiappuccis in one, a cooperative of Chiappuccis!'

Vona made it an Italian one-two, 1:34 down on Chiappucci, with Indurain third, another nine seconds later. 'I finished this stage very tired,' said Indurain. 'The hard course, the rhythm of the race and the heat exhausted me.' Indurain usually finished stages looking barely out of breath. Not today. 'It's the only day that I ever saw Indurain have trouble climbing the stairs in the hotel,' said his team-mate, Jean-François Bernard.

Behind Chiappucci, there was devastation. The crowds, high on Chiappucci's epic victory, did not calm down after he had passed. 'I remember asking Jean-François Pescheux, who was in the lead car, to do something about the crowds, to try and open up the roads,' said Laurent Fignon. 'It was the first time I ever saw anything like it. They scared me. Perhaps it was Chiappucci's exploit that made them like that.'

'When people ask me what was the hardest day on my bike, I say Sestriere,' said Stephen Roche, Chiappucci's Carrera team-mate. 'I've never been so exhausted. I spent 150km in the *gruppetto*. I'll never forget Gilbert Duclos-Lassalle's face. He said to me, "I can't see the 20km to go sign – where is it?" I dared not tell him that we still had 70km to do.'

Most poignant of all was the fate of LeMond, who hadn't even started climbing to Sestriere when Chiappucci was reaching the summit with his arms in the air. The three-time Tour winner was one of eighteen riders to finish outside the time limit; he was 130th, almost fifty minutes down. Did Chiappucci, once dubbed 'Cappuccino' by LeMond, enjoy that? 'I was already finished with him. After the 1990 Tour, he just didn't exist in my book. But it gave me a bit of pleasure to force him out. Yeah.'

He wasn't particularly enamoured with Bugno after Sestriere, either. Now he says: 'He gave Indurain a hand to chase. Indurain was on his own after Cenisio, but then they brought him back into the race. Why? I don't know, I've always wondered that. Maybe because I was Italian as well; maybe he thought, "It'd be better if a foreigner, a Spaniard, wins in Sestriere – at least that way he won't take any of my fame." I don't know. People were very upset with him. We never really had a chance to speak about it. For a long time we weren't talking, but now we hear from each other quite often. However, we have never talked about that day.'

Bugno's comments, immediately after the stage, sounded an oddly discordant note: 'Chiappucci's break is great but hard to believe in,' he said.

Gradually Chiappucci's ride, and its implications, were digested. In the short term, he was up to second overall in the 1992 Tour, behind Indurain. But the significance went beyond that. 'I didn't think it was possible to do such things in modern cycling,' said Felice Gimondi, the last Italian winner of the Tour, in 1965. 'It deserves to go down in the history of the Tour and of cycling.'

And yet against Indurain it was not enough. The Spaniard won in Paris, for the second of his five consecutive victories, while Chiappucci held on to second. But for Gianni Mura, writing in *La Repubblica*, 'Indurain is the winner but Chiappucci is the hero of the Tour ... the rider who lit up the race.' He had previously considered Chiappucci a glorious loser, another Raymond Poulidor, the so-called Eternal Second of the 1960s and '70s. 'Now I take off my hat and bow,' wrote Mura. 'What Chiappucci did on the stage to Sestriere is at the limits of credibility [and] is one of the greatest feats in cycling.' Little Claudio left the Tour 'enlarged by it'.

*   *   *

He had won stage nineteen, but Chiappucci looks reflective now: 'If there was one or two kilometres more, I could've won the Tour ...'

Typical Claudio, getting carried away. Always wanting more. Was the stage win, achieved in such extraordinary fashion, after seven hours, 44 minutes and 51 seconds in the saddle, mostly alone, not enough?

He springs out of the sofa, heads for one of his mother's cabinets and opens a drawer. 'Here, look at this photo,' he says. 'A fan took it from behind, as I'm crossing the line.' There he is, arms in the air, the vivid red polka-dots of his jersey standing out against the bright blue sky. 'It's beautiful, this shot. Not even taken by a professional.'

Not that you would know it now, in meeting the effervescent Chiappucci, but El Diablo's career ended ignominiously. In 1997, he twice failed the UCI's new 'health check', designed to control the scourge of EPO-abuse in the absence of a test for the drug.

The exact date at which EPO, which gave the body a magical infusion of oxygen-carrying red blood cells, entered the peloton is not clear, but most put it at some point in the early 1990s, and, if they were to identify a country of origin, it would be Italy.

By the mid-1990s it was ubiquitous. But in the absence of a test the authorities were powerless. The 'health check' was a compromise: if a blood test revealed a rider's haematocrit (red blood cell count) to be over 50%, he was forced to take two weeks off racing. It wasn't a doping ban, but a high haematocrit was prima facie evidence of EPO use. Chiappucci was one of the first to fail, initially at the 1997 Tour of Romandie in May, forcing him to miss the Giro, then again on the eve of the world championships. The test was, he said at the time, 'a scandal. I lost half my season because of that. The mentality of the sport has changed.'

Others have claimed that 18 July 1992 was the day the sport changed. A decade after Chiappucci's win at Sestriere, the French magazine *Velo* looked back on 'a day of madness', with Chiappucci cast as 'the bionic man'. 'Ten years later, what is the legacy of this day?' asked the magazine. 'Did it announce a new era, polluted by a miracle drug? Did it symbolise the start of the EPO years?'

'Sestriere symbolised the arrival of the heavy artillery,' was the coded verdict of one of Indurain's team-mates, Jean-François Bernard. 'A donkey will never be a racehorse,' said Roche. 'If you accuse Chiappucci, you doubt all the achievements of cyclists and athletes in general.' Fignon made

the point to *Velo* that Chiappucci's was not the only exceptional performance: 'Why not ask about the time trial in
Luxembourg, where Indurain takes three minutes out of the
second-placed rider, nearly four minutes out of Bugno, and
six minutes out of me? Nineteen-ninety-two was probably the
first year where we see lots of suspicious things and we get
clear confirmation in 1993. I will not say that I stopped only
because of this [Fignon retired at the end of the 1993 season].
I was finished. But riders who were not as good as me were
climbing much better than me. I regularly lost four or five
minutes despite riding well … I was becoming just another
rider in the peloton.'

In 1997, Chiappucci told an Italian prosecutor, Vincenzo
Scolastico, that he had used EPO since 1993, the year after
Sestriere. But later he retracted his statement.

Chiappucci was certainly part of what was described, at the
time, as an Italian renaissance, when their riders dominated
classics and the podiums of Grand Tours – only the presence
of Indurain prevented them hogging the top step. It was a
remarkable resurgence, one that coincided with the increasing prominence of Italian medics such as Professor Francesco
Conconi and Doctor Michele Ferrari, whose methods are now
well understood.

How did Chiappucci do it? How could he ride so hard, so
long, over five mountains, and hold off Indurain? 'Passion,
stubbornness, suffering and willpower. That is how I won on
Sestriere,' he says.

In 2012 Chiappucci was invited back to the mountain to
mark the twentieth anniversary of his defining achievement. With other cyclists, he rode from Cesana Torinese up
to Sestriere. 'It was a good party, we talked, and they gave me
a beautiful wood trophy – you want to take a photograph?'

The trophy is in Chiappucci's own apartment, so he leads
us back down the stairs. 'Time passes quickly,' says Claudio.
'I realised in my career, if I want to be different, I've got to do

it this way. Attack, cause trouble. And let me tell you, it's a lot more tiring. That's normal, otherwise everyone would be doing the same thing. I had the head for it, however. From the outside it looked like chaos, but it was planned.

'Okay, I could have just stayed and played the game and won many more races,' he adds. 'I would have won a hundred and fifty to two hundred races. There are many riders who've won that many races, but they lack character.

'I won eighty races; maybe I could have won more, but my victories have more value. And the people remember the way I won races, not the number of races won. The way you win. That's what's important.'

Classement

1 Claudio Chiappucci, Italy, Carrera, 7 hours, 44 minutes, 51 secs
2 Franco Vona, Italy, at 1 minute, 34 secs
3 Miguel Indurain, Spain, Banesto, at 1 minute, 45 secs
4 Gianni Bugno, Italy, Gatorade, at 2 minutes, 53 secs
5 Andy Hampsten, USA, Motorola, at 3 minutes, 27 secs
6 Laurent Fignon, France, Gatorade, at 5 minutes, 51 secs

L-R: Marco Pantani, Bobby Julich, Jan Ullrich

Chapter 12

SHOCK AND AWE

**27 July 1998. Stage Fifteen: Grenoble to Les Deux Alpes
189km. High mountains**

Marco Pantani bounced off the pavement on to the road,
like a kid out playing on his bike. I was walking behind him,
along the same pavement, in Dublin, on Saturday, 11 July
1998. Pantani had just ridden the prologue time trial of the
Tour de France, finishing 181st out of the 189 starters.

The sport's most exciting climber – the most exciting cyclist,
in years – seemed to be in Ireland for the craic, though his
distracted demeanour suggested he wasn't especially interested in that, either. Or in anything. Pantani had recently
won his home tour, the Giro d'Italia, and it had overwhelmed
him. The celebration parties drained him. The death of his
mentor, Luciano Pezzi, fifteen days earlier demotivated him.
He said he wasn't interested in the Tour; that the mountains weren't hard enough, and there were only two summit
finishes. In Dublin, he looked miles away.

The strangest ever Tour got underway, and still Pantani
showed no interest, even when, twelve days in, he won at
Plateau de Beille, one of the two summit finishes, in the
Pyrenees. 'Every day, including the stage to Plateau de Beille,

he was just sitting at the back with his team,' recalls Bobby Julich, the American who was fourth in the Dublin prologue. 'This is before race radios, and when you're going back to talk to the team car there's Marco sitting at the back, in last position.

'You think, well, he doesn't give a crap, he's just going for stages.'

After winning at Plateau de Beille, Pantani grudgingly admitted, 'Anything is still possible, but after all the stress of the Giro it makes my head spin when I think about the overall classification.'

The favourite and defending champion, Jan Ullrich, didn't seem any more comfortable. Still only twenty-four, the German described his Tour win as 'a nightmare for me. I didn't enjoy a single second of it.'

A month later, Ullrich stopped racing, ending his 1997 season early. He was suffering from stress and exhaustion. 'The physical and mental strain of winning the Tour took Jan to his limits and we have to protect him,' said his Telekom team manager, Walter Godefroot. 'He's still very young and we have to be careful.' At the end of the year, he was voted German sportsman of the year, bracketed among a small group of his country's über-stars that included Steffi Graf, Boris Becker and Michael Schumacher. But over the winter his weight ballooned from 72 to 83kg. All spring, in the run-up to the 1998 Tour, Ullrich battled to regain fitness and lose weight under the intense glare of a German media who declared his ample behind 'the most examined rear since Claudia Schiffer's'.

Ullrich and Pantani must be two of the most physically gifted but psychologically fragile athletes in Tour history. Yet in 1998, here they were, duking it out in a race that made everybody's head spin, which would surely have broken even the strongest of spirits ...

*   *   *

It was the best of Tours, it was the worst of Tours. The world was shocked as it came to terms with the revelations about the scale and systematic nature of doping on the world's top team, Festina. The riders were shocked, too. But for a different reason. If anything, they were shocked that the world was shocked.

It started with a small news item. As the Tour got underway, it emerged that a soigneur with the Festina team, Willy Voet, had been stopped on the French–Belgian border with a car full of banned drugs. He was en route to Dublin. The outside world paid little attention at first; it was a minor story, a sub-plot. But the riders' ears pricked up. 'I heard about it at dinner in our hotel in Dublin,' recalls Jörg Jaksche, a twenty-one-year-old German about to start his first Tour with the Italian Polti team. 'Word spread very quickly. Everyone was, like, "Holy shit. What are we going to do with our stuff?" It wasn't, "Fuck Festina, what assholes, they're doping."'

Everyone was using EPO, says Jaksche. 'Maybe not everyone, but it was a majority,' says Bobby Julich, who was riding his second Tour. The UCI had introduced a health check the previous year, designed to limit its abuse, but there was no test. It was banned, but undetectable. 'What should you do?' asks Jaksche. 'You could say that the UCI accepted the use of it, up to a certain level. I don't think that's true – they saw the problem but couldn't do anything about it with no test. At least they tried to do something about it. What more could they do?

'And what could the riders do? You know everyone's doing it, so you have to do it. If your contract is running out, no one's going to ask you, "Why didn't you perform well?" and give you a new contract if you say you didn't use EPO. But if you've been fourth in the Tour, they'll say: "Here's your contract."'

The Tour carried on as normal for its three days in southern Ireland, but Voet, in custody in Lille, was a ticking timebomb.

His initial story, that the enormous stash of drugs was for his own use, was patently ridiculous. There was a growing sense, among the riders and teams, that when the race arrived back in France – a country basking in the warm afterglow of not only hosting but also winning football's World Cup – there would be trouble. Across the Channel, storm clouds gathered. There were stories of drugs being dumped over the side of the boat that carried them to France from Ireland. 'At first we kept it,' says Jaksche of the doping products. 'I have to be careful. I kept my stuff. It was then thrown away in the second week.'

Voet changed his story on the Tour's first day back in France. He had been acting under team orders, he admitted. A day later, French police raided the Festina riders' hotel rooms. Now Festina was the story, the race was secondary. Journalists who had travelled to Ireland and then France to cover a sports event found themselves working as crime reporters.

As the race headed from Brittany to the heart of the country, the Tour de France was unravelling. The teams' world was collapsing as the outside world was afforded a glimpse inside, and recoiled in outrage and horror. Among the riders, there was confusion; on the one hand, they wanted to keep their secret; on the other, with the secret out, they couldn't understand what all the fuss was about. On some stages they were booed and jeered. *Libération* described the sport as a 'cesspit', adding, 'the giants of the road are dwarves of sporting morality'. The mood in the peloton was one of righteous anger, and hurt. Udo Bolts, a team-mate of Ullrich, protested, 'We are not criminals ... The booing was terrible, soul-destroying.'

The Festina doctor, Eric Ryckaert, summed up the ambiguity: 'I'm against doping. That much, I think, is clear. But there are questions you must ask yourself on the definition of doping. For myself, in the role of a doctor, I want to know where medical treatments end and where doping begins.'

A week in, after the Festina management admitted that the team organised a doping programme, their nine riders were thrown out of the race, including French darling Richard Virenque. The Tour director, Jean-Marie Leblanc, acknowledged 'a classic case of institutionalised doping within a team', which, he added, was 'a grave affront to the morality and principles of the Tour'.

That was the official line. Bernard Kouchner, the French secretary of state for health, struck a different note, saying, 'We are all accomplices in this huge hypocrisy. Everybody knows that doping reigns at the Tour de France.'

Amid the chaos, confusion and anger, the race continued. Pictures of riders celebrating stage wins seemed incongruous beside those of the police entering team vehicles and riders' rooms – the Dutch TVM squad was the next to be targeted – until finally, on 24 July, before stage twelve, the riders' patience snapped.

In Tarascon-sur-Ariège, the day after the first rest day, two days after Pantani's win at Plateau de Beille, they refused to start. Laurent Jalabert, France's second-most popular rider after Virenque, spoke for the peloton: 'Since the start, nobody has talked about cycling, only the Festina affair. We're fed up to the back teeth with it. They've treated us like cattle so we're going to act like cattle – we're not starting and that's final.'

Yet finally they did start, after a delay of close to two hours. And after the stage, Leblanc, Jalabert, Pantani, 1996 winner Bjarne Riis and French federation president Daniel Baal had a private meeting, following which it was reported that the Festina affair, and the allegations that doping was widespread, were 'likely to lead to a doping amnesty in professional cycling'. (It never happened, but was still being talked about sixteen years later.)

In Lausanne, meanwhile, the head of the Olympic movement, Juan-Antonio Samaranch, watched events with a sense of bewilderment. At its nadir, when the riders went on strike, Samaranch was in the company of a Spanish journalist who was shadowing him for the day. 'This is ridiculous!' said Samaranch. 'If it's not bad for the health, it's not doping.' (The furore that followed the reporting of Samaranch's words, which echoed those of Ryckaert and so many members of the peloton, forced the IOC to take decisive action: the World Anti-Doping Agency was formed a year later.)

*   *   *

Bobby Julich was a twenty-six-year-old from Texas riding his second Tour de France, his third Grand Tour. He had been 17th in his début the previous year. Now, a week in, he was third after the first time trial, won by Ullrich. Julich then moved up to second after the first day in the Pyrenees. It was tantalising; he could almost reach out and touch the yellow jersey. The only problem was that the rider in front of him was Ullrich, restored to a lean and muscular shape after a crash diet and a training camp in the Black Forest.

Julich had been the great American hope when he emerged in the early 1990s, becoming national junior champion, and the heir, perhaps, to Greg LeMond. At least, that was what Julich thought, until 'this triathlete kid came to our training camp'. Julich recalls: 'I was the hotshot junior at the time, and we went out and did two-man time trial efforts. Of course, they paired this triathlon kid, Lance Armstrong, with me. We did this five-minute effort, I was good for two minutes, then I was on the absolute rivet for the final three minutes. When the coach blew a horn signalling our effort was over, I was like, thank God, oh my God, this guy's so strong. And Lance just started yelling at me: "Come on, let's keep going," but throw in some expletives and you understand how worked up he was ... I was like, "No, Lance, that horn was the coach telling us to stop."

'Right there and then, I said to myself, "Man, if there are more guys like that in the world, I don't have a career." Because he was the strongest guy I'd ever seen.'

Julich and Armstrong might have been – should have been – riding the 1998 Tour as team-mates. They joined Cofidis when Motorola ended their sponsorship at the end of 1996, but Armstrong's contract was torn up by the French team as he received treatment for cancer. He missed the 1997 season but made a comeback in 1998 with US Postal. He and Julich rode Paris–Nice that spring. 'I was riding one day alongside [Armstrong's team-mate] Frankie Andreu,' recalls Julich. 'And we'd heard that Lance had dropped out and gone home. Frankie says, "Well, that's it, we'll never see him again."

'I remember thinking, nah, nothing's going to stop Lance.'

Julich had his own health problems. In 1996 he was diagnosed with a heart condition – known as RSVT, it saw his heart race at 250 beats per minute at rest, accelerating even more during exertion – but it responded to treatment and, after missing the Tour and Olympics, he was able to start his first Grand Tour, the '96 Vuelta. He was ninth, the highest ever finish by an American. The next year he was 17th in his first Tour. And in 1998 things got even better: in spring he won the Critérium International.

At the Tour, Julich's team leader Francesco Casagrande crashed out in the Pyrenees. It opened the door for Julich, still highly placed after his fourth place in the prologue. And, in this Tour of all Tours, he was focused on seizing the opportunity, despite the race appearing to be disintegrating, to be limping towards, perhaps even unlikely to make it to, Paris. Thinking about this now, Julich struggles to understand just how unfazed he was by all that was going on – the fact that, every day, bucketloads of shit were hitting wind-turbine-sized fans. 'I felt totally detached. Obviously there were a lot of guys in the race doing the same things that Festina got in trouble for, but the main thought that went through my mind was, if they stop the race now, do I get second place?

'I wasn't at all worried about getting busted and put in jail like the Festina guys, but at the same time you thought, wow, this is a nightmare. On the one hand, it was hard to stay focused, but when you're in that bubble and you've got your blinders on ... I just woke up every day ready to race.

'I didn't speak much French at the time. Kevin [Livingston, a fellow American and Cofidis team-mate] and I were room-mates and we would go to bed at 10.30, watch MTV, then get up the next morning, and everyone would have bloodshot eyes, and be, like, "Did you hear what happened?"

'We'd say, "What? No." Ignorance was bliss.'

At the same time, a little voice piped up in Julich's head: a voice he had, thus far, managed to ignore. Julich says that when he started doping in his second year with the Motorola team, in August 1996, he 'overrode' the inner voice telling him it was cheating (although this was the same year as his problems with his heart, there is no suggestion of a link; the heart condition was caused by a congenital defect or by a virus when he was young). As far as his doping went, he was able to rationalise it: 'We all knew everyone was doing the same things.' He was also able to justify it, and salve his conscience, by telling himself: 'I'm doing the minimum to be competitive. There are other guys doing much, much more.' There were, says Julich, 'all these rumours and innuendo in the peloton'.

Taking EPO was like drinking coffee, Julich told himself. But during the Tour, as fellow riders had their rooms turned upside down by police, and were marched into cells for questioning, Julich had a jarring realisation. 'I thought, this isn't like drinking coffee. This is something that's illegal. It was the tipping point, the moment you realised, that noise in the back of my head, this conscience I overrode, this is wrong. I'm never going to do this again. Look at these guys in jail:

that's never going to be me.' There was another influence on Julich: his fiancée (now his wife), Angela, who 'found out what was going on from another rider's wife. She confronted me on it and it was one of the most dreadful experiences of my life. She was never a part of this and I put her in a very difficult situation. She told me right then and there that if it ever happened again our relationship would be over.'

Julich allowed himself to think that ultimately the Festina affair would be good for the sport, and for him. 'Right then and there, I really felt the sport was going to change one hundred per cent. I thought, there's no one ever going to take a risk again. And I was happy. I was relieved. Coz, let me tell you, it wasn't fun living like that. I was like, thank God, we don't have to do this thing any more. We just have to race. I was confident I would still be competitive, because I felt I was doing the minimum. I thought the playing field was going to be more level.'

For the most part, Julich tried to keep his head down, to concentrate on the race. If the riders stopped to protest, he stopped with them, but he wasn't a ringleader, and he says he didn't feel the same sense of indignation or righteous anger as some. 'I felt like a nobody, yet I was in second place, and I remember Bjarne Riis coming up and telling me I had to go and speak to a commissaire on behalf of the riders. I told him, "Are you kidding? I'm nobody. You speak to him."'

There were moments of levity. Julich found that Ullrich, despite being defending champion, was also quite detached from the mood of indignation. He left the *patron* role to Jalabert and his senior team-mate, Riis. He had the ability, but not the ego for it. 'I really got to know Jan on that Tour,' says Julich. 'I was enamoured with him, I have to say. Humble, down to earth; a regular guy. I got to speak to him a lot on that Tour and we became good friends.

'One day, I was riding next to him and he had this nice Tag Heuer watch on. I was a big fan of these watches. I told him,

"Wow, I really like that watch." He said, "I have another one. Come to my hotel and I'll give you it."

'I was, like, who gives somebody a watch like that? I wasn't going to turn up at his hotel for the watch. But every day he would come up to me and say, "Sorry, I forgot your watch."'

*   *   *

Storm clouds loomed in Grenoble on Monday, 27 July. And for once, on this Tour, they were literal rather than metaphorical. They hung low in the valley, obscuring the mountains. It was gloomy and bitterly cold – 12 degrees C in the valley, 4 degrees C at the summits of the four mountains on the itinerary: the Col de la Croix de Fer, Col du Télégraphe, Col du Galibier and Les Deux Alpes. Hard enough without the cold and the rain.

It was the first of three days in the Alps, the second and final summit finish of this Tour: Pantani's last chance. Il Pirata was still a distant fourth, three minutes behind Ullrich, with Jalabert and Julich equal second, just over a minute down. But today would not be Pantani's day, as far as Julich was concerned – it would be his. 'I had a battle plan. I definitely looked on that day as my opportunity. I was so close to that jersey for two weeks and never got to touch it. This was the day I thought I had it.'

It was miserable in Grenoble and would be treacherous in the mountains. The riders were reluctant to leave the team buses, and when they appeared they wore arm-warmers, rain capes and gloves, with more layers stuffed in pockets. In subdued mood, they got underway, Rodolfo Massi leading over the top of the Croix de Fer, after 30km of climbing. By now conditions were deteriorating. The temperature plummeted and the rain turned to hail as they climbed towards 2,000 metres. And there was a crash, Daniele Nardello tumbling off the road, taking Pantani down with him – but he was quickly back up. Julich tried to use the climb as a launch pad for a long-range attack, believing that it was worth a tentative jab – that Ullrich and his team might not regard him as a serious rival, and let him go. But Ullrich seemed nervous; at his instruction, his Telekom team-mates brought Julich back. When Julich was caught, his Cofidis team-mate Christophe Rinero countered. He got away and was joined by three others: Massi, Marcos-Antonio Serrano and José María Jiménez.

Behind, Ullrich's Telekom team rode hard to control the race in the valley between the Croix de Fer and the Télégraphe, which acted as a first step to the monstrous Galibier. When the road began to climb again, Luc Leblanc became aggressive. And Ullrich seemed worried, reacting to his accelerations with nervous urgency. It was ominous: the final climb was still to come, yet here was the yellow jersey riding hard to chase down the thirty-one-year-old former world champion, whose best days were behind him. Clearly Ullrich was anxious. He was also now isolated, his team-mates having paid for their riding in the valley.

As Ullrich chased down Leblanc, Julich came up more steadily, followed by Pantani and the rest. There was a regrouping: eight riders bunched together, as though for shelter. It was a brief lull. The next to dart off the front was the Spaniard, Fernando Escartín. No reaction; the Ullrich group was still catching its breath after Leblanc's attack. They fanned across the road as more riders came up from behind to swell their numbers, including reinforcements for Ullrich and Julich in Riis and Livingston.

The climb eased. 'It was almost a false flat, but definitely still climbing – a bit of respite,' says Julich. 'And I remember Kevin, once he came back up to the group, going straight to the front. He started to go hard; instead of smoothly bringing it up, he kind of attacked. And I yelled at him, "Slow down!" And he looked back at me; he was in full race mode. He was kind of pissed at me.'

Leblanc went again, pressing hard on the front, stringing it out. Ullrich marked the move; Pantani tucked in behind. It was as close as Pantani had been to the front: he had been riding unusually conservatively until now.

*   *   *

Then he goes. With the muck and grime from the road clinging to his pale Mercatone Uno team clothing, Pantani looks like a little chimney sweep, with his goatee beard and bandanna, knotted at the back, and a small diamond-encrusted gold hoop in his ear. It was a carefully cultivated look, a disguise, a mask, amounting to an effort by Pantani to overcome years of self-consciousness about his appearance. His hair had started falling out when he was fifteen and he was conspicuously bald by his early twenties; his ears also stuck out, inspiring unkind nicknames, including 'Elephantino'. Eventually, he would resort to surgery and have his ears pinned back. But for now the bandanna did the job.

Implausibly, on this gloomiest of days, Il Pirata is wearing dark glasses with yellow frames, matching the flashes of yellow on his Bianchi bike and clothing, and his all-yellow shoes and tyres.

'He makes this jump,' says Julich. 'It's, like, come on! What? Here I am telling my team-mate to slow down and he just blasts past. He goes about fifteen pedal strokes and then he turns around and looks back and he has this ... smile on his face. I'll never forget it. This smile. And I thought, now he's going to slow up.'

Julich was wrong. Out of the saddle, hands on the drops, Pantani, having watched Ullrich use his strength to chase down Leblanc, sprints hard. He would use a single bullet, not a scatter gun: one devastating acceleration rather than a flurry of attacks. Eight seconds later he glanced back while still pedalling. Two seconds later he paused, freewheeled, stood on the pedals, twisted his body to the right, angling his head back down the road – a long, lingering glance.

He wasn't slowing down. He was surveying the wreckage. No wonder he was smiling.

Luc Leblanc tried to go after him. He almost made it. But there was no catching Pantani. Once on his own, Il Pirata removed his dark glasses and rolled down his arm-warmers: he was going to work. The loose ends of his bandanna flapped at the back of his head as he sprinted up the climb, hands in the hooks of the handlebars. There were 5.5km to the top of the 2,645-metre Galibier. 'Up there, I could see the weather setting in,' says Julich, 'and I thought, this is going to be nuts.'

Even in mild weather, the Galibier was fearsome. Jaksche had been given some advice by his team leader, Leblanc. 'Luc helped me a lot,' says Jaksche, 'and on the Galibier I came up to that front group before Pantani took off. Luc said: "Never look to the left or the right: just look at the road." I said, "Why?" Then I looked. "Ah, I see."'

The five riders ahead of Pantani – Escartín on his own, and ahead of him the four-man break of Rinero, Massi, Serrano, Jiménez – were his prey. Their laboured efforts reflected the dismal conditions while Pantani's defied them. Rain spattered the lens of the TV camera, distorting the image, turning the road slick and black, but Pantani appeared to be gliding up it. Behind, meanwhile, Ullrich sat at the front and looked around for help. Julich pulled alongside but offered none. Up front, Pantani caught and passed Escartín. Then Ullrich's team car accelerated to the front of the chasing group, warning the rider in yellow not to do too much work; there was still a long way to go, and the cold sapped strength and energy as effectively as the gradient.

Ahead, Pantani went through the breakaway like a hot knife through butter. Jiménez, the handsome and enigmatic Spanish climber known as 'El Chava', clung to his rear wheel. The image of this pair together on the upper slopes of this rain-lashed mountain is poignant because, these days, they are often mentioned in the same breath, as tragic icons of the destructive power of drugs. Like Pantani, Jiménez would enter a downward spiral of despair and depression. He died two months before Pantani, in December 2003. He was thirty-two, Pantani thirty-four.

Towards the summit of the Galibier, Jiménez was dropped by Pantani, who then caught Rinero; then El Chava got his second wind, and sprinted back up to Pantani's rear wheel – the effort visible in his heaving rib cage. But Pantani rose out of the saddle once more and crossed the summit of the Galibier alone, grabbing a rain jacket from one of his directeurs sportifs, Orlando Maini, who had jumped out of the car and was waiting for him. He tried to put it on, on the move, but couldn't and stopped, allowing Jiménez to pass him; they would team up again on the descent.

Julich crested the summit at the head of the chasing group, two minutes behind Pantani, knowing that the long descent would be more crucial than in normal conditions. 'Climbing the Galibier in that lead group, we were all just kinda stuck in mud. There were none of us who could do anything. Pantani was gone. We were just chopping wood trying to get up that climb.

'But I knew the descent was going to be important. And from the limited experience I had, I knew I had to get my rain jacket on before we started the descent. I had my Gore-Tex jacket in my back pocket; I had gone back and got it from the team car on the Télégraphe, before we started on the Galibier. I remember thinking to myself, OK, Bobby, if you have to stop at the top to put on your rain jacket then do it; and zip it up, make sure it's on.

'But I got caught up in the moment because guys were taking bottles and feeds, and we crested the top so quickly and you start the descent … So I thought, oh no, I'm not going to stop, I'll get this on while I'm riding.' That was easier said than done: Julich's hands were numb from the cold; he couldn't operate the zip, nor could he react quickly when he realised he was heading too fast into the first hairpin bend. Ahead of him was a campervan. He careered off the road. 'I almost ended up smashing into that campervan. I went round the front of it. I had my hands off the bars, and when I went to hit the brakes, in that weather the brake pads weren't working very well.

'I had meant to stop anyway, so I thought, I'll stop here and put it on. But then the guy who had the campervan, he jumped up and pushed me back on my bike before I was ready! I hadn't got my jacket on; I was still trying to zip it up. That made me panic a bit. Once I got going, finally I got it zipped up, and then I remember catching the group and looking over at Jan ...'

Ullrich, almost alone among the overall contenders, opted not to put on a rain jacket. 'He had these arm-warmers on,' says Julich, 'and this vest, and he had a bottle in his mouth: he was holding it with his teeth. I looked over at him and he looked absolutely frozen. I was freezing even with my jacket on. You couldn't go round the turns because you were shaking so bad.'

Now, says Julich, it was no longer a bike race. It was a game of self-preservation. A game that Ullrich was evidently losing. His upper body was locked, rigid. His face was puffy. Huge bags began to appear under his eyes.

Jörg Jaksche recalls, 'It was not really a race any more. It was just about trying to survive.' He says that his countryman Ullrich suffered even more in the cold because – ironically, given the attention paid to his weight – he was so skinny. But Jaksche has another theory about why Ullrich struggled so badly that day. 'It sounds silly, but the Italians didn't have only Power Bars for race food. This is a crucial moment,' says Jaksche. 'And Ullrich's team, Telekom, they had all this technical race food – the Power Bars. But they are shit when it's cold. You can't eat them. They turn into bricks.

'On the Italian teams, we ate small paninis with marmalade or honey or Nutella. Not so sophisticated, maybe, but better in those conditions. And I think this is one reason why Jan had such a bad time.'

Pantani rode most of the descent with Jiménez, though El Chava struggled for much of it with his rain jacket, trying to do the zip. Pantani urged him through as they plummeted together. Pantani drank from his bottle, and ate his paninis from his pocket: coal on the fire for later. He slipped his dark glasses back on. Further down they were joined by some of the other survivors from the break: Serrano, Rinero, Massi, and also Escartín. Strength in numbers. They were companions for Pantani to the base of the final climb, to the ski station at Les Deux Alpes. The gap opened to three minutes; it made Pantani maillot jaune virtuel: yellow jersey on the road.

Julich recalls, 'When you get to the bottom, there's a long valley with the tunnels before you get to Les Deux Alpes. By that time I started to get pretty warm; I had the jacket zipped up. And I was like, OK, it's on, here's the last climb, here we go. I was trying to get the guys to work but everyone was just frozen solid. I was with Jalabert in a little group at the base of the climb, and all of a sudden I saw him ripping off all his clothes, and I thought, I'm gonna do the same thing. It was like a garage sale at the bottom of that climb. Gloves, armwarmers, my Gore-Tex jacket, which had just saved my life. All on the side of the road.'

All except Ullrich, who had nothing to remove. Then, as if things couldn't get worse for him, he punctured. He pulled to the right side of the road, stuck his hand in the air, and his team car pulled up behind him. He was alone. There were no team-mates in his group. The timing was terrible. They were about to start climbing again. A similar thing had happened to Ullrich on the approach to Plateau de Beille, over a week earlier, and he had ridden hard to regain the group and move to its head – overdoing it, and paying for the effort later when Pantani rode away. Now, though, frozen to the core, teeth clamped shut to prevent shivering, it was impossible for him even to rejoin the group. He got back into the convoy of vehicles following Julich's group, but couldn't make contact. Later, he was joined by a couple of team-mates, Bolts and Riis. But he struggled to stay with them. He ripped off the yellow gilet he had put on as token resistance to the cold, throwing it angrily to the road, then tried to hold the wheels of his team-mates; the camera zoomed in on him, showing his puffy face, the bulging bags under his eyes.

Julich didn't know Ullrich had punctured. All he knew was that he had gone. Last he heard, Pantani was a couple of minutes up the road. Now the yellow jersey was his for the taking. 'Right away, I went. At the foot of the climb. I knew the climb. We had done it in a recon camp before the Tour. I knew it wasn't a very steep climb; that it was good for me. A minute later I took off my helmet, gave it to the motorcycle guy, the Mavic support motorbike. It's funny, my dad always told me to wear my helmet … Then I was just going in full time trial mode, just hoping Jan didn't come around me. I had no idea where he was.

'I was so cold, I could only push a massive gear. I couldn't spin, couldn't turn my legs fast, but it was just one of those times you felt: mind over matter. Mentally, it was, come on, all the way to the line, all the way to the line.' Julich felt that he was closing the gap on Pantani – or rather, that he must be, because he was feeling so strong. He was more concerned with the whereabouts of Ullrich than Pantani. 'I was thinking of Jan, because he was in yellow.

'No one passed me the entire climb and I felt like I was going, really going. I dropped everyone apart from [Michael] Boogerd, who came across and stayed on my wheel. I was thinking, holy cow. And when I came across the line, I thought I'd taken the jersey. I assumed I'd taken the jersey.'

Pantani had dropped his companions as soon as the road began to rise. They were blown away as he sprinted up the climb, hands on the drops, out of the saddle almost the entire way. Pantani appeared to flatten the gradient, going so fast into hairpins that he needed all the road. He reached the finish in 5 hours, 43 minutes, 45 seconds, sprinting all the way until just before the line, when he sat up, threw his head back, closed his eyes and spread his arms. He had crucified his opponents. But watching it now, this glimpse of Pantani in his Jesus-on-the-Cross pose is chilling: it is the defining image of Pantani, the one that, a few short years later, would be on the cover of the posthumous biography, *The Death of Marco Pantani*.

'When I attacked, I gave everything and risked everything,' said Pantani after the stage. 'It was incredibly hard. It's terrible to think afterwards about how much you suffer in an attack like that.'

He dedicated his win to Luciano Pezzi, his mentor, who had died, aged seventy-seven, just days before the Tour began in Dublin. The highlight of Pezzi's relatively modest racing career was a stage win at the 1955 Tour de France. Like Pantani at Les Deux Alpes, his success had also come on the fifteenth stage.

*   *   *

Julich crossed the line and awaited the congratulations: the stampede of reporters and photographers, the podium, the presentation of flowers, and the yellow jersey. None of it came. There was a soigneur with a towel and a long-sleeved Cofidis top. He had finished fifth, with Massi, Escartín and Rinero hanging on between Pantani and him. When he was told the gap to Pantani – 5:43 – he was stunned.

His shock, and awe, is apparent in his post-stage interview, just beyond the finish line: 'Incredible, Pantani. I knew he was very, very dangerous but I didn't know he could do what he did today. I mean, he just made us all look silly. The race isn't over yet … There's still quite a bit to go, and now his team has to take control, you never know what can happen …'

Julich was kidding himself, and knew it. Now, he says, 'I just assumed I'd taken the yellow jersey. I felt I'd done the best climb I'd ever done. But he put three minutes into me on that climb. Three minutes on an eight-kilometre climb! I just couldn't believe it. And the reality was, I remember thinking, this guy's going to win the Tour.'

It was the closest Julich ever got to the yellow jersey. Pantani did win the Tour, despite a show of defiance from Ullrich when the race resumed next day and he attacked on the Col de la Madeleine. It was a remarkable recovery twenty-four hours after the toughest day of his career (on Channel 4's coverage, Gary Imlach offered a wry summary of the slimline Ullrich's ride to Les Deux Alpes: 'The only excess baggage Jan Ullrich was carrying up the climb yesterday was under his eyes.').

When Ullrich attacked on the Madeleine, Pantani pounced after him and together they distanced Julich, with Ullrich winning the stage in Albertville. In Paris, Julich stood on the third step of the podium. Ullrich was more than three minutes down on Pantani; still only twenty-four, it was as close as he would ever get to adding to his one Tour win. He would finish second three more times, on each occasion to Lance Armstrong. Even though he wasn't there, the '98 Tour was pivotal for Armstrong in so many ways. In the short term, he went to the '98 Vuelta motivated rather than inspired by Julich's third-place finish. If the guy whose ass I kicked as a junior can finish third in the Tour, thought Armstrong, I can win it.

'It's funny,' says Julich. 'It's something I heard through acquaintances, that my result in the Tour was something that really motivated Lance to come back.'

As for Julich himself, 'I was never totally comfortable with that result, with third at the Tour de France. I knew I'd achieved it in a questionable manner. And listen, if those guys were in the race, I'd never have finished third and on the podium. I have to be honest with myself. That was an abbreviated version of the overall results. If guys like Virenque, Escartín, Jalabert had been there [Escartín and Jalabert withdrew when the Spanish teams pulled out en masse two days later, in protest at the continuing police attention], I wouldn't have been in that position.

'The year before I was 17th, and my best years after that I was 17th to 20th,' Julich continues. 'I was never third again. I felt I kind of got lucky. If I'd backed it up in other years, I'd be more proud of that. It was always in parenthesis for me. Especially now.'

Julich insists he never used EPO after the 1998 Tour. But the ghosts of that race came back to haunt him and others fifteen years later, when, as part of a wider inquiry, the results of urine tests (conducted in 2004 using the test for EPO that was developed in 2000) were disclosed by the French Senate. Julich was in the 'suspicious' category. Among the positives from the 1998 Tour were Pantani and Ullrich.[4] In *The Death of Marco Pantani*, which tells of Pantani's psychological disintegration following his failed 'health check' at the 1999 Giro, ending with his lonely, cocaine-fuelled death in an out-of-season hotel in Rimini on Valentine's Day, 2004, Matt Rendell asserted that Pantani's 'entire career was based on EPO abuse'.

---

4 Julich says he stopped taking EPO during the Tour, and the retrospective tests of his 1998 urine samples, published by the French Senate in August 2013, do not contradict his claim. Only one of his tests, after stage 11, was deemed 'suspicious'. The tests confirmed that Pantani and Ullrich were using EPO throughout the race: Ullrich was positive after stages 12, 14 and 21; Pantani was positive after stages 11, 15 (Les Deux Alpes) and 16.

Still, the 1998 result stands.

'I put that whole period of my life in a box in my mind and only recently re-opened it,' says Julich. 'Because it was a period when I was doing something I knew I shouldn't be doing, you compartmentalise things. It feels like a lifetime ago. It feels like a different person. I have a picture going down to my basement: a fancy framed photograph that Oakley gave me from the prologue in Dublin. And I look at it and go, "Oh my God, that's me." It feels so separate.'

While Julich says he changed, he admits the sport didn't. 'It was the turning point for at least fifty per cent of the peloton. But for the rest, it drove it underground. One thing I do agree with: after that, Marc Madiot [Française des Jeux team director] coined the term "cyclisme à deux vitesses": cycling at two speeds. It definitely was the beginning of that era.

'But, you know, it was a great race. Despite everything. And if there's one day I remember more than any, it was to Les Deux Alpes. It was probably the most epic day I've ever been involved in, in racing.'

Given what they had been through – the scandals, the hostility from the media and public, police raids, the conditions on the stage to Les Deux Alpes – it was something of a miracle that the Tour made it to Paris. It was a depleted peloton: only ninety-six riders. The irony was that they had rarely been so united. They were cheered on to the Champs-Élysées, noted *The Times'* sportswriter Simon Barnes, by a public who perhaps, in the end, admired their fortitude, or maybe, mistakenly, believed the bad apples had been thrown out, that the riders left in the race must be clean. 'The riders of the Tour have their own ethic,' wrote Barnes. 'It is them against the organisers, them against the media, them against the world.' Pantani punctured on the way into Paris, but nobody took advantage because, Barnes added, 'It wouldn't be right.'

There is another enduring memory for Bobby Julich from the 1998 Tour, from the night the race finished. 'I was in the hotel that everyone goes to, the Concorde La Fayette, all dressed up. I was with my mum and dad and my dad is, like, "Oh my God, there's Jan Ullrich." And there was Ullrich with his girlfriend, Gaby, and a million people around him. He was going to the Telekom dinner, I was going to the Cofidis dinner.

'Jan spots me. He races up, says, "Wait right there." He races through the people, all trying to get a piece of him, and back up to his room. In a few minutes he's back with this beautiful Tag-Heuer watch. I still have it to this day.'

Classement

1 Marco Pantani, Italy, Mercatone Uno, 5 hours, 43 minutes, 45 secs
2 Rodolfo Massi, Italy, Casino, at 1 minute, 54 secs
3 Fernando Escartín, Spain, Kelme, at 1 minute, 59 secs
4 Christophe Rinero, France, Cofidi,s at 2 minutes, 57 secs
5 Bobby Julich, USA, Cofidis, at 5 minutes, 43 secs
6 Michael Boogerd, Holland, Rabobank, at 5 minutes, 48 secs

Urs Zimmermann, 2013

Chapter 13

WHAT ABOUT ZIMMY?

17 July 1991. Rest day: Pau
0 (zero) km

The Tour de France is the circus that everybody thinks they would love to run away with. Colourful, exotic, glamorous, the allure for those outside its bubble is as strong and appealing as the idea that everybody inside it is as one. An impression of cohesion and unity is reinforced by the peloton itself, one of sport's most powerful symbols of togetherness.

When the riders, lean and tanned and at the peak of their athletic prowess, step out of their team buses and climb aboard their gleaming bikes, on which most cut such graceful figures, it can be difficult not to feel a twinge of envy. But there are around 180 riders at the Tour. Of the 180, some will be highly motivated. Some will not. Some will be at war with their team-mates. Others will be at war with themselves. Some will be confident. Others will be terrified. The Tour amplifies problems: physical, psychological, political.

People love sport because it offers an escape from reality. But what if it *is* reality? Despite what many might like to believe, what might be called Andre Agassi syndrome is not uncommon in elite, professional sport, even if Agassi is an extreme case. 'I play tennis for a living, even though I hate tennis,' said Agassi, 'hate it with a dark and secret passion and always have.'

*   *   *

It wasn't that Urs Zimmermann didn't like his fellow cyclists. It was just that, after two weeks in their company, he felt like he needed a change.

Actually, Zimmermann thinks again, sometimes he really didn't like his fellow cyclists.

He was always a little different. Zimmermann was not someone who grew up dreaming about riding the Tour de France. He wasn't even aware of it. By nature, he was not competitive; he began cycling by riding to school, because it was the only way to get there. He was a farmer's boy from the village of Mühledorf, near Bern in the German-speaking part of Switzerland. When he was fifteen, he earned a place in a school for smart kids. It was 15km away, and, 'I always went there by bike because of money and time.'

From riding to school, Zimmermann graduated to cycle-touring with a friend and they rode all over Switzerland. He fell into racing, and found he was good at it – especially, with his long, lanky frame, climbing. He turned professional for a small Swiss team in 1983 and in his second year won his country's biggest race, the Tour of Switzerland. It was a huge achievement, but Zimmermann, as he recalls it, looks haunted. 'For me, it was perhaps too big,' he says. He made his début at the Tour de France that same year, finishing 58th, then moved to the Italian Carrera team for 1985, riding the Giro d'Italia, finishing 50th.

Zimmermann was striking looking, with his dirty blond hair, hollow cheeks, sunken eyes and rangy limbs. The haunted look that flits across his face as he recalls specific episodes conjures up memories of him in his pomp, climbing to a metronomic rhythm, hands in the centre of the handle-bars, face down, glazed eyes focused on the road just in front, sweat dripping from his nose.

Already stick-thin, Zimmermann shed more weight after going on an extreme diet in the winter of 1985 – though this coincided, he points out, with moving out of his parents' house. The next year, he finished third in the Tour de France, one of the greatest Tours of all time, behind the warring team-mates, Greg LeMond and Bernard Hinault.

Yet even then Zimmermann seemed awkward and uncomfortable, as though he didn't really belong in their company. Part of the reason was that he spent much of that Tour arguing with his Carrera team director, Davide Boifava, over his tactics. Boifava thought he wasn't calculating enough; that he was reckless in attacking too often and at the wrong moments. It was Zimmermann's nervousness that partly explained his attacking style. Like a lot of climbers, he didn't like being in the peloton: he would rather be up the road, preferably alone.

Meeting him twenty-five years later, in Lausanne, he still seems like a man apart. He is edgy and nervous, and barely involved in the sport of cycling these days, though he has written a novel, *In the Crosswind*, about an ex-cyclist who is brooding, melancholic and finds himself caught 'in the cross-winds' of life.

It was Zimmermann's desire to be apart, his reluctance to spend more time than was absolutely necessary in the company of his fellow cyclists, that led to his involvement in one of the stranger episodes in Tour history. It was halfway during the 1991 Tour when he was disqualified for travelling by car rather than plane from Saint-Herblain in the Loire-Atlantique, in north-west France, to Pau, in the south-west: some 565km. Few riders in the history of the Tour had been thrown out of the race – at the time, even a doping infraction would often result in a paltry fine and time penalty.

It seemed a ridiculously excessive punishment for such a crime. Particularly when it was explained, in his defence, that Zimmermann was scared of flying. Zimmermann smiles at the memory. 'I wasn't afraid of flying. If I was afraid of flying, why did I go to the airport to fly home?'

*   *   *

After his breakthrough at the 1986 Tour, Zimmermann's career began to flounder. It had much to do with a broken heart. The year he finished third in the Tour, he had been in love with the daughter of a cycling coach. Everything in his life fell into place: 'I felt like I was in another sphere.' Suddenly, he could follow the likes of Laurent Fignon, somebody he previously regarded almost as an alien being. In 1986, Zimmermann was twenty-six: he should have had his best years ahead of him. But his obsession with his weight overwhelmed him. 'I was fighting not to take even one extra gram over the winter. I thought, maybe if I lose one more kilo, I can win the Tour de France. I kept thinking, one more kilo, and that's it. But in the spring [of 1987], instead of growing stronger, I was going slower.

'I had major problems. I had the illness of models.' Anorexia? 'Yeah, and maybe I was also too low in iron.'

He lost much of 1987 to illness. But in 1988 he recaptured his old form: he was third in the Giro, behind a rider who would become one of his few friends in the peloton, as well as a future team-mate, Andy Hampsten. At the same time, Zimmermann resisted pressure from his team, Carrera, to move to Italy, where doctors were assuming greater importance than coaches. He was vaguely aware that they, and other riders, might be involved in doping. 'I fought to have distance from that,' he says.

In 1989 he joined a new team, 7-Eleven. 'It was a new start for me. I loved the American guys and the way it was in the team. It was relaxed. I said I was a vegetarian and they said it was no problem. People had responsibility and freedom, compared with Italian teams.

'But I had problems in my relationship, and that was really eating me.' By now he was suffering from depression, though he only realised that later. He believes that this partly explains why he struggled to recapture his 1986 form. 'I started to suffer with depression in the winter in 1988. I think one part of me is a little bit manic. So if everything is going well, you lose yourself in that, and you are successful.' But it was different 'in the winter, when there's no racing, no structure'.

Would he, I wonder, have suffered from depression had he not been a professional cyclist? 'No,' is his emphatic response. 'I think I wouldn't have come to the bottom of my personality. This [depression] is something that's inside me, and it could have come out, but I don't think so. But I don't know.'

By 1991, Zimmermann was still with the same American team, now sponsored by Motorola. It was strange that he was still racing: he had intended to retire the previous year, when he was still only thirty and his contract ended. 'I just had enough. I had no team and I had these problems in the winter.' His relationship ended, and, 'I was in deep trouble because of this, and I started to travel. I went to Australia for one month and it opened my mind. But I also thought, you can't solve your problems by being in Australia.

'I came back, and I started to ride a bit and I started to feel strong. And it turned out I could ride a bit for the team.' Jim Ochowicz, the 7-Eleven and Motorola team manager, offered him an unusual deal: essentially, he hired him as a freelancer. 'I had no contract. They just paid me 3,000 bucks every month I raced. I played a different kind of role; I just worked for Andy [Hampsten]. That was kind of fun. There was not the same pressure as before.'

*　　*　　*

Zimmermann was selected for the Motorola team for the 1991 Tour. But by now he felt a different atmosphere in the sport. He didn't like it. By the halfway point he was fed up. The stages had been hard and fast. Charly Mottet won the eleventh stage into Saint-Herblain. Thank God, thought Zimmermann, the next day was the first and only rest day, though this brought its own challenges. It involved an air transfer. They were always tiring and stressful.

'I had started to feel that the Tour de France was like a prison,' Zimmermann says. And he was sick of the company of his fellow inmates. 'So I said, "If there is an opportunity, I would like to go in a car instead of taking the plane." The team said that was okay, because the big boss wanted to fly. So we swapped. I went in a car with the mechanics. And we drove 300km to a small village, had dinner, drove some more, then I did the last 60km by bike.'

He rode from near Aire-sur-l'Adour down to Pau, where there was an unexpected welcome party. 'I get to the hotel and there are some journalists saying: "You are out of the race. You should have been on the flight."'

Uh-oh, thought Zimmermann, *I'm in trouble here.*

'That evening they told me: "You are out of the race." But the team said, "Come to the start and do everything as if you are starting and we will fight for you at the team meeting."'

In the pre-stage meeting, Ochowicz fought for his rider. Zimmermann was afraid of flying, he explained. Curiously, Pascal Richard, another Swiss, had also missed the flight. His excuse was that he had to visit a dentist. There was sympathy for Richard from the Tour organisers, but not for Zimmermann. Ochowicz came to find him, and told him: 'I'm sorry. You have to go home.'

There was sympathy from the peloton, however, even as Zimmermann was driven from the start in Pau to the airport – to fly home. When the riders lined up, and the flag was dropped for the start, they didn't move. The organisers tried several times to initiate a start, but they wouldn't budge. 'It was spontaneous, not planned,' said Gilbert Duclos-Lassalle, one of the most senior and respected French pros. 'We wanted him to start. This isn't the army. If he doesn't want to take the plane, why should he?'

The Tour organisers, headed by race director Jean-Marie Leblanc, had a problem. Reluctant to yield to rider power, adamant that their rules should stand, they faced a dilemma. It might have seemed petty, but there was a reason for the rule that all riders should travel together: it was to prevent some gaining an unfair advantage. It was to stop star riders taking a private jet or catching a helicopter off the top of a mountain. But Zimmermann's case was different: few could see what advantage he had gained by sitting in a car for 500km.

Zimmermann didn't actually believe his fellow riders were striking on his behalf, except perhaps for his own team-mates. He thought he was a convenient excuse for the riders to register their displeasure at something else. 'They were also protesting because of the helmet rule,' he says. It was the first time helmets were compulsory. 'They didn't want to wear them in the mountain stages. But when they were about to go [after making their point about helmets] my team-mate Phil Anderson said, "What about Zimmy?"'

There was a standoff. With no Zimmermann, there would be no race, said the riders. The organisers couldn't be seen to cave. So they reached a compromise: Zimmermann would be reinstated. But the Tour seemed to need somebody to blame for Zimmermann missing his flight, and expelled his manager, Ochowicz, instead.

By now, Zimmermann was at the departure gate at Pau airport. He received the news of his reinstatement with mixed emotions. But he had little choice other than to race back into the town centre to start the stage, 192km in the Pyrenees, to Jaca. He changed into his racing clothing in the car, and arrived in Pau ready to join his peers. Finally they

got underway, forty minutes late (and with only forty-seven
riders wearing helmets. The fines gave the UCI a £16,000
windfall). 'And a few minutes later, I was in the breakaway,'
laughs Zimmermann.

It's true: by the foot of the first climb, the Col de Soudet,
Zimmermann was one of twenty-two riders in the early break,
along with Hampsten, Maurizio Fondriest, Pascal Richard
and the Uzbek sprinter Djamolidine Abdoujaparov. There
were only six still in the break at the summit. Zimmermann
was among those dropped on the climb.

He finished the Tour: his final one. Nevertheless, in the
short amount of time he spent out of the race, thinking he
was finished with it and waiting at the airport to fly home,
he experienced an epiphany. 'I became suddenly aware: I am
far away from the race, and I don't care too much if I stay in
or not.'

*   *   *

A year later, Zimmermann retired for good. He was aware of
talk in the peloton of 'new things', and of the racing being
faster and harder, and of riders who previously were not
climbers beating him in what should have been his terrain.
The rumour was that some were using EPO. 'I read in a newspaper about some deaths in Holland [linked to the drug] and
I was shocked. I started to be really annoyed. And I thought,
this is not my sport any more.'

He struggled to adapt to life post-cycling. 'I was sick for
maybe a year and then I started to [reach] the bottom. Then
I worked in a bike shop and I started writing my book.' He
didn't want to write a standard autobiography, 'like everybody does'. Instead, 'It's really about depression and what
you're going to do about it' – though cycling does feature,
as does a traumatic break-up. It took him six years to write,
and finding a publisher was not easy. Throughout this period,

'I did almost nothing. I lived from what I earned before and I lived in a really simple way.'

The book was published in 2001, and in the same year he and his new partner had a daughter, Rosa. Then Zimmermann began riding his bike again. Now he finds that cycling helps him to 'forget about thinking. For the last six years I go out once, two, three times a week. After a few years, I felt stronger and more relaxed.'

As he talks, Zimmermann glances at his watch; he wants to get home so that he can meet Rosa from school. 'I don't have to, but I like to,' he explains. I leave him at the railway station in Lausanne, where, with his long legs, he lopes across the large concourse, head down, as though not wanting to attract any attention.

José Luis Viejo, 2013

Chapter 14

THE UNKNOWN WARRIOR

6 July 1976. Stage Eleven:
Montgenèvre to Manosque
224km. Mid mountains

His is a name that is only ever mentioned in connection with one obscure but impressive achievement. Otherwise, it has faded from the cycling record books; and in any case, it was never in bold type. A career, in short, that passed almost without note or notice.

Apart from one stage.

He meets you at the train station in Azuqueca, a dormitory town thirty minutes east of Madrid. He is not tall but wiry, grey-haired, wearing silver-rimmed spectacles and a striped shirt. He drives you in his modest car to his modest first-floor apartment. And in his living room he shows you his trophy cabinet, which is large and has pride of place, and suggests the record books might be lying; or at least not telling the full story. There is a glut of silverware; three shelves, packed with trinkets, ribboned medals and big-eared cups. A bronze medal from the 1971 amateur world road race championship, where Freddy Maertens was second; a trophy for winning the amateur Tour of Poland, the only Spaniard ever to do so;

awards for stage wins in the week-long stage races that pepper the Spanish calendar.

Now in his early sixties, José Luis Viejo can also boast of a fifth overall finish in his national tour, the Vuelta, in 1977. But that is not what he is known for. Instead, his fame, if it can be called that, is of the pub quiz variety. The biggest winning margin by an individual rider on a stage of the Tour de France? That would be José Luis Viejo, on stage eleven in 1976.

It is a historic feat, yet one that earns only a couple of pages in Geoffrey Nicholson's wonderful *The Great Bike Race*, a book that tells the story of the Tour through the reporter's travels on the 1976 race. Nicholson's book is all the more remarkable for it being a pretty unremarkable edition of the great bike race. In fact, Viejo's achievement was one of the most notable things to happen, but Nicholson doesn't dwell on it; he wasn't to know that the record would endure into a fourth decade, and is unlikely ever to be beaten. For Viejo himself, it is the source of great pride, but also frustration. Not least because the true story, or his story, is not the official one.

'José Luis Viejo is not a name that anyone has bothered to conjure with so far in the Tour,' writes Nicholson. He mentions a couple of minor placings, 'but the proper function of this long-faced, twenty-six-year-old Castillian has been to cater for the needs of the two Super Ser stars, Luis Ocaña and Pedro Torres.' Which, says Nicholson, 'is not a particularly thankful job when the stars themselves are waning.'

Viejo's best performances – the 1971 worlds, the Tour of Poland – were as an amateur. As a professional, his problem was that he was good at everything rather than excellent at any one thing: 'a proficient climber, sprinter and time triallist – a *coureur complet*, if not of the highest rank'.

The stage began on top of Montgenèvre, where the previous day, a stage won by Joop Zoetemelk, had finished.

It looped south, through the Hautes Alpes and Alpes de Haute Provence, with four category-three climbs in its 224km. It was a classic transitional stage after two tough days in the Alps; it would be followed by a rest day and then four days in the Pyrenees. It's a stage that is wedged in between these decisive and difficult days, which perhaps offers a partial explanation for the strange events of 6 July 1976.

Nicholson described the scenery, spectacular and ugly at the same time – 'an oppressive landscape of rocks striped like cross-sections in a geology textbook. Pipes the size of brick-yard stacks ran down the mountainside with no attempt at concealment; red and white pylons marched brazenly down the valley; the Durance was flowing like lava' – but concedes that it is a day when not much is expected to happen. This might explain why he and other reporters race ahead and stop for coffee in Embrun. It means they miss 'the start of a puzzling sequence of events'.

Freddy Maertens, in the midst of winning eight stages, claims the hot spot sprint in Embrun after 54km. Nicholson reports an attack at this point by Viejo's team-mate, José Casas, his second attempt of the day. Eight riders try to fol-low, 'including the unknown warrior, Viejo'. Then Nicholson tells us that Viejo goes alone, and bridges up to Casas, join-ing him as they ride through the feed zone at Savines-le-Lac after 64km.

For 10km, the team-mates ride together, says Nicholson, building a lead of four minutes. Which is unusual enough: a breakaway consisting only of team-mates. But then some-thing odder happens: Casas sits up. He is not dropped; he voluntarily returns to the peloton. It leaves Viejo on his own with 160km to go. 'A pure suicide mission,' as Nicholson puts it.

The climbs lie ahead of him: the Col de Saint-Jean at 97km, where Viejo's lead has increased to twelve minutes; La Javie, 40km later, where he is twenty-one minutes ahead;

Poteau de Telle after 183km; and finally Mont d'Or on the six-kilometre finishing circuit. In Digne, a little before the third climb, his lead stretches to twenty-seven minutes. He had started the day seventy-seventh, forty minutes down, so he poses no threat overall. And behind him the peloton switches off. Nicholson again: 'The race was quietly getting on with its own business and making no demands on anyone, but the Spaniard was moving along in a world of his own.'

Up front, our lone leader rides powerfully, even brilliantly. Observers are forced to admit that even if he has been let go, he rides with strength and grace, 'dancing round the corners' on the Poteau de Telle. At one point he punctures, 'which costs him precisely 22 seconds,' writes Nicholson. When he arrives in the finishing town of Manosque, he still leads by over twenty minutes. The peloton is still more than six kilometres from the town, where they will have to ride the six-kilometre finishing circuit.

Viejo's ride around the finishing circuit could be a lap of honour. He crosses the line with both arms in the air. Then he stands 'on the platform and watches the peloton pass through like any other spectator'.

Finally, twenty-two minutes and 50 seconds later, the other riders finish. Twenty-two minutes and 50 seconds: the biggest winning margin by a single rider in the history of the Tour then, and still a record to this day.

The inquest followed. The reporters spoke to the riders, directeurs, and tried to piece it all together. 'It was only afterwards that we found the explanation,' wrote Nicholson. The race thus far had been a disaster for Viejo's team, Super Ser. Ocaña, the winner in 1973, was past his best. Torres had been King of the Mountains the same year as Ocaña, after so many battles with Eddy Merckx, finally triumphed. But neither Ocaña nor Torres was performing well in 1976.

Now, according to Nicholson, the management 'delivered an ultimatum; unless the team put on a show before Manosque, it would be withdrawn'. Ocaña and Torres, though below par, would not be allowed any freedom. And so Casas and Viejo were 'detailed ... to do or die this day'.

Nicholson writes: 'The rest was diplomacy. As the bunch rolled along, Ocaña explained the team's predicament to Van Impe and the other leaders; and though he may no longer be a contender, he remains a person of influence among them. Casas they would not accept; although 29:32 down overall he could still cause some upset if his escape got out of hand. But they could see no possible harm in Viejo ... If he went off alone, they agreed not to make things too difficult for him.

'So Viejo was given his freedom, but no more, it seemed, than the freedom of a condemned man to choose his last breakfast.'

*   *   *

Thus was written the official story of Viejo's stage win. There was no asterisk next to his name, but there might as well have been. He had been gifted the stage; it was a consolation, an example of solidarity by the peloton; a charitable donation to a team in trouble.

Only, this is not quite how Viejo remembers it. Even the reported length of his escape, he says, was wrong. He says he was away for 194km, not 160.

It is true he was under orders to attack. His directeur sportif, Gabriel Saura, had ordered aggression. 'He said the Tour was over for Luis, and that we had to go for stage wins,' Viejo says. 'So I attacked after thirty kilometres.'

What about Casas, the team-mate with whom he was reported to have joined forces? Casas attacked before the first feed station, confirms Viejo. But he had been brought back by the time he launched his own bid for freedom. Viejo attacked through the feed station, he says. Etiquette dictates that the racing is neutralised here, as the riders collect their musettes, so was that fair? 'Hey, everything's fair in racing,' protests Viejo. 'In fact, Merckx used to do that, pick up his food before the feed station and then attack so that his rivals wouldn't get the food. And so did Maertens in the Vuelta he won [1977].'

Yet Viejo's break was pre-arranged, wasn't it? 'No,' says Viejo, with more than a hint of indignation. So there is no truth to the story that Van Impe allowed him to go, as a favour to Ocaña? 'None whatsoever.' Nor, he adds, is it true that he was ever with Casas. 'There was a guy chasing behind me, some Dutch guy not on our team, but they caught him on the big climb [the Col de Saint-Jean]. I attacked alone, and then I kept going and for about thirty kilometres I was at a minute, a minute and a half, and Van Impe's team wouldn't let me go.

'Finally, I ended up getting half an hour's advantage, and my time gap would have been bigger but I punctured on a seventeen-kilometre climb, a front wheel puncture. It took a long time to repair, because my team car had dropped back at that point to try and find out what the time gap was. I was so far ahead that the race radio frequency had dried up. So I lost a lot of time waiting for them to come back up to me, and change the wheel. Maybe a minute and a half.'

It is the idea that his escape was easy, that he was simply allowed to go, that most frustrates Viejo. Especially the story that he was given a pass by Van Impe. Of all people, Van Impe! 'Just look at how the bunch was a minute and a half behind me for thirty kilometres,' he says. 'There were times when I could see them, just behind me; I could actually see them chasing, and I thought, "These bastards are going to get me."'

So why did they eventually give up – as they must have done, given the way his lead expanded so dramatically? 'There was a small classified climb and Van Impe lost a lot of team-mates there and that's when they sat up. And from then on, I got time. But the stage was not easy at all. About fifteen or sixteen riders were eliminated; they missed the time cut. And it came right after the Alps, so everybody was tired.'

Behind Viejo, in the Super Ser team car, were his team's assistant directeur sportif and Jaime Mir Ferri, a mousta-chioed, larger-than-life character who became a feature on the Spanish scene in the 1970s. He was part soigneur, part public relations man. But he was also an actor, appearing in 125 movies, mainly crime films, between 1970 and 1994 (with his moustache, he also made a convincing Mexican bandit). Four decades on, Mir Ferri is still around; him and his moustache, still larger than life.

On the day of Viejo's great escape, Mir Ferri was in the team car, yelling encouragement. 'Mir kept on telling me, "Take it easy, you've got it won!" But I didn't believe him, and in fact nobody knew what the time gap was, because the race kept on splitting up behind. Even so, I didn't feel weak, not at all. I was on such a good day that day and I'd been strong all the way through the Tour.'

Viejo says he had seven minutes' advantage after the first climb, the Col de Saint-Jean, not twelve. 'I thought the big names would attack there and start to pull me back.' But his lead kept building, and building, and building. Yet, through-out, he was oblivious because the radio contact was so patchy – partly, though he didn't appreciate this at the time, because he was so far ahead. Even on the finishing circuit he wasn't sure he would hang on. 'There was a climb in Manosque, through the town, which we had to do twice. It was maybe three and a half kilometres or four and starting in the city, but a real wall. It was tough.

'And just coming over the top of that climb was where I thought, for the first time, I could win it. By that point we'd completely lost contact with Radio Tour, even when the car dropped back. It only went back so far before they had to come back to me again. It was only when a race motorbike which used to buzz around with food and water for the riders crossed the divide between me and the chasing teams and told us what the gap was, that I realised I was going to win.'

Second time up the climb he knew, for sure, he had it. The peloton hadn't even reached Manosque yet. Still, 'I wasn't interested in starting the celebrations early. I wanted the win too badly and I wanted to be sure of it before I did.' Viejo admits that his stage victory 'saved my team's Tour. It happened on 7 July, which was the day of San Fermín, so that was good, too.' San Fermín is the patron saint of Pamplona, where Super Ser had their headquarters.

What should we make of the inaccuracies in Nicholson's – and others' – reports? The truth may lie somewhere between Viejo's and the reporters' versions of events, since what is clear is that the information on the day was jumbled. If Viejo himself didn't know what was going on, or how big his lead was, then how could reporters (especially if they had stopped for coffee in Embrun)?

Inadvertently, the episode highlights one of the most challenging yet also fascinating aspects of covering the Tour, especially in the pre-Internet, pre-live television feed age. The close relationship between newspapers and cycle racing was forged in the earliest days when the written word was the only medium by which the action could be conveyed. Unlike other sports, held in self-contained arenas, road races happened largely out of sight. It meant they were perfect for newspapers; it is no accident that the Tour de France, and so many other races, were founded and organised by newspapers, in the Tour's case the precursor to *L'Equipe*, *L'Auto*. The reports of road racing were dramatic, poetic, florid; full of epic deeds, tales of suffering and heroism; and frequently speculative. They relied on the testimonies of participants who could, of course, be unreliable witnesses, because there was no way anybody could know everything that had happened. For years, writing about the Tour could be as much the work of the imagination as the reporting of hard and verifiable facts – hence novelists, playwrights and poets were sent by their newspapers to cover races such as the Tour, Giro d'Italia and Paris–Roubaix.

It's what makes cycle racing such a rich subject for writers. A goal in a football match can be pored over; the build-up can be analysed; its context can be understood by watching the rest of the match with your own eyes. In a road race, despite the probing gaze of television cameras and photographers' lenses, much remains unseen and unknown, even to many of the participants. The mystery is a big part of the appeal. It also means that the reports are not always accurate, and that the full truth sometimes does not emerge until later. Years, or even decades later. Or not at all.

*   *   *

What of the man who holds the record for the biggest margin of victory on a stage of the Tour de France?

The impression one has, speaking to Viejo, is that he looks back on his career with some disappointment; that he feels he did not fulfil his potential, either because of wrong decisions, a lack of confidence or flaws in his character. He wonders what else he might have been capable of, even at that 1976 Tour. 'It was clear I was pretty strong because the next stage [after his win] finished at Pyrenees 2000 and I got eighth. In about ten stages I finished in the top ten, including eighth on the Champs-Élysées. And now that time's gone past, I realise that if I'd worked more for myself, I'd have done a lot more.'

Viejo had started cycling at sixteen. 'There was a village bike race here and I rode it on my family bike, which was a racer, just for a laugh. And I won. After that, I bought a better bike to race as an amateur. The following year they offered me a place in Federico Bahamontes' [amateur] squad,

La Casera-Bahamontes.' Bahamontes, known as the Eagle of Toledo, was Spain's first Tour winner, in 1959, and the winner of the King of the Mountains six times.

'I won quite a lot of good races,' Viejo continues. 'The Vuelta a Navarra, the Vuelta a Toledo, some of the best in Spain, the Valenciaga, and in the international sphere I won the Tour of Poland and in the GP William Tell I twice got second – and that's the hardest race there is out there [for amateurs] because at that point in the season everybody is building towards the world championships.'

There is another unforgettable, harrowing memory from his amateur days. 'I took part in the Olympic Games in Munich, and from our building you could hear the shots when the Palestinians kidnapped the Israelis.'

But it is his Tour of Poland win from the same year, 1972, that stands out. He is still the only Spaniard ever to win, and to go there in the midst of Franco's dictatorship cannot have been straightforward. Yet going was the easy part, says Viejo. 'On the last stage, where I was winning everything, the mountains, the points, the lot, I had a thirty-seven-second advantage on a Polish rider, and the Polish national trainer got all the riders from the different regions together and told them to race against me. And they were pushing him along, pulling his saddle so he'd not have to pedal so hard, and it was so obvious what they were doing that the Swiss and the Italians opted to help me, just because they didn't like it.

'The race itself was very well organised, although I remember the food and conditions were awful. We got an invite as the Spanish selection, and to tell the truth it was pretty rough. It was very flat, minus a couple of short hilly stages, four or five kilometres long, but there were a heck of a lot of cobbled sections and a heck of a lot of people. We got to stadiums for the finishes and they'd be packed.'

It was Bahamontes who became the dominant influence on Viejo's career, but not a positive one. 'In La Casera-Bahamontes,

Bahamontes was the technical director. He had a lot of character and I don't really think he was a good director because of his personality. He wasn't cunning enough to handle a team of amateurs. Then I turned professional with [the professional version of the team] La Casera-Bahamontes and that was the worst thing that he did to me, because he made me turn pro with his team even though Dalmacio Langarica [the KAS directeur sportif] came down here to Madrid and wanted me to sign with them. The problem was Federico made me keep my word. I'd promised to turn pro with him and when I told him that KAS wanted me, and for a lot more money, too, he wouldn't let me go, he said I'd made a promise. And I hadn't signed with La Casera, but I couldn't break my word, either. Which was a mistake on my part.

'The problem was that there was a pre-established hierarchy at La Casera. It was like doing military service: the more experienced were automatically superior to you. I had done some good rides as an amateur, even against riders like Freddy Maertens. But in La Casera, even though I was better than guys like José Luis Abilliera and Andrés Oliva, I had to work for them because I was younger.

'I won a couple of races, and then I went for Super Ser [1975] and I raced the Tour. I finished the Tour but there were people with more reputation and prestige like Ocaña and [Swiss rider Josef] Fuchs you had to work for. There were team-mates who would pretend they hadn't seen when the big guys punctured; but I did, I always waited for them, I'd be the first to do that.'

His stage win in the 1976 Tour was certainly the high point of his career. Viejo finally got his chance with the KAS team the following year, and finished fifth in his national tour, the Vuelta. The next year he won a stage in the Vuelta Ciclista al País Vasco, but abandoned his final Tour in 1979. Then he spent a couple of seasons with Teka before joining Zor for his final year, in 1982, 'a much more modern team, and

Pedro Muñóz was the leader. And Pedro had a good chance in the Vuelta, but, as for me, I went down with gastroenteritis, and after a few bad days I had to abandon. I won a stage of the Vuelta a Asturias, but I went down with brucellosis and I went to the Midi Libre before being really cured of the illness and I had to abandon. Then I went down with another illness, typhoid fever, and that was enough. I decided to quit.'

In retirement, he ran a bike shop in his village, which closed in 2008. Now he has an office selling lottery tickets – a common occupation in Spain – which employs his daughters. He has four daughters and one son, who isn't interested in cycling.

His stage win at the Tour remains in the record books. His twenty-two minutes fifty-second margin of victory may never be beaten. But it didn't change his life. It didn't even do much for his career. Geoffrey Nicholson's description was apt; then again, he is one of many unknown warriors.

'No, it didn't change my career,' Viejo says. 'But it's the biggest stage race in the world, and that does make me proud. Proud that the record has stood for so long and proud I got there alone. Because going away in a group of three or four riders would be very different. They could get a half-hour lead easily.

'But one rider? I don't think so.'

Classement

1 José Luis Viejo, Spain, Super Ser, 5 hours, 42 minutes, 34 secs
2 Gerben Karstens, Holland, TI-Raleigh, at 22 minutes, 50 secs
3 Freddy Maertens, Belgium, Velda-Flandria, at 23 minutes, 7 secs
4 Wladimoro Panizza, Italy, SCIC-Fiat, same time
5 Gianbattista Baronchelli, Italy, Bianchi-Piaggio, s t.
6 Raymond Delisle, France, Peugeot-Esso, s.t.

FREDDY MAERTENS

Chapter 15

CHAMPAGNE FREDDY

28 June 1981. Stage Three: Martigues to Narbonne 232km. Flat

As first encounters go, it couldn't have been less auspicious. It was May 1987 and Freddy Maertens was the star name in a race being held in an unlikely location: a park in Dunfermline, close to my home city of Edinburgh.

Maertens was thirty-five and had not won a race of note for years. His name meant little to me, but his CV sparkled. He had won some of the great races: Classics, stages of the Tour de France, two world titles. Yet the trajectory of his career was erratic, to say the least. There were gaps that were more like black holes. He was brilliant then terrible, then briefly brilliant again, before he all but disappeared – only to pop up, on a miserably cold day, in Pittencrieff Park in Dunfermline.

Five years after his last flashes of brilliance, this Belgian once-upon-a-time star brought continental allure, even if his star had actually faded to a point where it was barely visible. Even in Dunfermline.

Maertens was hopeless. Humiliated by a bunch of Scottish amateurs, he quickly fell out of contention on the narrow, twisting and rutted park lanes. He failed to finish. But he did pick up his appearance money, courtesy of a local double-glazing magnate, which is why he was there in the first place. He needed the cash.

Two decades later, I encountered Maertens again, once more in curious circumstances, at the 2006 Tour de France. We were in Gap for a stage start, snaking out of town as part of the large convoy of vehicles that precedes the race. The stage was due to start in fifteen minutes. But as our press car jostled with the other vehicles for a place in the line of cars, a figure materialised. He was walking quickly towards the traffic, on the left side of the road, waving his hands, imploring each vehicle to stop. He looked frantic, manic and dishevelled. Everybody ignored him. But as we got closer he began to seem familiar, the face, in particular the lips, unmistakable. It was the rider known cruelly as 'Fat Lips' – Freddy Maertens.

We slammed on the brakes, to a cacophony of horns from the vehicles behind, and Maertens jumped into the back seat, expressing gratitude and relief in a thick Belgian accent. He explained that he was there as a guest of one of the Tour's sponsors, but his vehicle had left without him. He didn't know how to get in touch with the driver. He phoned his wife, Carine, who clearly had experience of bailing her husband out before.

For the rest of the journey, Maertens leant forward, like a little boy, and talked earnestly, and compellingly, about his strange career. He seemed a sad but sympathetic figure; boy-like, with a friendly, open face and a remarkable facility with languages – he was fluent in about five.

Seven years later, after our encounter at the 2006 Tour, I meet Maertens for a third time, this time by prior arrangement, in the Flanders Centre. It's a large, modern visitor attraction in Oudenaarde that, in a sign of how fervent Flandrians are about their cycling, is entirely dedicated to the Ronde van Vlaanderen, the Tour of Flanders. It is where Maertens now works.

We are supposed to meet at eleven, but there is no sign. 'Where's Freddy?' I ask at reception. The girl doesn't know, so she phones a colleague: 'Where's Freddy?'

The colleague appears, shrugging. She asks another colleague, 'Where's Freddy?'

'Where's Freddy?' is a refrain that might echo around the Flanders Centre on an hourly basis. It would perhaps have made a fitting title for his autobiography. Instead it is called *Fall from Grace*, which is also apt. Because that, certainly, is what Maertens did.

*　　*　　*

The town of Narbonne, nestled in the wine-rich Languedoc-Roussillon region in the south of France, is a place of faded glory, but it is close to the Mediterranean beaches that stretch for kilometres. It was a stage – stage three of the 1981 Tour – which hugged that coastline after heading west from Martigues, 40km north-west of Marseille; a stage, finishing on Narbonne Plage, that was made for sprinters. 'It was five or six kilometres, along the beach, a straight line,' Maertens says. He knew it well. And he liked it. 'Because it was by the sea. And I was born by the sea, in Nieuwpoort, so it was special to me.'

Being born and living by the sea also, says Maertens, made him an outsider, even an outcast. He believes that he didn't receive an official reception from the King of Belgium after either of his world titles, 'because I came from the coast, while Eddy Merckx was from Brussels'.

When the Tour visited Narbonne in 1981, Maertens had done his homework. 'I had studied the finish.' He had been there a few weeks earlier, having failed to finish the Midi Libre – one of many races he failed to finish in 1981 – when it used the same finish by the beach. 'I sat on a terrace bar studying events closely,' writes Maertens in his book.

On that day, weeks before the Tour started and with his own place in the team far from certain, Maertens watched as the riders appeared, noting that the road widened and narrowed, observing the wind direction, and that the sheer length of the finishing straight confused riders, tricking some into making their effort too early.

It is a powerful and arresting image: Maertens sitting on the terrace of a bar – if anyone spotted him it would have fuelled rumours that he had a drink problem – and studying the road below, looking to the outside world like the fallen star everybody thought he was.

To understand why Narbonne in 1981 meant so much to Maertens, you have to understand what he went through to get there.

                              *   *   *

It was so different in 1976, Maertens' first Tour. His was a long-awaited, much-anticipated début. Maertens had been brought up by his father, Gilbert, to be a cyclist. Gilbert took his obsession with his son's career to ridiculous extremes: on one occasion, when he caught his teenaged son walking hand-in-hand with a girl, he raced home and took a saw to his bike, cutting it in two. But perhaps, as Maertens acknowledges today, his father needed to be strict. He had a boyish sense of mischief, loved pranks and had a general air of haplessness. At least two of these traits are still evident today.

Throughout his career, Freddy was guided, or kept in check, by father figures. After his own father it was Lomme Driessens, who became his directeur sportif at the Flandria team in 1976, in time for his Tour début. Known by some as 'Lomme the Liar', he 'lived in a fantasy world', says Maertens, though it was true that Driessens had directed Merckx (he had also worked with Fausto Coppi, and another great Belgian, Rik van Looy). The cigar-smoking Driessens hitched his wagon to Maertens just in time. According to Maertens, 'he could motivate like nobody else. Even when you felt terrible because you were riding badly, he could almost make you believe you were the best rider in the race.'

Driessens was overbearing, and a constant presence in Maertens' life, visiting his home and standing over Carine as she cooked, telling her what she should be making her husband; specifically how she should prepare Freddy's minestrone soup, which Driessens believed to be the staple of a cyclist's diet. The impression formed of Driessens is that he was all – or mainly – bluster. Maertens and the team-mates to whom he was closest, Michel Pollentier and Marc Demeyer, behaved like unruly children at a boarding school, with Driessens in the role of strict but hapless headmaster. On one occasion they trapped him in a sauna for an hour, until he 'looked like a boiled lobster'; on another they put crushed sleeping pills in his beloved minestrone soup; and on another they cut the legs off his suit trousers as they lay draped over a chair.

Maertens, Pollentier and Demeyer called themselves 'The Three Musketeers'. They trained together most days, practising lead-outs; Maertens was an impressive all-rounder – he could time trial, he could climb – but his most powerful weapon was his sprint finish. There is a belief, in some quarters, that the first lead-out 'train' was Jean-Paul van Poppel's Superconfex 'green train' in the late 1980s, copied by Mario Cipollini's Saeco 'red train' a decade later, and perfected by Mark Cavendish and his HTC team another decade later. Maertens laughs at the idea. 'I wasn't even the first sprinter to have a lead-out,' he says. 'Van Looy did, too.

'For sprints, we talked about it and we trained for it, too,' Maertens continues. 'They think now they are the first to have a lead-out train! Ha ha ha! There is nothing new. We trained almost every day together, me, Pollentier and Demeyer. We did this in training, many times in each ride.

And at the finish of a race, the lead-out was first Pollentier, then Demeyer, then me. Demeyer was bigger, which was good for me. Michel was a good climber, but very strong on the flat as well. We trained hard. If we were training for the Tour of Flanders, which was 280 kilometres, we went out for 310 to 320 kilometres. For the Tour de France we raced a lot: Midi Libre, Tour of Switzerland, and then the Tour.'

Maertens wasn't overawed by the Tour when he finally made his début in 1976. He wasn't particularly impressed, either. Asked what he remembers of his début, he screws up his face: 'Everything. A lot of the time we slept in school. French schools with dormitories. The food was the same every day. Mashed potatoes, haricots verts, and little bits of meat. Steak, but not good steak. The potatoes came out of boxes, already mashed. But every day was the same. Breakfast was the same: bread and honey. The caterer travelled with the race. When you saw the food, you said: "It's better at home." But [despite that] the Tour was good for me from the start ...'

Maertens won the prologue time trial in Saint-Jean-de-Monts in the Loire. Next day, he won the first stage to Angers. He wore the yellow jersey for ten days, into Belgium, and won stages in Le Touquet–Paris-Plage (a 37km time trial: his favourite of his eight stage wins in 1976), Mulhouse, Langon, Lacanau, Versailles and another time trial, into Paris, on the final day. He was eighth overall and won the green points jersey. But it was his eight stage wins that marked his début and put him in the company of just two other riders: Charles Pélissier in 1930, and Maertens' countryman, Merckx, in 1970 and 1974.

'It should have been nine,' Maertens says. 'I gave a stage to Jacques Esclassan.' It was stage eight, Valentigney to Divonne-les-Bains; a flat 206km, made for sprinters. Made for Maertens. 'I was winning a lot of stages,' he explains, 'and Peugeot [Esclassan's team] didn't win anything. They came to ask me for help. Peugeot were going to stop their sponsorship, and so the evening before, in Mulhouse, they came, Maurice De Muer and the boss of Peugeot, to see Driessens and me. Pollentier was there too. I didn't want to speak alone. And we made an agreement.'

For money? 'No, for friendship,' says Maertens, who senses my scepticism because he repeats: 'Really, friendship.'

Maertens' penultimate stage win in the 1976 Tour was extraordinary, even by his standards. It was a 145km road stage from Montargis to Versailles. It was bucketing down, and he attacked with another Belgian, Ferdinand Bracke. 'I was attacking to get on the podium, because that was still possible. I could still finish third, though [Lucien] Van Impe had won, more or less.'

If Maertens was still in contention for the podium, why was he allowed to escape? 'Because it was raining and we had our rain jackets on,' he says. 'And the rain jackets of the '70s are not the rain jackets of now. You couldn't see what jersey you were wearing, or what number you were. And there were no radios. So nobody knew I was away. At a certain moment in the race they said our numbers, the others realised and started to chase, but by then we were 15km from the finish …

'Anyway, Bracke and I were away, but suddenly, on a corner, Bracke's wheel slips, I touch it, and I go down. My chain was off and I had to wait for the car with my other bike. I waited, the peloton raced past, I got my other bike and then I caught the peloton again. I still won the stage. It was a sprint. But if I had stayed away with Bracke, if I hadn't crashed, I would have had four or five minutes.'

* * *

'Deals, doping and near-death experiences' might also have been the title of Maertens' autobiography. Sometimes they were wrapped up together. As a baby, he had a lung infection that saw him hospitalised for six months. The nurses injected medicine into his bottom. 'I suppose you could say that was my first experience of doping,' is his wry observation on page two of his book.

It wasn't the last. 'Anyone who says they can do it naturally is a liar,' says Maertens, meaning racing without drugs. He used amphetamines in kermesses, 'but never in the Classics or Tours,' though he lost the Tour of Belgium in 1974 after testing positive. He also tested positive in some big races in 1977, the season after his great year: at the Flèche Wallonne, Tour of Flanders and Tour de France. In those days it didn't result in expulsion, far less suspension, far less disgrace: the standard punishment was a time penalty, usually of ten minutes.

There was one doping scandal that did provoke a sense of outrage, and Maertens was closely linked to it. It was his great friend, fellow musketeer and room-mate, Pollentier, who, during the 1978 Tour, was caught trying to cheat a drugs test. It was at the summit of l'Alpe d'Huez, where Pollentier had won the stage and taken the yellow jersey. As he went to give his sample, the drugs-tester became aware of some apparatus: a length of tubing containing ('clean') urine, which Pollentier was holding alongside his penis.

In reports at the time, and since, it was said that the tubing was connected to a bulb in his armpit. But Maertens corrects that now, when I ask him if it was a trick he ever pulled: having 'clean' urine in a bulb – often a condom – in his armpit. 'It was not there,' Maertens says. 'No, it was here,' and he points to his behind. The urine was in a condom in Pollentier's bottom? 'Yes.' And did Maertens himself ever do this? 'In kermesses, yes. When the police did the controls, no. There were a lot of people who did that. But not in the Classics; not in the Tour. It wasn't possible.'

After Pollentier's expulsion, he and Maertens spent the night in their room, trying to keep the press at bay. Pollentier was concerned about how he would be received back home in Belgium. He needn't have worried. As Maertens recalls:

'During his suspension, when he appeared at criteriums to give the start signal, it was not unusual for him to receive more applause than any of the riders.'

Maertens' own problems were just over the horizon. With Pollentier having departed, he was unhappy with his Flandria team in 1979, sensing a plot against him, suffering with an injury to his wrist, and only winning two minor races. He had fallen a long way from his eight stage wins and world race title of 1976. Three years later, he could barely finish races: 'Depression was looming just around the corner.' On the advice of his team boss, Paul Claeys, he travelled to the USA, to the school of medicine in Philadelphia, for tests. He claims he almost died before he even got there. Throughout his flight across the Atlantic, he was disturbed by a strange noise from the engine on the left wing. When he mentioned it to his companion, his companion told him to shut up.

Maertens disembarked in New York, and the plane, an American Airlines DC-10, took off for Chicago. From Chicago it took off for Los Angeles, but moments later one of the engines – on the left wing – came off. The plane crashed, killing 273 people. Until the 9/11 terrorist attacks, it was the worst air disaster in American history.

Maertens stayed in Philadelphia for several weeks. He was under the care of a Dr Fischer, who ran a series of physical and psychological tests. In Belgium, the rumour was that he had been committed to a mental hospital. Meanwhile, in Philadelphia, all the tests were clear: Maertens was told there was nothing physically wrong with him, although Dr Fischer did suggest that his psychological problems were due to 'the problems he has had in relation to drugs'. He added: 'Though I suspect he will be tempted to use stimulating drugs when he is under competitive pressure, I think he has the inner strength to resist the temptation.'

Still Maertens could not rediscover his old form. Still he struggled to finish races; winning was out of the question. The rumours intensified: he was an alcoholic; a drug addict; he had a nervous breakdown. It was none of these things, Maertens says now. It was all a big misunderstanding. He did have a problem, and it completely derailed his career. It was financial. The taxman was after him. 'Nineteen seventy-seven was good,' he says, 'and '78 was OK, but then began the problems with the taxes. It was the biggest problem I had in my career. But in the winter of 1980 my wife and I talked. She said, "You have to do it like you did it before."' She meant training: focusing solely on cycling. 'She said, "When it comes to speaking to the accountant, the lawyer, the court, I will do it. You have to train and nothing more."' Carine shielded her husband, intercepting mail, phone calls and even visits from the taxman.

At the start of the 1981 season, Maertens had a new team, Boule d'Or, and, with Pollentier and Demeyer no longer by his side, he had two new musketeers: Ronald De Witte and Alain De Roo. He was also reunited with his old director, Lomme Driessens, who had been sacked after the 1977 season. But a return to his previous form seemed impossible. Although still only twenty-nine, Maertens was seen as a spent force. Whatever his problems, he had shone too brightly, too young, and burnt out.

*   *   *

Maertens wishes to correct one point. 'I was not an alcoholic. The problem is that when they see you drinking one beer, people think you are an alcoholic.'

He did use alcohol, though. He used it as a performance aid. But only champagne. 'It was Lomme who said to try it. Seventy-six was the first time; you have to try it in training, not racing. That was the mistake Pollentier made. He tried it before the Baracchi Trophy and his legs were like that' – Maertens shakes his legs and they wobble like jelly. 'Everything new, you have to try it in training.

'Once you know it works, then the fortnight before, you do not drink alcohol. No! Or the champagne has no effect. When the legs weren't good, I didn't drink it. But in big races I left the bottle in the car.'

A whole bottle of champagne? 'No, no, no – half a bottle. In a cool box. A team-mate went to get it for me at 30km from the finish.' Who? 'Normally it was Herman Beyssens who went back, because he would have a drink also.' By the time it reached Maertens, with Beyssens having had his share, it was 'more like 33 centilitres'.

'It was in a bidon, mixed with some sugar and some caffeine.' He would drink it in three or four gulps. And the effect was like dynamite. Comparable to amphetamines? 'Yes,' nods Maertens. 'Like amphetamines, yes. It was like a legal high.'

What happened to the rest of the champagne? 'Lomme finished off the bottle while driving the team car.'

But in 1981 even the champagne didn't seem to be working for Maertens. Nor did his renewed partnership with Driessens, who was back standing over Carine, telling her how to make minestrone soup. Maertens says that he overtrained at the start of the season. Then he crashed, breaking two fingers in his hand. He came back but kept crashing. He fell off in virtually every race he rode in the spring; plus, despite Carine's reassurance, the tax problems weighed on his mind. He became 'apathetic' about racing. 'Psychologically, I was at a low ebb.' In May he went to the Midi Libre, run in 'tropical heat, and which had never been one of my favourite races,' and climbed off on the second stage.

He elected, however, not to go home. Instead, he stayed with the team. He rode each stage ahead of the race. And for the stage that finished at Narbonne Plage he sat on the balcony of a seafront bar and waited for the finish. And studied the long stretch of road, knowing that stage three of the Tour de France would also finish there – and that it would almost certainly end in a bunch sprint.

Maertens insists now that his habit of not finishing races was all part of a grand plan. 'I stopped races because I was preparing for the Tour de France and world championships.' He was confident? 'Sure. I didn't finish the race, but then I rode in the car for a bit, then stepped out and rode 100 or 120 kilometres on the bike. Nobody knew I was doing that. But that was my plan.'

Not that Maertens' selection for the Tour was guaranteed. In fact, it looked as though he would be left out, until he made a pleading phone call to Driessens' wife, Maria, who always had a soft spot for Maertens and 'mothered' him (it isn't difficult to imagine; even now in the Flanders Centre, where he works, his colleagues seem protective of Maertens). Maria Driessens convinced her husband that he should pick Maertens. Driessens relented, but Maertens went to the Tour as a team member, with no 'privileged status'.

While warming up for the prologue time trial in Nice, he crashed into a woman who was crossing the road. He was late to the start house and finished 66th. 'The press had a good snigger about that,' Maertens writes in his book.

But the next day, over hilly and wet roads around Nice, the first road stage burst into life with an attack from Bernard Hinault, who escaped with Jean-René Bernaudeau and one of Bernaudeau's Peugeot team-mates, Charly Bérard. Hinault's companions slid on a corner and both fell; then Hinault fell, and then Bernaudeau fell a second time, and with that all momentum was lost. They were caught, and the stage came down to a sprint.

It was a short stage, just 97km, but the rider who emerged at the front surprised everybody. It was Maertens, who came off Sean Kelly's wheel to win his first stage in three years. 'I have always said that I would bring Freddy back,' said Driessens, basking shamelessly in the reflected glory, trying to claim as much credit as possible, even telling the journalists that he had stopped Maertens drinking.

'Very satisfying,' says Maertens of his win in Nice. 'It was hilly, short, and before the race all the journalists laughed at me because my weight was a bit over – only one or two kilogrammes. They said I was lucky.'

Many remained sceptical, and unconvinced that the old Maertens was back. It had only been 97km – hardly a real road stage. It was a one-off, a fluke, a brief flash of the old genius. As one journalist put it, when the race got properly underway, with the 232km third stage from Martigues to Narbonne, 'Maertens will be ridden into the ground.'

*   *   *

The stage began in the 'Venice of Provence' in lashing rain and wind as the riders cut up from Martigues and headed north-west, through the Camargue, where cross-winds can play havoc. The wind whipped across plains populated by white horses and flamingoes, but it was too early in the stage for the race to split into echelons. They skirted Montpellier, heading for Béziers via a detour to the north, to Roujan, and into more rain. The race sparked into life. Ludo Peeters went clear after an intermediate sprint and was joined by Phil Anderson, the Australian poised to become the revelation of this Tour, as well as Daniel Willems, Gerrie Knetemann and Jean-Luc Vandenbroucke: a dangerous quintet, all strong *rouleurs*, threatening to rule out a bunch sprint.

Maertens sat in the bunch, thinking about that long straight at Narbonne Plage. It was tantalising. Should he get his team to work and bring the break back? It was complicated: he wasn't the leader. And yet he had been promised, by Driessens, support in the finale, if it looked like ending in a sprint. And he had support before that – he sent Alain De Roo back to the team car with 30km remaining to collect the bidon containing his legal drug, his champagne. 'I knew I needed it,' Maertens recalls, 'because I knew it was my stage.'

Maertens' team did some work at the front, but it was another team that closed down the move. Hinault instructed his Renault squad to chase; they did so with ruthless efficiency. It was back on for Maertens.

The dangerman was Urs Freuler, a moustachioed Swiss better known as a track rider and signed by Peter Post, the director of the TI-Raleigh team, to win bunch sprints on the road. Freuler won the first intermediate sprint on this stage, at Raphele-les-Arles after 34km, from Maertens himself. But Maertens was confident he had the beating of him when it counted, on the long straight by the beach at the end.

When the riders finally appeared on that long, long straight, it was messy, as sprints tended to be. There was no organisation, just chaos. The road was wide, the surface uneven, and there was – contrary to what Maertens tells me – little evidence of any lead-out for him on this occasion. By the final 800 metres, he was on his own. The riders fanned across the road, and then there was a surge down the left, before momentum swung back to the right. All the time, Maertens remained in the middle, hiding in the wheels, holding back, waiting. He remembered his homework: that this straight was longer even than it looked.

Freuler led the charge on the right, Maertens tucked in behind Jos Jacobs, who in the final 200 metres suddenly emerges into clear space. In doing so, he unwittingly provides an effective lead-out for Maertens, who appears late, in the middle, head down. Maertens, short, stocky, with thick, muscular arms and shoulders, sprints like a charging bull. Once in front, he veers from left to right, head still down. He also seems to engage a higher gear: when he kicks again his speed over the closing metres takes him up to Freuler. He draws level. Then he edges in front just centimetres before the line. And he throws his arms up. Maertens always celebrated in the same style: arms flung in the air, elbows locked, palms facing forward, fingers spread; often gurning, too, with his tongue hanging out, leading to some cruel descriptions.

The bunch sprint at Narbonne Plage was, as *Cycling Weekly* reported, a 'charge', or a stampede, but 'Maertens moved as if on rails, accelerating, gathering speed until he put in that special effort that we thought we had seen the last of. He thundered across the line ... it was a spectacular, dangerous final sprint.' And it represented a 'miraculous return to form of former world champion Maertens'.

Phil Anderson had opted out altogether. 'It was too dangerous for me. I was on Maertens' wheel when I got stuck behind Sean Kelly, who was giving a sling to Eddy Planckaert.'

Kelly, a former team-mate of Maertens, was becoming one of the fastest sprinters in the world, but Maertens didn't fear him. Who was faster, him or Kelly? 'Me,' he says quickly. 'Me, me.'

'This win in Narbonne, it was really the most satisfying,' he says now. Why? 'Because Peter Post had taken Freuler to his team to beat me. I also liked winning by the sea ... But that day the whole team arranged for me to arrive at the finish for the sprint. They set it up for a sprint. You don't see that in the final, but they had done their work earlier. It was a long, long finish – five or six kilometres along the beach. But I knew it very well. And I didn't fear anybody.'

*   *   *

Maertens went on to win three more stages, including the final one into Paris, and the green jersey. He also won his second world title later the same year, in Prague. His comeback was the story of the year, and explanations were sought. 'He's riding two gears higher than the rest of us,' one unnamed rider said in a story in a Belgian newspaper. Another rider, Fons De Wolf, pointed to his renewed association with Driessens: 'Lomme knows how to deal with certain types of people.

Remember, he has been with him since October and love can work at once.'

But 1981 was Maertens' final hurrah. Though he raced another five and a half years, he hardly had a result of note. It is one mystery among many concerning Maertens. The rumours at the time were that he was using a new 'wonder drug'. 'Yah, yah, they said I had a new drug,' he tells me. 'But as I told you, in cycling, people talk a lot. No, my doctor prepared me well. And I ate well. I ate a lot of fish.'

So what happened – why did he never hit those heights again? After all, he was still a young man, only twenty-nine. 'I said to my wife, "When I become world champion again, I'm finished." I said the same to Bernard Hinault.' The only reason he didn't retire, he adds, is because he needed the money. He finally cleared his tax debts in 2011. 'It followed me for thirty years. Thirty years! I feel much better now, and my wife, too. Thirty years! It's not possible, eh?'

For many, Maertens, despite a career trajectory that resembles the profile of a Pyrenean stage, is the fastest sprinter in history. Those who saw him at his best – rather than in a park in Dunfermline – say that at his best he was electrifying, with a kick that could destroy opponents. But in recent years another sprinter has emerged to lay claim to the title of fastest ever. At their best, who would win, Maertens or Mark Cavendish?

Maertens gives the question serious thought, chewing his full lips. 'Can we arrange it that I am thirty years younger?' he says.

'Imagine you are both twenty-seven,' I tell Maertens. He continues to chew his lips, and now furrows his brow and stares at his clasped hands. 'There are similarities, yeah. He doesn't always need team-mates, he is good at positioning himself – like me. And he is able to jump twice – go, and go again. I could do that, too. Yeah, Cavendish is very fast.

'But I was very fast, too.'

Classement

1   Freddy Maertens, Belgium, Flandria, 6 hours, 33 minutes,
    50 secs
2   Urs Freuler, Switzerland, Bilta-Echter Glarner-Chämi Salami,
    same time
3   Jos Jacobs, Belgium, Capri Sonne, s.t.
4   Eddy Planckaert, Belgium, Wickes-Splendor, s.t.
5   Walter Planckaert, Belgium, Wickes-Splendor, s.t.
6   Yvon Bertin, France, Renault-Elf, s.t.

L–R: Jan Ullrich, Lance Armstrong, Iban Mayo

Chapter 16

HONOUR AMONG THIEVES

21 July 2003. Stage Fifteen:
Bagnères-de-Bigorre to Luz Ardiden
159.5km. High mountains

Lance Armstrong is angry.

'I mean, listen, look. Travis Tygart and his band of haters can say what they want. Those Tours happened … it was an unfortunate time, most of us if not all of us played by the same set of rules … I consider myself the winner of those seven Tours.'

We had been talking about a stage that officially didn't happen, ten years after it didn't happen, one year after it has been deemed not to have happened. Armstrong is talking as he drives to the golf course, forty minutes from his house in Austin, Texas. It is almost a year since he was officially stripped of his seven Tour de France titles and banned from competitive sport for life. He gets angry when he talks about Travis Tygart, the man at the head of the US Anti-Doping Agency, who led the investigation into Armstrong and his US Postal team, eventually describing the set-up as 'the most sophisticated, professionalised and successful doping programme that sport has ever seen'. (To which Armstrong responds: 'You can't say that one team has the most sophisticated programme in the world when you don't look at the other nineteen teams. You have to look at all twenty before you make that claim.') But otherwise Armstrong seems remarkably relaxed. The fact that he is on his way to play golf suggests that he is holding it together; that he is not in the midst of a breakdown.

On the contrary, Armstrong says he is well. 'Yeah, y'know. Just dealing with a little drama here and there, but otherwise not too bad.' The 'little dramas' include an insurance claim of several million dollars, and a federal case that might cost him up to $100 million, to name just two.

Yet in one sense Armstrong is certainly right. Those Tours did happen.

*   *   *

It was the year Armstrong was bidding to join The Club. The Club of five-time Tour de France winners, whose members were Anquetil, Merckx, Hinault and Indurain. But, in the months leading up to his bid to join The Club, things and events, which had always been tightly controlled and micromanaged by Armstrong, seemed to unravel.

First, his marriage ended in the winter. Armstrong has never said exactly what happened, but in January, as he and his wife, Kristin, strolled along a beach in Santa Barbara, he told her that it was over. It seemed a characteristically clinical, ruthless decision, and yet it wasn't quite as simple as that. Their three children – son Luke and twin girls Grace and Isabella – complicated things, and Armstrong was distracted in the first months of the season, travelling between the USA and Europe to spend time with them. It meant he raced a lighter programme. He didn't appear to be his usual, hyperfocused self. Indeed, it is perhaps a sign of how out-of-sorts he was that, as the Tour got underway, Armstrong was making a doomed attempt at reconciliation with Kristin.

There were other rumours about Armstrong in early 2003: that he was distracted, living the high life, drinking alcohol, and generally not as committed as before. Tyler Hamilton, Armstrong's former team-mate, who now led the rival CSC squad but still lived in the same apartment block as Armstrong in Girona, suggests as much in his book, *The Secret Race*. It was said that Armstrong would 'ghost in and ghost out' of Girona, and that team-mates joked they were most likely to find him 'on television'.

Armstrong dismisses such rumours. 'Ah, well, I haven't read Tyler's book, but I wouldn't put a lot into what Tyler and Dan Coyle [Hamilton's ghostwriter] have to say. They're too … committed to tearing somebody down and it really clouds reality.

'But, you know, there's no doubt, the winter before, we had split up, then we got back together. And even though we got back together, it hadn't gone that well. But that … I don't … when I think of 2003, and what went wrong, or what was the problem, that doesn't cross my mind. There are other factors that went into it.'

The drinking? 'I was still pretty strict. I didn't start drinking a glass or two of wine at dinner every night until 2004. And that year I definitely, almost every meal, would have a glass or two of wine – every meal. Before that, from February to August, I didn't drink.'

There were other distractions, though. Throughout 2003 the Irish journalist David Walsh was investigating Armstrong's then rumoured doping, seeking witnesses. Armstrong knew what Walsh was doing and was almost as busy as Walsh in making his own inquiries about Walsh's inquiries (Walsh's book, *L.A. Confidentiel*, would be published a year later, on the eve of the 2004 Tour).

It's ironic that, as suspicion around Armstrong intensified, he might have been losing his edge when it came to doping, too. Hamilton thought that the peloton was 'catching up'.

As he wrote in his 2012 book: 'Good information is hard to keep underground ... Innovations can't help but spread.' In early 2003, that meant 'talk about artificial haemoglobin', masking agents, new types of EPO, blood transfusions. Germany's Jan Ullrich, who finished second to Armstrong in 2000 and 2001, was returning from a short ban imposed for testing positive for the recreational drug ecstasy, and had started working with Hamilton's trainer, Luigi Cecchini (once a colleague, now a rival of Armstrong's trainer, Michele Ferrari). Like Hamilton, Ullrich was also working with Eufemiano Fuentes, a Madrid doctor who ran a blood-doping ring, organising the storage and transfusions of hundreds of bags of athletes' blood (blood transfusions now being preferred to EPO, for which there was a test).

In *Wheelmen*, the 2013 book about Armstrong's downfall, the authors claim that Ullrich returned stronger 'thanks to a renewed commitment to doping. Ullrich and his trainer had backed off doping after the Festina scandal [in 1998], on the assumption that everyone else in the field would, too; but they realised, after the 2002 race, that their logic was flawed ... They were playing doping catch-up, but they were confident that they were closing the gap on Armstrong.'

The theories of Hamilton and *Wheelmen* are dismissed by Armstrong, who says there never was a 'gap'. What he and his team, US Postal, did in terms of doping was 'pretty fucking normal', he tells me. 'It was not the most sophisticated doping programme in the history of the world. It was pretty conservative. Ferrari was a very, very conservative guy, he was risk-averse. His athletes had the bare minimum, and these other idiots like Floyd [Landis] and Tyler can attest to that because they went out and started to take exceptional risks.'[5]

---

5   Tyler Hamilton tested positive for blood doping in 2004, while Floyd Landis, a team-mate of Armstrong in 2003, would later test positive for testosterone while winning the 2006 Tour. The risks were also in

*   *   *

Armstrong's opponents were well known to him, and he had the measure of them (with Ullrich, his strategy was to praise him, calling him the most naturally talented rider of his generation. As Armstrong's chiropractor, Jeff Spencer, told Coyle: 'He understands that what Jan doesn't like is pressure. If you want to get into his head, praise him to the skies.')

But in 2003 another rival emerged as if from nowhere – or the Basque Country, which amounted to much the same thing as far as Armstrong was concerned.

Iban Mayo was as proud, unpredictable and obstinate as the region he came from. Armstrong faced this mercurial climber at the Dauphiné Libéré, just weeks before the Tour got underway – it was his last tune-up before the big one. 'I always used the Tour of Switzerland or the Dauphiné, and most of the time we used the Dauphiné, as final prep for the Tour,' Armstrong says. 'For 2003 I did the Dauphiné. Before

---

evidence at the 2003 Tour, though few realised it at the time. On stage seven, the first in the mountains, a little-known Spanish rider, Jesús Manzano, began to weave across the road before collapsing and being air-lifted to hospital. Manzano later claimed that he had been injected by his team with Oxyglobin, a blood substitute, and that he almost died of dehydration as a result. In his book, Hamilton writes: 'Over the following days the truth came out through the peloton grapevine. Rumour was, something had gone wrong with his BB [blood bag] … I felt grateful to have professionals working with me.' Manzano would later become the whistleblower who began the police investigation into his Kelme team's doctor – the same Eufemiano Fuentes whose clients also included Hamilton and Ullrich. Manzano listed the numerous products he said he was forced to take by his team, including Actovegin, extracted from calves' blood, and Oxyglobin, which helps treat anaemia in dogs. As Manzano said, 'We used to joke about it. Some days we would go out barking and others we would go out mooing.'

that, I was riding very good. I was in the [leader's] jersey. One of the days, I had a really bad crash. We never really figured out what happened, but my bike just basically locked up and I went sliding on a fast downhill; really messed up my arm, lost a ton of blood, had stitches and a bunch of stuff through the night. I wanted to stay in the race and everybody else told me to drop out. Ferrari said, "You gotta drop out. You're riding good, just go home and rest."'

'But Iban Mayo was in second,' Armstrong continues. 'He was attacking me all the time. And, let me tell you, I was not a fan. I was *not* a fan of Mayo. I thought he was a little punk. We were all sort of … dirty, but I viewed him as being a lot dirtier than us.'

Mayo was certainly intriguing and enigmatic. As such he was an archetypal climber: slightly built, quirky, erratic, and capable of devastating accelerations in the mountains. But Armstrong's description of him as a 'little punk' seems fitting for other reasons, too. He had two hoop earrings in one ear, and straggly, shoulder-length hair. Handsome, with his dark eyes and sharp nose, he seemed the heir to Marco Pantani, the little Italian climber who Armstrong might also have described in less than friendly terms as a 'punk'.[6]

And that was the point. If Mayo was the new Pantani, Armstrong had every reason to be worried (and so, perhaps, did Mayo). It was Pantani who got under Armstrong's skin, especially in the 2000 Tour, with his erratic, unpredictable,

---

6 Pantani had been a thorn in Armstrong's side, but as Iban Mayo's star rose the Italian's plummeted. Despite having finished 14th in the 2003 Giro d'Italia, Pantani was locked into a deathly spiral; as the Centenary Tour de France got underway in Paris, he was checking into a clinic in Padova that specialised in the treatment of nervous disorders, drug addiction and alcoholism. The 2003 Giro would prove to be his last ever race; eight months later he was dead, aged thirty-four.

explosive attacking. Ullrich had always been his strongest rival on paper, but Armstrong knew where he stood with Ullrich. The German was as good-natured as he was strong; too nice, too compliant, without Armstrong's ruthlessness or Pantani's subversiveness. When Armstrong allowed Pantani to win the stage at Mont Ventoux in 2000, the Pirate threw the gesture back in his face. Ullrich would have been grateful for the gift. Pantani was offended by the charity.

Like Pantani, Mayo seemed uncontrollable. Thus he could unsettle Armstrong. Which is why Armstrong says of the 2003 Dauphiné, 'I wasn't going to let Mayo win.' And yet it was only the Dauphiné; only a warm-up for the Tour. When Ferrari and others advised him to forget about Mayo and the Dauphiné, Armstrong told them, 'No way, because if I go home this punk wins.'

'So I stayed in,' Armstrong says, 'and he kept attacking me, attacking me hard over the Galibier. And it just fucking killed me to stay with him … but I wasn't going to let this little punk win.' When Armstrong caught Mayo he gave him a look – or 'the look', which he had used to intimidate Ullrich on l'Alpe d'Huez during the 2001 Tour. He also indulged in some trash talk. Mayo remembers, 'On the last day Armstrong came up to me, drew level with my handlebars and said to me, "Iban, can't you go a bit harder than that?"

'So that day I went so hard, I kept attacking and attacking, and Armstrong came up to me again and said, "Is that all you've got? Can't you go any harder?" And so we'd do it all over again and again, each time Armstrong asking me, "Can't you go any harder?" and me attacking again.'

Mayo wasn't aware, at the time, how much he annoyed Armstrong. 'People told me afterwards. Maybe I was more unpredictable than Ullrich, I could attack on other climbs, because I could go all out in one place or another, whereas Ullrich would not surprise him; he'd be a guy who would go for him in the time trials. I could surprise him.'

Armstrong won the Dauphiné, but not without cost. 'It took too much out of me. I had two weeks between the Dauphiné and the Tour. And I just didn't recover. I came into the Tour behind, and tired and depleted.

'I mean, so much has been made about, y'know, doping and blood [transfusions] and etc, etc,' Armstrong continues. 'But I'll never forget, I started – in those years they did the pre-race screening and haematocrit test, etc – and I started the Tour at 39 [per cent] haematocrit. And I remember thinking, oh fuck. Huh!' Armstrong laughs: 39 was low; it meant his red blood cells were depleted. Hamilton, who took a blood transfusion on the eve of the race, started with his at 48.

'And it didn't start good,' Armstrong continues. 'I had a bad prologue. I was used to winning those prologues and I barely made the top ten. It was just a rough start and a rough three weeks. I had to get lucky.'

*   *   *

Since his first Tour win in 1999, Armstrong had never had to 'get lucky'. He never crashed. Never punctured. Never fell ill. Never had a bad day – minor dips in form, but not a really bad day. He even felt that his Tour wins were 'dialled in'. There was precious little drama, excitement or suspense, apart from when Pantani launched his (self-)destructive attacks. Otherwise, the Armstrong Tours were as predictable as the Indurain Tours.

Until 2003.

The bad luck started the night before the race started, when the hip Armstrong had landed on in his crash at the Dauphiné seized up. He couldn't walk until his chiropractor, Spencer, performed a ritual called 'the shotgun', pulling the leg as though wrenching it from the socket. This produced a shockingly loud crack. But it worked. Armstrong could move the hip again. But his luck didn't turn. After his disappointing prologue time trial in Paris, where he was seventh, on the next day's first stage, to Meaux, he was bothered by a stomach upset. (Tyler Hamilton was even more unlucky: he crashed at the end and fractured his collarbone. But he strapped it up and carried on.)

The first serious test was l'Alpe d'Huez, a week in. And, six kilometres from the summit of the Alpe, there was Mayo, taking off alone and flying up the mountain, his orange Euskaltel jersey open and flapping like Superman's cape. Mayo had struggled on the lower slopes of the Alpe as Armstrong's team led the leaders at a ferocious pace into the first of the twenty-one hairpins, as though to terrify the others. It was a bluff that almost worked, but Mayo battled back, and watched Armstrong, now isolated, struggle to chase Hamilton and Joseba Beloki, another Basque climber. Mayo went as soon as Beloki came back. 'I attacked because it was the moment. Attacking is often a question of knowing it's the right moment rather than feeling strong, and having this' – Mayo points at his groin. Balls.

Although Mayo was coming from way back after a typically dismal performance by his team of fellow Basque climbers in the stage four team time trial, it was uncharacteristic of Armstrong to not at least try and chase a rival. Here on l'Alpe d'Huez he seemed to simply let Mayo go.

Mayo won alone at the summit, a minute 45 seconds in front of Alexandre Vinokourov, over two minutes ahead of Armstrong, who sprinted in for third. 'If you had asked me a month ago if I was going to suffer that much on l'Alpe d'Huez, I would have said "no way",' said Armstrong at the summit. 'So let's hope that things get better and not worse.'

Next day, he was shadowing Beloki on a descent close to the finish in Gap. Beloki went too fast into a corner, locked his back wheel, and slammed on to the tarmac. Armstrong just avoided him, but left the road, riding across a field, cutting out a hairpin, and bouncing back on.

It was an incident that encapsulated Armstrong's good fortune and skill: an extraordinary near-miss and an equally extraordinary demonstration of improvisation, not to mention bike-handling ability. As he returned to the road just in front of the main group, containing Ullrich and Mayo, Beloki lay motionless on the road above, his elbow and wrist broken, his femur fractured in two places. He had finished third at the Tour in 2001, second in 2002, and looked stronger in 2003. But his career was as good as over with this crash. He never returned to the same level.

Armstrong was holding his luck, but there were odd, almost unimaginable things going on, which again now seem symptomatic of a year in which Armstrong's focus went awry. As his mechanic, Mike Anderson, watched the Alpe d'Huez stage on television, he thought that Armstrong's bike didn't look right: that the forks were too small. Armstrong also discovered that his brake blocks were rubbing against his rear wheel, the last thing anyone needs. If a gap had been closed by his opponents, Armstrong thinks, it wasn't in doping but in equipment, a realisation that would prompt an urgent, angry post-Tour review with Trek, his bike sponsor.

*   *   *

Despite defeat on l'Alpe d'Huez, despite stomach problems, hip problems, bike problems and the near-miss on the road to Gap, Armstrong was still in a position to win. The race would be decided in the Pyrenees, the second mountain range, by which point, in other years, Armstrong had it more or less sewn up. Not this year. Ullrich, riding in the celeste green of Bianchi, seemingly channelling the spirit of the Italian bike-maker's greatest champion, Fausto Coppi, on a time trial bike that was superior to Armstrong's dated model, was resurgent. He destroyed Armstrong in the stage twelve time trial in the stifling heat of the Tarn, where the champion suffered as never before. Armstrong finished severely dehydrated and over a minute and a half down. He was in yellow but with Ullrich on his shoulder, only 34 seconds behind. Then there was Mayo, down in sixth with over four minutes to make up, but about to enter his playground, filled with his people, preparing a rowdy welcome party for him and a hostile reception for Armstrong.

Day one in the Pyrenees confirmed that Armstrong was not the Armstrong of old. He was sluggish and conceded seven seconds to Ullrich on the climb to Ax-3-Domaines. The next day, to Loudenvielle, he lost time to Mayo. 'I can't exactly say why,' Armstrong told reporters, 'but I wouldn't argue with people who say I'm declining. This is a sport where you can not only look at the differences between other riders, but you can look at the times on certain climbs. If you look at the times on l'Alpe d'Huez, that's four minutes slower, so it doesn't take a rocket scientist to figure out that that guy is not as strong as he was two years ago. Something is not clicking.'

The 'queen' stage was the next day, stage fifteen, 159.5km between Bagnères-de-Bigorre and the summit of Luz Ardiden. There would be three mountains in the final 80 kilometres: the Col d'Aspin, Col du Tourmalet, then Luz Ardiden. On the Tourmalet, there were echoes of Alpe d'Huez. Armstrong lost all his team-mates. He didn't look too good himself, either. 'Armstrong was at his weakest on the Tourmalet,' Mayo recalls. 'I attacked, then Ullrich came across and went for it, then there was [Mayo's Euskaltel team-mate Haimar] Zubeldia and Armstrong behind. At one point Ullrich was ahead, then Armstrong was 50 metres back, then me another 50 metres back, then Zubeldia. I remember thinking, Ullrich should stop. Finally he did, and the four of us joined together.'

It was unusual for Ullrich to attack so far out. It briefly rattled Armstrong, then, paradoxically, reassured him. 'At that point, when he went, we were all broken up, there was no

team left, it was every man for himself, basically,' Armstrong
says. 'Ullrich went up the road. I was just behind him, maybe
five–ten seconds. And I just kept him there. At that point I
was actually glad he did that. I thought, that's too early. If
you feel good and you want to make your move in the race,
that's too early to go. I kept him there, I let him hang a little.
He was going fast, he was going hard, it was hard for me to
keep him at a stable distance, but it was better that I let him
burn some matches on the Tourmalet so that he didn't have
'em on Luz Ardiden.'

Armstrong made contact with Ullrich over the top, as the
two Basques, Zubeldia and Mayo, joined them to make four.
To Mayo's frustration, Ullrich and Armstrong then eased up.
'They weren't interested.' Not in reaching Luz Ardiden as
a foursome; they didn't care if others, including Hamilton,
still struggling with his broken collarbone, caught them.
Armstrong was concerned mainly with Ullrich now, with the
threat posed by Mayo receding.

Armstrong, for all that he seemed weaker than the rider
who had won the last four Tours, was still there, still in yellow. He was still in a position to win. And yet he has said that
he started the race with a haematocrit of only 39. Had he not
artificially boosted this, his red cell count would surely be
further depleted by week three; he wouldn't even have been
in contention.

The cat is out of the bag – I mean doping. What was it
this time? 'Well, the usual,' Armstrong replies sheepishly. 'I
mean, that year was no different to the years in and around
that. I mean, yeah, we did what the whole world now knows
we did, but it was also what all of us … I wouldn't say that
the *Lanterne Rouge* [last man] was having a transfusion, but
certainly any and all GC contenders were.' Armstrong is still
reluctant to go into specifics (though he says he would if a
'truth and reconciliation' process was established by the UCI:
'I'm on standby. If I get the call, I'll be there.')

Yet all the doping products and blood transfusions in the world could not have prepared Armstrong for what happened next, high on Luz Ardiden, on slopes packed with orange-clad Mayo fans. They were desperate to see Armstrong collapse ... but not like this. Not at the hands of a child wielding nothing more threatening than a canvas bag ...

With the group swelling in the valley, with Hamilton and Armstrong's team-mate Manuel Beltran among those to regain contact, Mayo was the first serious attacker as the mountain reared up. Armstrong, looking fresher, stronger and more alert than he had appeared on the Tourmalet, immediately went after him. He didn't want a repeat of l'Alpe d'Huez. He caught Mayo. 'And he went right past me,' says Mayo, who dug deep to stay with him. Ullrich lagged behind, apparently beginning to struggle, finding the small gap to Armstrong and Mayo unbridgeable. Armstrong sensed it; he pressed on, out of the saddle, sprinting, hugging the right-hand, fans-lined gutter, with Mayo grimacing as he tried to hold his wheel.

'I was too close to the side,' Armstrong says, 'which I had a tendency to do. A lot of times in time trials, Johan would say over the radio: "Watch the fucking side of the road. There's debris over there; there are people there." I was always trying to get as close to the side as I could because any kind of protection from the wind is good. But who knows, some lunatic ...' Armstrong's mind drifts towards doomsday theories – a punch, a knife, a gun – before he catches himself: 'But this was no different to normal. I just got too close.'

Now he is sprinting, hard. Mayo remains behind, Ullrich a couple of bike lengths further back. And then it happens: Armstrong goes down as if hit by a sniper. His bike stops dead as though pulled by a trip wire. He is flung forward; doesn't even have time to unprise his hands from the brake hoods. Mayo has nowhere to go and lands on top of him. Ullrich's eyes widen to saucers as he steers his bike into the middle of the road, around the tangle of bikes and bodies, and carries on.

'It was a little boy,' Armstrong says, 'probably a ten- or eleven-year-old kid, whose parents had bought a commemorative musette from the concession stand. And he was kinda flapping it back and forth. And he timed it just right, caught my handlebars, and down I go.

'The kid must have had a firm grip. He was, like, "Look, I don't wanna lose this thing!"'

There was no time to check the bike. Armstrong's mechanic, Chris van Roosbroeck, sprinted out of the car, carried out a quick visual inspection, then pushed him so hard that he was almost immediately back with Mayo, who was also back up quickly.

Ahead, Ullrich rode at the front of the group, but was he going hard or soft-pedalling? He pulled a couple of lengths clear but kept glancing round as if unsure what to do. Hamilton, who benefited from the chaos by rejoining Ullrich and co, sprinted to the front and took control, turning and gesturing for Ullrich and the other rider at the front, Ivan Basso, to slow down and, out of a sense of fair play, to honour cycling's unwritten rules, wait for the yellow jersey.

Mayo had another take on Hamilton's intervention. 'I was up the quickest and rejoined the group ahead of Armstrong, and Hamilton was there, saying we should wait for Armstrong.' He grins. 'Hamilton wasn't on a good day, that is my impression.'

The question of whether Ullrich waited or not would erupt into a controversy, but not immediately. 'It was correct that when Armstrong crashed I didn't attack, because cycling is a fair-play sport,' Ullrich said after the stage. Armstrong was initially grateful. But perhaps he studied the footage afterwards, because later he criticised Ullrich for not waiting. There was no intended irony in the words of Ullrich, Hamilton or Armstrong. Each had a strong sense of fair play.

As Armstrong says, he believed most if not all of his rivals were doping. That was okay. Taking advantage of a rival's misfortune on the road was not. There was, after all, honour among thieves.

Back down the road, Armstrong had more to worry about than whether Ullrich was waiting. Again, something wasn't right with his bike. As he sprinted out of the saddle to try and regain contact with the group, his chain jumped and he lurched forward like a drunk, sprawling onto his top tube as his right foot became unclipped from the pedal. He had just passed Mayo, who had another close call, just avoiding hitting Armstrong a second time. He sprinted ahead to avoid any more trouble, which is how he managed to rejoin the leaders when Hamilton was urging them to wait.

This time, Armstrong was soon back in his rhythm and chasing with relentless fury. As for the damaged bike, it was Mayo who had done for him after all, albeit inadvertently. 'It turned out, with the crash, with Mayo falling on me and the bike, that the chainstay area was cracked. When I slipped again, it had something to do with the bottom bracket being a little compromised. We didn't know until after the stage when the mechanic put the bike on the car on the roof rack. At that point the crank and bottom bracket were at eye level and he said, "Fuck, look, this bike is cracked!"'

At the time, chasing the Ullrich group, stopping to change bikes was simply not an option. 'I knew after that, I had to go there' – Armstrong means into the red. 'It was too close. I didn't want to go into the final time trial [four days later] and leave Jan that close. A, I wouldn't have slept at night, and B, based on my condition, he would probably have got me.'

With the help of his team-mate Chechu Rubiera, Armstrong caught Ullrich's group. On his radio, Bruyneel urged: 'Lance, recover a little bit.' He wanted him to ride with the group, to find again a steady, manageable rhythm. Armstrong wasn't interested. Adrenaline was pumping, as it always is after a crash. And something else goaded him: the little punk wasn't going to wait to find out if Armstrong was OK. There was a lull as the others fanned across the road, with Ullrich still glancing around, still unsure what he should do.

So, as soon as Armstrong makes contact, Mayo goes.

Armstrong had been out of the saddle, sprinting, almost since the moment he remounted after his first crash. Now he moves ominously up the outside of the group as Ullrich glances around again; is he waiting for permission from Armstrong? Armstrong goes after Mayo. He brings him back, only for Mayo to jump again.

Iban, can't you go a bit harder than that?

Is that all you've got?

Can't you go any harder?

Can't you go any harder?

Armstrong gives Mayo a look – *the* look – as he passes him. He pulls ahead, and Mayo digs deep to try and hold on. Armstrong looks furious, as though he might punch someone. Ullrich is again being left behind, fading into the distance. Armstrong's head is down, his jaw clenched, his eyes narrowed and squinting angrily up the road. Mist envelops the peak of the mountain, and ahead of Armstrong is a rider who is the only survivor of a long breakaway, a young Frenchman, Sylvain Chavanel. He had about four minutes at the foot of the climb but Armstrong is eating into that with each stamp of the pedals. He reels Chavanel in, easing off to pat him on the back as he passes: a fluid motion that barely interrupts his rhythm. And he reaches the summit alone. There's no celebration as he lunges for the line. Just a twenty-second bonus to add to the forty he has claimed on Mayo, who sprints in for second.

The anger that seemed to propel Armstrong up the climb continued to simmer as he went through the podium ceremony and dope control, before setting off in a team car. When he was in yellow Armstrong often arrived at the team hotel after the others, but this time he wanted to catch the bus and join his team-mates. One of them, his Colombian domestique Victor Hugo Peña, would later recall: 'It was the most euphoric day for Lance since I've known him. I've seen him happy before, but never like this. He stormed up and down the aisle, punching the seats and shouting, "No one trains like me. No one rides like me. This jersey's mine. I live for this jersey. It's my life. No one's taking it away from me while I'm around. This fucking jersey's mine."'

Armstrong told reporters: 'This has been a Tour of too many problems; too many close calls, too many near misses … I just wish the problems would stop. Many of the problems I haven't discussed, but there have been a lot of strange things that happened this Tour de France that I need to stop having. Some of them were evident like the stage to Gap; other things were not talked about. It's been a very odd, crisis-filled Tour. But it was a good day today.'

Armstrong led Ullrich by one minute, seven seconds. It would be enough for the final time trial, especially when Ullrich crashed in the wet conditions. Tour number five was in the bag. More importantly, so was membership of The Club.

*   *   *

Armstrong started his own club with wins number six and seven, both far less complicated and easier than win number five. And then he would lose them all. His surprise comeback in 2009 began a chain of events that led to a federal investigation into allegations of doping, prompted in part by claims made by Floyd Landis and then backed up by Tyler Hamilton. When the federal case was dropped, it was picked up by Travis Tygart and the US Anti-Doping Agency. And in 2012 Armstrong was formally charged with doping and stripped of all seven Tour titles.

The process of grief for Armstrong seems, thus far, to have been roughly as follows: denial, defiance, contrition, anger. As time has gone on, his bitterness seems to have grown, especially over the fact that he was singled out. As he says, none of his old rivals has stepped forward to claim any of the seven Tour titles that will, as the authorities have decreed, be left permanently vacant, including the 2003 runner-up Ullrich (who was eventually charged with doping, too, but only stripped of his results since 2005, so he retains his 1997 Tour and 2000 Olympic gold medal).

There remains honour among thieves. Although Armstrong later chastised Ullrich for not waiting for him after his crash on Luz Ardiden, as he had waited for Ullrich when he crashed a couple of years earlier, and expressed his gratitude to Hamilton (texting Hamilton's wife, Haven, that night: 'Tyler showed big class today'), these days his scorn is reserved for Hamilton, his respect for Ullrich.

'Did Ullrich wait?' Armstrong repeats my question. 'Huh! It's one of those things people will debate forever. You know, I got to know Jan a little more after that, and getting to know him more, and realising the man that he is, I would be inclined to say now that he did wait ... He may not have pulled over to the side of the road, but he wasn't pedalling hard, let me put it that way. He eased up for sure. I've never asked him, but to me, that's the man he is. I've got a lot of respect for him, I like him a lot, and I think he probably played it fair and waited for me to come back.'

As for Mayo, he is not untypical among riders of his generation – those that contended for major races, at any rate – in believing that Armstrong has been unfairly treated, that he was the best rider of his generation and deserves to be recognised as the winner of seven Tours. 'My memory of Armstrong hasn't changed,' Mayo says. The revelations of his doping didn't surprise him? 'It doesn't change what happened.' Mayo's own career was effectively ended by a positive test for EPO in 2007. With evident pride, he adds, 'I lived with him – nobody can take that away … But the difference between Armstrong and the rest of us was enormous. He was way superior to the rest.'

Armstrong is adamant that 'his' Tours should still count, because they happened, and people haven't forgotten them. If he regrets something, it is his behaviour off the bike, not his doping. Few are sympathetic, but some are. Scott Mercier, a former US Postal team-mate who refused to dope and lost his contract and career, has been reconciled with Armstrong. 'You hear about what a bully he is,' Mercier said, 'and now he's the one getting bullied.' Armstrong is certainly intelligent and charismatic; traits he can use to charm, or manipulate. 'He might be playing me, I don't know,' Mercier added.

How does Armstrong feel now, reflecting on days like the stage to Luz Ardiden, arguably the most dramatic and important single stage in his seven Tours? Does he ever watch the footage on YouTube? He is characteristically decisive, if not entirely convincing, on this question, insisting: 'No, I'm not that guy. That was a different part of my life, and I've moved on. I've retired now. I don't get real sentimental about that shit. I get mad and upset that I'm in the position I'm in now, and perhaps paying a heavier price than everybody else combined. And honestly, I wouldn't have talked to you about this, for this book, if you hadn't asked me about 2003, and the fact that you want to talk about something that a bunch of dickheads swear didn't happen, um, that convinced me that I should talk to you about it.'

It is at this point that Armstrong's tone changes, and darkens, his anger bubbling to the surface. 'I mean, listen, look. Travis Tygart and his band of haters can say what they want. Those Tours happened, Richard, and uh, y'know, the fact that they've not been awarded to anybody else, and that none of my peers have stood up to claim them, it really says it all.

'The races happened, it was an unfortunate time, most of us if not all of us played by the same set of rules, and um, it is what it is. And, look, I consider myself the winner of those seven Tours.

'Period.'

It's difficult to see where Armstrong goes from here, other than to the golf course. Some athletes thrive on competition, while others find motivation inside themselves. Bernard Hinault was a boxer in need of an opponent, while Greg LeMond's main opponent was always himself. Armstrong is squarely in the Hinault camp: opponents became rivals became enemies. It was all about beating people, and not just beating them, but 'kicking ass'. As his one-time coach, Chris Carmichael, once said, he was less interested in how many titles he won than in 'going to go to the Tour and kick[ing] the shit out of everybody'. Indeed, he almost lost the 2003 Tour because he had been so determined to kick the shit out of Iban Mayo at the Dauphiné.

When doping charges were finally brought against him, in August 2012, Armstrong was deep into training for Ironman triathlons. Into his early forties, the urge to compete is an itch that cannot be relieved. He has described his lifetime ban from competitive sport as a 'death sentence'. It might not be as hyperbolic as it seems. In the meantime, he is reduced to hacking round a golf course. It is hard to believe that it scratches that itch.

'Hold on a second,' Armstrong says. 'I gotta go through the gate here.'

Armstrong has arrived at the golf course. 'Hey, how are ya?'

'Good,' replies the gate man. 'How are you?'

'Good. I'll see you tomorrow morning, too.'

Classement

1 Lance Armstrong, USA, US Postal, at 4 hours, 29 minutes, 26 secs
2 Iban Mayo, Spain, Euskaltel-Euskadi, at 40 secs
3 Jan Ullrich, Germany, Team Bianchi, same time
4 Haimar Zubeldia, Spain, Euskaltel-Euskadi, s.t.
5 Christophe Moreau, France, Credit Agricole, at 43 secs
6 Ivan Basso, Italy, Fassa Bortolo, at 47 secs

MARK CAVENDISH EMBRACES BERNHARD EISEL

Chapter 17

UNTOLD STORIES

**20 July 2010. Stage Fifteen: Bagnères-de-Luchon to Pau
199.5km. High mountains**

Climbing the Col du Tourmalet, Mark Cavendish slips out
the back of the group. His loyal team-mate, Bernhard Eisel,
remains at his side and tries to encourage him.

'Big effort, Cav, come on, stay with the group.'

Cavendish screws up his face. 'Bernie, I can't do it.' He is
suffering a thousand agonies. He wants Eisel, his best friend,
to shut up. But Eisel knows how critical it is that they stay with
the *gruppetto*, the group that rides a shadow Tour de France in
the mountains, out of view of the television and photographers' lenses. For Cavendish, a prolific winner of flat sprinters'
stages, stages like this are the B-sides to his hit singles, songs
that no one hears.

Today, the top of the Tourmalet is not the end of the stage:
there is a fourth Pyrenean climb, the Col d'Aubisque, and then
60km of flat, valley roads to the finish in Pau. Manageable in
a group, impossible as a duo. He and Eisel will almost certainly miss the time cut and be out of the race.

Cavendish is ill, feverish, and in a desperate bid for marginal
gains he removes all extraneous items: sunglasses, food from

pockets, even *bidons*. Still Eisel cajoles him and Cavendish snaps: 'Don't nag! Just let me fucking ride,' he says. *Fuck you, then*, Eisel thinks. He could ride back up to the group and leave Cavendish to his self-pity, to stew in his petulance. But he doesn't. He sticks to the task, which means sticking with Cavendish, but pointedly veers to the other side of the road.

On they ride up the Tourmalet, 'together' but not together, Cavendish hugging one side, Eisel the other, shutting each other out, not speaking a word, sulking like a married couple.

*   *   *

For the majority, the Tour de France is not about winning. By the third week, it has nothing to do with winning. An example: with two days to go, the 2008 Tour was on a knife-edge. It was so close that either Cadel Evans or Carlos Sastre could still win. The time trial on the penultimate day would decide.

It was thrilling; the watching world was transfixed. On the eve of the decisive time trial, David Millar, not a bad time triallist himself, was asked how he thought the race would go and who he thought would win.

'I don't give a fuck,' said Millar.

The great myth of the Tour is that the riders are all engaged in the main narrative, the battle for yellow. Yet those transfixed by the duel in 2008 did not include most of the riders.

Two years later, on stage nine of the 2010 Tour, a week before Cavendish and Eisel's turmoil on the Tourmalet, Millar was engaged in his own, very different and very personal narrative. He had crashed on the Tour's second day, breaking a rib – though he did not know that at the time. He persevered, with the help of painkillers that 'dulled everything, all sensations'. He decided not to take any when the race entered the Alps. It was the ninth stage to Saint-Jean-de-Maurienne, taking in one of the longest climbs in the Alps, the Col de la Madeleine. Millar began to struggle just fifteen minutes into the stage, on an uncategorised climb. He was then dropped for good on the Col de la Colombière and rode for over four hours on his own, eventually coming in 42 minutes behind the winner, Sandy Casar. The penultimate finisher was a full seven minutes ahead of him; Millar just scraped inside the time limit.

It is unusual for a rider to spend all day on his own like that. It is even more unusual for him to survive and avoid elimination. The *gruppetto*, containing the non-climbers, forms in the mountains, usually with a leader, somebody well respected and good at maths who can calculate how hard they need to ride to make the time cut. It acts as a safety net. But if you are dropped from the *gruppetto*, you might as well wave good-bye to the Tour de France. Millar explains: 'What happens is a hard stage will start and there are a number of guys, the super domestiques of each team, who will make a calculation: "We've got thirty-five minutes today," or whatever. "We can hang on to the penultimate climb and then let go."

'Then, when you get to that penultimate climb, they drop back, shout *"Gruppetto!"* and everyone says, "OK", and the *gruppetto* forms, with the super domestiques, or very experienced, very charismatic guys, in charge. The *gruppetto* goes hard through the valley, in through-and-off formation, the riders rotating at the front as in a team trial, then they find a comfortable pace on the climbs and ride like banshees down the other side: they know that's where they can make up time. The idea is to make it inside the time limit. But they know there's power in numbers; that if 40 per cent of the peloton is there they're less likely to be eliminated.'

On a typical day in the mountains, the *gruppetto* can number between around thirty and eighty. On this particular day, with Millar dropped on the Colombière with the Madeleine still to come, it hadn't even formed yet. When it did, it comprised fifty riders. Behind them was Millar.

That evening, scanning the results sheet, and seeing Millar's name marooned at the bottom, so far behind the *gruppetto*, it was clear that something exceptional had happened. There was a story here, perhaps more interesting than what had gone on at the front, given that it had turned into a fairly routine day for the overall contenders. And so the next morning I positioned myself by Millar's Garmin team bus and waited for him to emerge. First, a gendarme appeared and spoke to the team's press officer; he was looking for David Millar, too. Oh, dear. Millar had, infamously, been in hot water with the French police before, when he was busted for doping in 2004. But this gendarme's demeanour did not suggest that kind of trouble.

When the door hissed open and Millar's lanky frame filled the space, he spotted the gendarme and they embraced, then chatted like old friends. Then Millar went back inside, re-emerging with a Garmin shirt, which he signed and presented. The gendarme accepted it as he would a precious gift and left smiling.

What had that been about, I asked. 'That was the gendarme who was with me yesterday,' said Millar. 'I spent the whole day, five hours, on my own. And he was fifty metres in front of me the whole way. A few times he dropped back and handed me his water bottle. "Here, have a drink." Then he'd buzz off again. He crawled up the mountains ahead of me, making sure the road was clear because the fans thought all the riders had come through. On the descent of the Madeleine, I knew I could make up time so I really went for it, and he started going nuts, honking, clearing everybody out the way, scraping his bike on the road on the corners. He got really involved in my pursuit. So I just wanted to say, "Thanks for saving my Tour de France."'

The gendarme had not been allowed to help in a practical sense, but he kept Millar going. By his mere presence, he had helped him to finish the stage and stay in the Tour. An unlikely bond had been forged. It was quite a story, yet it had been witnessed by nobody. Nobody except Millar and the policeman.

*   *   *

Millar's day of solo survival was unusual principally because it is the *gruppetto* that holds the key to survival for the non-climbers in the mountains. And with this in mind, I was keen to speak to Cavendish, the greatest sprinter of his generation, about this aspect of his Tour: the shadow Tour. Days in the *gruppetto* are Cavendish's most difficult, the suffering of a different order to the days in which he fights for position and follows his lead-out train, then sprints for the win at the end. Those days, in the full glare of the TV cameras, involve courage, skill and the sharp pain of a flat-out effort (or several). Days in the mountains, away from the glare, involve pure suffering.

When asked to nominate his single toughest day in the mountains, Cavendish struggles. 'All of them?' he suggests. Perhaps they seem a long way away from where we are sitting, in a deserted hotel on the Costa del Sol in Spain in January, during a pre-season training camp. How about Hautacam in 2008? 'That was pretty hard coz I crashed,' Cavendish recalls, almost nostalgically. 'I hit a football. A football in the middle of fucking nowhere!

'But nah, there have been harder ones. Oh, I tell you. There was one I was ill, it finished up the Tourmalet. We only did the Col d'Aubisque and Tourmalet but I had fever. I suffered that day. I was way off on the Aubisque with Bernie, but we got back on the descent. Then I suffered up the Tourmalet …

'But no, that wasn't the hardest … I don't know. Days like 2012, the ring of fire: Aubisque, Tourmalet, Aspin, Peyresourde. That was bloody hard.

'No!' Now Cavendish is sitting forward in his chair. 'When we did that ring of fire the other way, in 2010. That day was fucking …' he trails off, shakes his head.

It was dubbed the Circle of Death (rather than ring of fire) when this circuit of the Pyrenees, including four major climbs, first featured on the route in 1910 and the riders feared bear attacks, among other things. A century on, the same route, in reverse, was stage sixteen of the 2010 Tour, over 199.5km.

Cavendish, who was enduring a difficult season after complications following dental surgery over the winter, was ill. He was coughing and feverish in the morning when his main rival for the green jersey, the Italian sprinter Alessandro Petacchi, paid a visit to the bus of his team, HTC-Columbia. Petacchi wanted to discuss how to ride the stage. With the climbs at the beginning rather than the end, and that long run-in from the Aubisque to Pau, it was more complicated than, say, a summit finish.

They started in the pretty spa town of Bagnères-de-Luchon. 'It started right at the bottom of the Peyresourde,' Cavendish recalls, 'literally at the foot of the mountain.' And because it started with a climb, riders could be seen doing something they rarely did: warming up. One, Julian Dean of Millar's Garmin team, started to ride up the Peyresourde, on the course itself, but was mistaken for a fan by an over-zealous gendarme. He was told to get off his bike and push it: an instruction he ignored, provoking the anger of the gendarme, who wrestled him to the ground. As if the race wasn't hard enough for a sprinter like Dean, he was starting it with fresh crash wounds.

'It was supposed to be neutralised going up,' Cavendish remembers, 'but I was dropped right at the start. It was just me, Bernie and [Bert] Grabsch [another HTC team-mate]. And who's that French guy who crashes a lot? Lloyd Mondory, that's him.'[7]

Cavendish was in the process of rescuing his dismal season at the Tour, winning three stages in the first two weeks, but

7 On the eve of the Tour, Mondory had been in another incident with Cavendish, when he came down in a horrific crash at the Tour of Switzerland for which Cavendish was blamed. 'If you look at that, he was nowhere near me!' Cavendish says now. 'He just can't handle his bike.' It was a year in which Switzerland seemed cursed for Cavendish: earlier, at the Tour de Romandie, he was sent home by his team after winning a stage and celebrating with an 'Up Yours' V-sign, a gesture apparently directed at his 'critics'.

on the Peyresourde, so early on stage fifteen, it didn't look as though he'd make it to Paris.

He takes up the story: 'So there's us four, we're dropped on the Peyresourde, and there's the *gruppetto* ahead, with Petacchi. They hear we're behind, so they try to eliminate us. They start riding full gas so we can't get back.' So much for Petacchi's pre-stage chat: all's fair in love and the Tour. 'It's the four of us,' Cavendish continues, 'and we go down the descent from the Peyresourde and then start climbing the Aspin alone. Jens [Voigt, the veteran German] had crashed; he comes flying past on the Aspin, we can't stay with him, but then we descend the Aspin like mad dogs, and drop Grabsch.'

The small group now comprises Cavendish, Eisel and Mondory. They were a mere 42km into the stage by the time they crested the summit of the second of the four mountains, the Col d'Aspin. Still to come was the monster, the Tourmalet. Eisel, whose job was to accompany Cavendish and make sure he finished in the time limit, reckoned they had to make contact with the *gruppetto* before the Tourmalet – otherwise their task would be far more difficult, perhaps impossible.

After a flat-out chase from the summit of the Aspin, they made contact. Cavendish remembers: 'We caught the *gruppetto* at the bottom of the Tourmalet, by which point all the glycogen has gone; I'm finished. Ivan Basso was ill, so he was in the *gruppetto*.' Basso, usually an overall contender, was unused to being with the back-markers, which caused a problem. 'Normally the *gruppetto* rides steady up the climbs but Basso was panicking because he thinks we're not going to make the time cut, and he starts riding up the Tourmalet fucking full gas. I was, like, "Bernie, I can't do it!"'

As Cavendish slid out the back, Eisel urged him on. 'Cav, I know you're ill, mate, but we can't fuck around here. We have to go faster than this. Come on.'

'Don't nag me,' said Cavendish. 'Just let me fucking ride. Fucking leave me alone.'

So Eisel shut up. Cavendish was angry. Eisel was furious. And so they rode on up the Tourmalet, side-by-side but on opposite sides of the road, not speaking.

*   *   *

It was unusual for Eisel to sulk. He has been called a 'one-man morale boost'. Permanently upbeat, always smiling, he comes from a small Austrian village near Graz. Eisel was a few years older than Cavendish, but they had hit it off immediately when they became team-mates at T-Mobile in 2007. As that team morphed into HTC-Columbia they grew closer; they were often room-mates, confidants and companions in the mountains. They compared themselves to a married couple. But on days like this, Eisel was more like a big brother.

He was an important member of Cavendish's lead-out train, but it was in the mountains that he really earned his corn. His job went well beyond that of an ordinary domestique or *gregario*. And yet the strange thing about Eisel, and his faithful service, is that he was better than this; unlike some other *gregari*, he did not depend on Cavendish for a professional contract. He could win races in his own right – the biggest being Ghent–Wevelgem earlier that same season, 2010.

Eisel's sacrifice owed something to loyalty, something to pragmatism. It helped, too, that his ego is the size of, say, a category-four rather than an *hors-categorie* mountain. He had been a professional for seven years when he and Cavendish became team-mates, with Eisel having started out at Mapei, then the world's biggest team. He was smart; he realised early that the peloton was divided into very good riders and stars (there were no bad riders), and he learned that a good rider could do one of two things: keep trying to be a star, or accept that he was just a very good rider. 'I could see straight away that I was competitive,' says Eisel, 'but to win the race takes so much more.'

When Mapei folded, Eisel moved to Française des Jeux in 2003, from the world's number one team to a resolutely French outfit run by Marc Madiot, whose first instruction to Eisel was to move to France. 'I said, "No way." They wanted you to live in some holiday chalets in the middle of nowhere. I managed to put it off, started getting some really good results, and after Milan–San Remo, where I was 12th, I said to Marc: "Look, I'd love to stay in Austria. I'll bring you results." Finally he said OK.'

Still, this was Eisel's chance to become a leader, a star. He had the physical attributes: he was strong and fast. 'I had one year when I thought I'd be the bunch sprinter,' he says. 'One day I would lead Baden Cooke out, the next day he'd lead me out. But it was a mess. Never put two sprinters together. Me and Cookey still talk, but we could have been best mates. We never really had a problem, but we both knew it just couldn't work.'

Eisel moved to T-Mobile in 2006. He was still ostensibly a sprinter and he won stages at the Tour of Qatar and Three Days of De Panne. He was also more than a sprinter: he was fifth in Paris–Roubaix. 'Then Cav came,' says Eisel. Cavendish was twenty-one, but even then, in 2007, had the self-belief of a champion. 'I saw in the training camp that he was quick – we had a lot of fast guys there. We had André Greipel as well.'

But it was Cavendish who, in his first full year as a pro, beat a field of fast sprinters to win the Scheldeprijs semi-classic in Belgium. Eisel didn't go for the win that day: he made a late decision to help Cavendish instead. 'I can remember just being tired in that race, having done Flanders and Roubaix. I knew I wasn't going to win that day. I thought I'd give him a chance and he brought it home. We'd done some lead-outs in the training camp. In the first one he was quick, but in the second one, I'd never seen anything like that from a young guy.'

Cavendish was brash, confident – arrogant, some thought. 'I mean, Cav didn't show all that much respect, but if you're as good as him it's a lot easier,' says Eisel. 'If he'd behaved like he did and not won anything, he'd have landed on his nose sooner or later.

'But I liked him,' Eisel continues. 'He was a good kid.'

*   *   *

Eisel was never officially assigned to the role of Cavendish's personal escort in the mountains. It just seemed to happen. It helped that he was vastly experienced in the *gruppetto*, as his finishing positions in his ten Tours de France, from 2003 to 2012, suggest: 131st, 143rd, 107th, 121st, 144th, 150th, 148th, 155th, 160th, 146th. Consistent, if nothing else.

'I understood how to ride in the mountains, and how Cav had to ride and how he had to be brought over the climbs,' says Eisel, 'but in the first few years it wasn't calculation; it was just like survival.'

They perfected the survival technique together, he adds, summing it up as, 'steady on the climbs, hard on the descents'. And eventually that technique came to be about more than survival. It was with the next flat stage – the next sprint stage, so the next Cavendish victory – in mind. As Eisel explains: 'The idea was to help him get through these stages, so he would finish fresher than he would have been if he'd just been scrapping on his own. He would sometimes try to hold the wheel in front. But it would mean killing himself' – the benefits of sitting behind another rider on a climb, where gravity rather than wind resistance is the main limiting factor, can be negligible. Eisel adds, 'The fresher he could come out of these stages, the better chance of winning the next day.'

Despite his anger at Cavendish's petulence, Eisel kept this in mind as he rode up the Tourmalet on the opposite side of the road to his team-mate. The next day was a rest day. If he could only coax and cajole Cavendish through this one ...

On they rode up the Tourmalet, still not speaking. 'There were many stages where we'd argue,' says Eisel. 'This wasn't the only time I'd ride up one side, him up the other, not talking to each other. Sometimes, it was because I was on my limit, rather than Cav.'

Could he be hard on him, like an elder brother? 'That was really rare. Most of the time I'd be telling him, "Dude, we are this much behind, we need to keep riding."' Eisel was in charge of the calculations, and he had this down to a T. 'It's an easy calculation on a normal climb: you lose a minute every K at a certain speed. So, you keep that speed. And you know how far down you are at the top. Then, on a 20k downhill, if they don't race full gas at the front you can bring back a minute or two. If it's hard rain or slippery, we can bring back five minutes.'

It sounds like they take risks on the descents, but Eisel and Cavendish both say no. Eisel explains: 'Over the years, I remember a lot from previous years; I really know most of the descents very well. Maybe not every corner, like a MotoGP rider, but I remember the important ones, where you have to be careful; the rest we can go full gas. Also, you have to trust the motorbike in front of you. We always have a motorbike in front. If he doesn't touch the brakes, then you don't touch yours; if you see his brake lights, you touch your brakes.'

Eisel and Cavendish's fall-outs followed a typical routine. 'He'd come up with a can of Coke in his hand to say sorry,' says Eisel. 'That's how it went.' He laughs. 'Like feeding apples to an elephant.'

*   *   *

So it goes: as they continue up the Tourmalet, Cavendish drops back to the team car and gets Eisel a can of Coke. They're friends again. 'After 4k of the Tourmalet, with 18k left, we're losing about 10 seconds a K [on the *gruppetto*], but I know we can make it back on the descent,' says Cavendish, 'especially with Basso there.' Basso was strong uphill and notoriously slow going down. 'We ended up losing two and a half, three minutes on the Tourmalet. And we caught them back half-way down.' Cavendish's eyes sparkle as he recalls the pursuit. 'We were on the edge, like, down that descent – on the edge.'

There was still another climb, the Col d'Aubisque. As well as Eisel, Cavendish now had another team-mate there, Tony Martin. 'I got a little bit of help from Tony. He was carrying my bottles. Then I took my radio out. I was, like, fuck ... I took it off to save weight. I was like, I needed to lose *every* bit of weight; no sunglasses, nothing.'

Cavendish survives up the Aubisque. Basso seems less anxious here, more confident that his continued participation is not at risk. The *gruppetto* is unusually large, almost ninety riders. It is another factor in their favour: even if they finish outside the time limit, will the officials be brave enough to expel half the field?

'It was a big long run-in to Pau and I was just swinging, really struggling to hang on,' Cavendish says. 'I'm sat on the back and, next thing, with 10k to go, we're quite close to the time limit, and I puncture. I haven't got my radio, have I? I'd given it to Tony to save some weight on the climb. I'm on the back on my own; the guys – Bernie, Tony, Bert [Grabsch, who had rejoined them] – are on the front riding hard to make the time limit.

'I put my hand up. No team car comes up.

'I drop back through the convoy. No HTC car. Allan Peiper [his directeur sportif] had at that moment stopped for a piss. And no fucking car wanted to help me until the last car, Astana, stops and gives me a wheel. That saved me. I got back on. But, yeah. Fucking, yeah.'

On the Place de Verdun in Pau, the Frenchman Pierrick Fedrigo sprints in at the head of a small group that includes Lance Armstrong. Armstrong had been trying to salvage a stage victory from what had otherwise been a disastrous final

Tour; in Pau, he can only manage sixth. 'It's a very, very beautiful day,' says Fedrigo, for whom it is the third stage win of his career. Behind him, Alberto Contador and Andy Schleck roll in almost seven minutes later. Another large group comes in 23 minutes down. Finally, eleven minutes later, comes the *gruppetto*: 34 minutes and 48 seconds behind Fedrigo. Eighty-three riders make up the group, including David Millar as well as Cavendish and Eisel.

Cavendish and Eisel were sharing a room, and Cavendish went to use the bathroom first. 'Ten minutes later, Bernie wondered why he hadn't heard the water running. He stuck his head around the door ... I was sitting, cross-legged, fast asleep in the bottom of the shower.

'Bernie has a photo of me asleep in the shower. I didn't eat that night. Didn't have a massage. It was the rest day the next day, but I was so ill, I had fever; I couldn't get out of bed. I was gobbing up this orange shit.'

The next race day, Cavendish survived another climb of the Tourmalet. He finished 164th, in a seven-man group with his three amigos, Eisel, Martin and Grabsch. Millar, still surviving with his broken rib, was just behind. He was ill, too.

The following day, into Bordeaux, was a classic sprinters' stage. Cavendish was still rough; still coughing. 'What I remember most is that I had this square stem on my bike,' he says. 'At one point in the stage I coughed up this orange ball, spat it out, and it landed on the stem. It just sat there.'

Four and a half hours later, when Cavendish sprinted into Bordeaux at the head of the peloton, the orange ball of phlegm was still there. He won the stage. And he won again two days later, this time on the Champs-Élysées for the second year in a row.

Few knew how close he had come to not making it to Pau, never mind Paris. It was, like Millar's ordeal in the Alps, one of the Tour's untold stories. Another B-side that nobody heard.

ANDY SCHLECK

Chapter 18

PLAYSTATION CYCLING

21 July 2011. Stage Eighteen:
Pinerolo (Italy) to Col du Galibier
200.5km. High mountains

It was a stage destined for the history books. But that was the whole point. On the hundredth anniversary of the Tour's first expedition into the Alps, the eighteenth stage finished at the top of one of the most mythical of mountains, the Col du Galibier.

The Galibier featured in 1911, but almost didn't. The road was finished just in time. Although to call it a road is pushing it a little: from the old pictures of riders pushing their bikes up the rough, rutted surface, the Galibier pass resembled a goat track.

A hundred years later, the Tour's fifty-seventh visit to the Galibier was to be its first finish. At 2,645 metres, it would be the highest ever. And this eighteenth stage of the 2011 race included two more brutes: the 2,774m Col d'Agnel and 2,360m Col d'Izoard. Then the Galibier. (Officially, the finish would be listed as Serre-Chevalier, the name by which the southern Hautes-Alpes valley's enormous winter sports resort is known: a disappointing but hardly surprising prioritising of commercial interests over heritage.)

The Galibier, when it first featured, was remote, desolate and soared higher into the sky than the Pyrenean climbs, prompting Henri Desgrange, the Tour's founder, to consider other mountains in a diminished light. 'Oh! Sappey! Oh! Laffrey! Oh! Bayard! Oh! Tourmalet! I will not fail in my duty by proclaiming that beside the Galibier you are but pale and vulgar beer: before this giant, there is nothing to do but tip your hat and bow very low!' Given such an endorsement, it is fitting that Desgrange's memorial now sits close to the summit: a towering, pale stone monument, cylindrical in shape, like a lighthouse.

The Tour's founder seemed to enjoy inflicting pain and suffering on the riders; as far as he was concerned, this was its *raison d'être*. The Tour was all about incredible feats that captured the imagination and explored the limits of human endurance. Desgrange would have enjoyed stage eighteen of the 2011 race.

*   *   *

'Don't give me credit,' says Andy Schleck when he sits down, eighteen months after the event, to talk about the Galibier stage. 'But the idea was mine.'

In 2011 it was all going wrong for Schleck. Or Baby Schleck, as he was disparagingly known. He had other nicknames, none of them flattering: Schleck Minor, Andy Pandy. Which was odd, in some respects, because Schleck was a likeable, goofy, buck-toothed Luxembourger who seemed perpetually trapped in a younger self. Skinny-limbed and size-zero gangly, Schleck was the child prodigy who never grew up, and seemed permanently on the cusp of greatness. But never quite there. He was a pure climber in the classic mould: lightweight, angular (surprisingly tall, at 1.86m), with an upright riding style in the mountains, a little like – though not quite as bolt upright as – the Eagle of Toledo, Federico

Bahamontes, the great Spanish climber of the 1950s. Indeed, in the modern era, which favoured all-rounders, Schleck was a throwback. Like old-school climbers, he seemed incapable of producing anything approaching a decent time trial. If he deserved mockery for anything, it was for his haplessness in this discipline.

The Baby Schleck nickname was particularly unfair, because Andy's palmarès was better than that of his older brother, Fränk. Yet Andy, for all his apparent class on a bike, appeared to lack something, and the 2011 Tour seemed to be exposing that quite brutally. He had finished runner-up for two years, both times to Alberto Contador, though he would eventually inherit the 2010 title when Contador tested positive for clenbuterol. In the official history, the winner of that Tour is Andy Schleck. But it doesn't count, insists Andy. He wants to win on the road; to enter Paris in yellow and be crowned champion on the Champs-Élysées.

In 2011 Contador was back, not because he had served his suspension, but because his doping case from 2010 was still unresolved. He had ridden the Giro the month before the Tour, and won, but in doing so dug deep into his reserves.

It should have meant that the race was on a plate for Schleck. But as the first two weeks unfolded, and they entered what should have been Schleck's hunting ground, the Pyrenees, something was wrong. It was as though he missed his duels with Contador; as though the Spaniard had drawn something out of him that he was incapable of finding within himself. Without Contador – or with a diminished Contador – Schleck seemed diminished himself.

In previous years, whenever Contador had jumped away in the mountains, Schleck had gone with him; they kept each other company on these steep climbs, at times seeming too cosy. In 2010 the denouement was their 'showdown' on the Col du Tourmalet. But they rode up side-by-side, keeping a cautious eye on each other, sparring rather than going for the knockout. That was fine by Contador: he was in yellow. But Schleck needed to do something, at least to show aggression. As the Tourmalet wound up, his final chance to dethrone the Spaniard vanished in the fog that enveloped the summit. Defeat was conceded not with a bang but with a whimper (maybe this fact, too, has affected Schleck's response to being named 'winner' of that Tour; perhaps, deep down, he feels that he doesn't deserve it).

It seemed to confirm Schleck as a nearly man: brilliant, talented, precocious, but not a champion. And yet he was a member of that rare breed – Anquetil, Merckx, Hinault, LeMond – who had finished on the podium in his début Grand Tour (second at the Giro in 2007, aged just twenty-two). So what was the problem? That he was too nice? That he didn't have the required ruthless streak?

There was 'chaingate', an incident earlier in the 2010 Tour, when Schleck attacked towards the summit of the Port de Balès, opening a gap of around ten metres before he unshipped his chain. Behind, as this happened, Contador was reacting to Schleck's attack. And as he caught the Luxembourger, it was clear to everybody – and must have been clear to Contador – that the rider in the yellow jersey was suffering a mechanical problem. As Schleck fiddled with his chain, and had to dismount, Contador spread his wings and flew. Schleck gave chase on the descent – not his forte – but was 39 seconds down at the finish. He was furious; wide-eyed with indignation. 'I have anger in my belly,' said Schleck.

By the next morning – after Contador had posted a video on his website apologising for taking advantage of his rival's misfortune, insisting that he hadn't realised Schleck's chain had come off – the fire had gone out. On the start line Schleck shook Contador's hand. All was forgiven. And, as though decreed by fate, Schleck went on to lose the Tour by the amount of time he lost on the 'chaingate' stage: 39 seconds.

So here we are in 2011. Week three. The Alps. It has come to the point where Schleck has to do something, because people are mocking him. In the Pyrenees, where he and Fränk had been expected to tear the race to pieces, they failed. Worse, they hadn't even seemed to try. They prevaricated. On Plateau de Beille, the final Pyrenean climb, Andy launched a series of attacks, but no sooner had daylight appeared than he would glance back, seeing what damage he'd done.

Andy's attacks were head-turning, all right. But the only head that was turning was his. In the French press he was given another nickname, 'Torticollis' – a reference to a condition in which the sufferer has a stiff neck, forcing their head to one side. He seemed to ride up Plateau de Beille with his head cocked, keeping an eye behind him, searching for his brother Fränk.

*   *   *

At the summit of Plateau de Beille, Schleck entered the Leopard team bus and slumped in his leather-upholstered chair. Twenty minutes later, Stuart O'Grady, his friend and team-mate, entered. O'Grady was perhaps feeling a bit silly, too. Their team had been launched with such fanfare, based in Luxembourg and built around the Schleck brothers, with a portentous pledge inked on the side of the bus: 'True Racing'.

True racing? Today, at the summit of Plateau de Beille, that looked more pretentious than portentous. And O'Grady had contributed his own hubris, mocking the Europcar team defending Thomas Voeckler's yellow jersey. 'Gonna be fun watching Europcar trying to control the race,' O'Grady had tweeted.

Now, as he sat with Andy at the end of the stage, he could reflect on the fact that Europcar *had* controlled the race. And that Voeckler was still in yellow.

'OK, Stuey, here is what I'm going to do,' Schleck told him. 'I feel strong, but I haven't shown it yet, so on the big Alpine stage I'm going to go early. Not leave it to the Galibier, but go on the Izoard. If I come over the top with a minute and I have help in the valley, I will go to the finish.'

'Mate, if you do that ...' O'Grady didn't even finish the sentence.

Schleck was aware of the criticism. 'It's what people do, it's natural,' he says when we meet in southern Spain eighteen months later. 'It's like me watching a football game; I criticise. When you're in the race, there was not an awful lot more I could do. At 300 metres to go on Plateau de Beille, I went all out, and people say: "Look how strong you are." But I gained nothing. They said I should have attacked earlier, but I had already attacked so many times. And there was a headwind: people don't see this. And maybe I didn't have the right legs that day.

'Anyway, I don't mind when people criticise, because it means they don't forget you.'

He wasn't waiting for his brother? 'No, no. That's silly. Of course we are better together, but ...'

It didn't get any better for Schleck after Plateau de Beille. Three days later, at the end of a stage to Gap, it got worse. On a relatively minor climb, the category-two Col de Manse, Contador used the rising road, tackled in torrential rain, as the launch pad for an audacious bid to haul himself back into contention. Cadel Evans was able to follow him, but both Andy and Fränk Schleck struggled to respond. They were distanced on the climb and fell further back on the descent, which Andy tackled like a startled deer.

He lost a minute that day. The stress was showing. 'Is this really what people want to see?' asked Schleck in Gap, referring to the descent, which he felt was dangerous. He said that he was worried about the next day's 'mortally dangerous' downhill finish into Pinerolo. If he wanted to offer encouragement to his rivals, and to suggest where he might be vulnerable, he could hardly have been more obliging.

And yet, despite some nervous moments on the twisting descent into Pinerolo, Schleck finished with Cadel Evans and Contador. It meant that on the eve of the Galibier stage he was fourth overall, two and a half minutes behind Voeckler, with Fränk third, almost a minute and a half down.

'We talked about specifics that night,' recalls Luca Guercilena, one of two Leopard directeurs sportifs, along with Kim Andersen. 'On the morning, we got down to the fine details.'

'At the team meeting in the morning, the plan was made,' says Brian Nygaard, who was the team manager. 'Andy had been talking about it, he told me a couple of days before, and he was extremely confident. I hadn't seen him that confident since he won Liège–Bastogne–Liège in 2009. Three days before Liège he had said: "No one's going to follow me on Sunday." The thing with Andy is, he's either really chilled out or he's excited. He was really excited for Galibier.' Partly, admits Nygaard, that owed to his frustration at the criticism: 'Criticism doesn't really bother him, but once in a while he has what I would say is a really useful sense of pride. Then he reacts.'

The first part of the day's plan was to put two riders in the main breakaway. There were four candidates: Maxime Monfort, Joost Posthuma, Jakob Fuglsang and Linus Gerdemann. O'Grady would keep an eye on things, and try and infiltrate the break if the quartet failed – because making the break is not as simple as it sounds.

'Kim Andersen explained it to me,' says Monfort. 'We had had some bad days, especially into Gap. Andy losing a minute for nothing. We were all really disappointed. And Kim told me, "We have a plan for Galibier."

'When he told me what it was, I didn't believe it.'

The plan was for two riders to go up the road with the break; for Schleck to attack from behind on the Col d'Izoard;

for one of his team-mates in the break to drop back and help him; then for the other Leopard rider to pace him along the long valley road, where the wind can make it hard. Finally, Schleck would take off up the mountain. As he told O'Grady in the bus at Plateau de Beille, he believed he needed a minute on his pursuers at the summit of the Izoard.

Monfort was sceptical: 'I said, "This is Playstation." It was Playstation cycling. I told Kim, "It's not going to work." It was nice to hear that the team was ambitious, but this, I thought, was too much. Modern cycling does not work like this.'

*   *   *

The stage rolled out of Pinerolo, with a long run-in to the Agnel, the road rising gradually from 46km, the climb proper starting 40km later, crossing back into France at the summit. The pace was high from the start; with the climbs back-loaded, it was an opportunity to get in a break on what was being called the 'Queen Stage'. There was an intermediate sprint after 46km, just before the climbing started, and that helped to glue the race together as Mark Cavendish's HTC team, in the hunt for points towards his green jersey, led the peloton.

Then, unexpectedly, a seven-man break formed just before the sprint. 'I was trying from the beginning to get away,' says Monfort. 'Jump, jump, jump. Then I stopped, because it didn't make any sense. It's always the same story: you fight, but everyone fights, until eventually everyone has had enough and riders need a break or they stop for a piss. On this day, though, no riders were getting away.'

No surprise, with the speed at 50kph. Then came the lull, just before the sprint, and seven slipped off the front. Joost Posthuma was the only Leopard rider in the break. 'I could see them with fifteen, twenty seconds,' says Monfort, 'and I jumped. I gave it all I had. Joost was there, but I gave it everything. I was strong, but a bit lucky, and I caught them. So I was in the break.'

Others jumped across until it contained sixteen riders. They included the Irishman Nicolas Roche, the highest-placed rider on GC in 21st, the Kazakh Maxim Iglinsky and a rider who seemed to suffer a nervous disposition that made him unable to sit in the peloton, and prompted him to seek to be part of every break in every race he rode: Johnny Hoogerland. The sixteen committed to the task in hand, working together. The peloton relaxed. After a 50kph first hour, in the second the average speed dropped below 35. The lead kept building: as they began the Agnel, it was almost nine minutes.

The pace behind was slow. It wasn't exactly fast in the break, either. 'On the first climb, the Agnel, we were so slow, too slow,' says Monfort. 'I was a little bit stressed by that. We had to maintain the right gap between the breakaway and peloton. We wanted it not too big, not too small: about seven minutes. But they were slow behind as well.'

Halfway up the climb, Schleck dropped back to the team car, to chat to Kim Andersen. Luca Guercilena was in the other car, behind the break. By this point Schleck had realised that he'd made a mistake. He was wearing the wrong shirt; it was Monfort's. This was typical Schleck. 'I've never known Andy to have an orderly suitcase,' says Nygaard. 'He regularly forgets bike shoes. He had done that on this Tour, earlier in the race: left his shoes at the hotel. Somebody had to go back and pick them up. Fränk is the polar opposite, very organised.'

Dropping back to speak to Andersen in the team car on the Agnel, Schleck checks that everything is OK up front. He is concerned that his group is going too slow; that the gap will be too big to bridge. It is an indication of how slow they are riding that he can drop back like this on a climb. 'Don't worry,' Andersen tells him. 'The break isn't going especially fast, so you don't have to worry about that. But use a couple of team-mates in the peloton, make it a bit faster.'

Schleck speaks to O'Grady, who moves to the front, upping the pace. At the summit they are five and a half minutes behind the break, led by Iglinsky. Posthuma has been working hard on the Agnel and to the base of the Izoard to keep the speed high. The Izoard is a brute: 14.1km at an average gradient of 7.3 per cent, with much steeper sections halfway up and close to the summit. From the southern side they ride through the barren, spectacular outcrop known as the Casse Déserte. The Izoard is etched into the history books as the scene of famous exploits and battles involving Coppi, Bobet, Bahamontes, Merckx ...

And now Schleck attacks, jumping up the outside, flying into a hairpin so fast that he almost has to brake. He glances back and sees Pierre Rolland, the young Frenchman, trying to follow, but Schleck's eyes lock on the road in front and he doesn't look back again. Rolland does not make contact and gives up.

'I knew the corner where I was going to attack,' Schleck says, his eyes flaring as he recalls his move. 'Having two guys up ahead was ideal. Or I wouldn't have attacked: it would have been stupid.' His one fear was that Bjarne Riis, his old manager and now Contador's directeur sportif, would know what he was up to. 'Bjarne's a clever guy, but what could he do when Contador wasn't so good? So I knew it was my moment.

'When I attacked ... I had been waiting three days to do that. I went from second, from behind Stuart, and I just went with everything. You have to. I looked around after 200 metres and thought: now I have got to go. I went up there hard, and later, when I saw it back on TV, I could see they were nervous behind. There was still a long way to go, and they were maybe thinking I was going too early.'

Posthuma, who had done so much to ensure that the break had a seven-minute lead as they began the Izoard, was dropped on the climb. Two kilometres after breaking away,

Schleck had 45 seconds on his pursuers. Just over a kilometre later he caught Posthuma. It gave him a breather: Posthuma dug deep, using what strength he had left to pace Schleck for as long as possible. With Posthuma's help, Schleck's advantage stretched to two minutes. And then Posthuma was done: he swung over as Schleck continued up the climb.

Up ahead, Monfort heard what was happening from Guercilena, in the car following him. 'The goal was that I would reach the top of the Izoard with Andy,' says Monfort. 'But the gap was about two minutes; I was a little bit too far ahead so I had to ease up and almost stop. That was great! For the last 500 metres of the Izoard I could take it easy. I had two [energy] gels, two bidons, and I could really rest for two minutes. I knew he was coming. I had Luca behind me, who was hearing from Kim. Luca said, "Max, you have to stop, you have to stop." I got to the top and then did the first two corners alone and then Andy was coming.'

'I felt I only needed a minute at the top,' Schleck says. 'I knew that if I came over the top of the Izoard with a minute and had help in the valley that I could go to the finish alone. I said, "If I go on the climb, then it's only the leader of another team who can go as fast as me. If they have to work hard, that suits me. And if they catch me, then Fränk can go."

'I met Max, he was waiting, and he was really on a mission: he needed to do the time trial of his life. He's a super team-mate, super loyal.'

Ahead, the original breakaway had splintered. Schleck and Monfort caught Roche and another two survivors, the Dutchman Dries Devenyns and Russian Egor Silin. Iglinsky was ahead. Schleck's problems of the last few days, into Gap and Pinerolo, had owed much to his apparent lack of descending skill, as with the loss of those 39 seconds to Contador in 2010. But with Monfort leading him down the Izoard, choosing the lines around the hairpins, and with Schleck putting his trust in his Belgian team-mate, they dropped like stones.

In the valley, into the headwind, Monfort sat on the front and dragged the group along. Schleck helped, Roche and Silin contributed little, but Devenyns seemed a willing worker, perhaps helping Monfort, a fellow Belgian. Monfort barely noticed. 'I couldn't speak in the valley,' he says. 'I couldn't hear. I was just full, full, full gas.'

'I told Max he had to do the time trial of his life,' Guercilena says. 'We were playing to win the Tour. We knew in the valley the wind would be bad, but the goal was for Andy not to work too much and save his biggest effort for the climb. In the car, following, it was really thrilling. I can say I saw Andy incredibly focused on the race. I have told him many times since, that at the moment he joined the breakaway it was like he entered a tunnel and could only see the finish line in his head.'

Presumably, Monfort could tell his leader was in the form of his life. 'Actually, no. Only afterwards I realised. He helped me a little in the valley and we had some help from Devenyns. That was nice, it meant Andy could have twenty seconds easy and I could take a drink.'

The valley was hardly a valley at all: the road dropped into Briançon and then began to rise steadily for 15km before they began the Galibier, via the Col de Lautaret. The climb to the finish was really 23km. 'There was a false flat in the town of Briançon,' says Monfort. 'It was a crazy headwind. Luca was in the car, and said: "OK, Max, you're a time triallist now; you go to the point where you can see the summit is in 23km," at the foot of the Galibier.

'But when I got to there, I thought, I'm OK. Exhausted, but still OK. I'll try to get to 20k to go. That was my next goal.'

Schleck's lead stuck stubbornly at two minutes. There were 40km left. Still the chase was disorganised; riders were rolling through, keeping the gap respectable, but not riding hard to close it. Cadel Evans's BMC team was working, but without going all out, perhaps because sitting behind Evans was

Fränk Schleck. They didn't want to give Fränk a free ride, to tow him up to his brother only to watch him fly away. All the way through the valley, to the base of the Galibier, the older Schleck shadowed Evans, then, as the slope started, he switched his attention to Contador, the more explosive climber. In the valley, Contador and his fellow Spaniard, Samuel Sánchez, sat together at the back of the group talking, as though hatching a plan. Then Sánchez's orange-clad Euskaltel team-mates appeared at the front with Contador's Saxo Bank lieutenants, and began to chase.

With 30km remaining, Iglinsky was finally caught by the Schleck group: now there are six. Five kilometres later, Schleck's lead has grown to 3:10. Devenyns has been doing a lot of work but doesn't last much longer. And then, with 17km remaining, Monfort is finished. A few hundred metres later, so is the Russian, Silin. 'I got to 20km to go, and I had some energy left,' says Monfort. 'Then, suddenly, I was empty.'

It is easier to empy yourself for someone else, says Monfort, a rider who seems happier in the role of domestique. 'When I knew I had Andy on my wheel, I could really kill myself without even thinking about making it to the finish myself. I had a real role. It was important for the team, and there was a plan, a tactic. And it was Andy's last chance.'

As the climb began, Schleck's lead shot up. On the shoulder of the Lauterat, with 15km to go, the trio of him, Iglinsky and Roche had almost four minutes, but the work was all being done by Schleck. 'It felt like I had wings,' says Schleck. 'They stayed on my wheel but as soon as I hit the hill, when it started to get steeper, I didn't want them there any more. I didn't think about that because when you think about that you lose the concentration. I just rode hard and I knew that I was strong and they wouldn't be able to hang on.'

Guercilena, in the following car, tried to keep Schleck in the moment, focused on the effort, not letting his mind wander, or start making calculations about how much time he had, how much he needed to claim yellow, or how much he wanted if he was to keep it to Paris. 'We kept telling him: "Don't think about the gap." We had told him from the moment he attacked: first, reach the breakaway; second, ride to the bottom of the climb without using too much energy, using Max; third, try to win the stage at the top; fourth, check the gap. If you're fighting for the time gap, the stress is too high. We weren't giving him information on the gap to the others.'

On his own, with Iglinsky falling back, and riding through banks of supporters at the summit of the Lauteret, Schleck's lead grows to four minutes, 24 seconds. Here you can see the dark clouds above the Galibier, the snow-capped peaks surrounding it, and the thin road slashing up its slopes. When Iglinsky finally could hold on no longer, Schleck glanced round once, twice, then lifted himself out of the saddle and pressed on. Never mind the stage, he could be winning the Tour today.

Finally, Evans realises that his Tour is slipping away. He looks around at Voeckler and Pierre Rolland, the Europcar riders, gestures with his hands, asking, 'Why aren't you working?' When they don't respond he looks disgusted. Then he attacks. Rolland follows, and Voeckler, in yellow, follows Rolland. Others claw their way back up after Evans's brief surge. He's a diesel, not a sports car. But what's surprising is how far back Contador is. Fränk Schleck still shadows him, but it is obvious now that Contador is not on a good day.

The contrast in styles between Andy Schleck and Evans is striking. Evans is scowling and snarling, baring his teeth like an angry Jack Russell. Schleck, though he is suffering, is far more fluid and graceful. His upper body is so skinny you can see his ribs through his (well, Monfort's) shirt. Evans's grinding performance brings the gap inside four minutes, though this also owes something to the fact that up ahead, where Schleck is, the road has steepened.

Schleck, with his sunglasses perched on his helmet, grimaces. It's him versus Evans, and the gap, as the Australian leads the others over the Lauterat, is three minutes, 30 seconds. Schleck keeps getting out of the saddle, trying to find a rhythm. Behind him, the red Tour director's car has Eddy Merckx in it, and Merckx squeezes his ample frame through the sun roof. For a short time, as they inch up the mountain, he looms over the slight figure of Schleck like a colossus should. Merckx takes a special interest not only because it is a performance that is reminiscent of one of his own, but because the Schlecks' father, Johny, was one of his domestiques.

The lead reduces to three minutes. Still no sign of Contador. And Sánchez has been dropped. All that Schleck remembers of his effort, at this point, is the wind. 'The headwind was all day, 65km into the wind. You could see the flags. There were lots of Luxembourg flags on the Galibier but all I could focus on was that they were blowing towards me, because of the headwind. It was so strong. It made it very, very tough.'

Crawling towards the summit, the stage win in the bag, Schleck finally lets it out. His celebration is primal: a release of all the pent-up frustration at his own performances and the criticism that had followed. He raises his arms, opens his mouth, as though screaming – he looked angry rather than happy. But now, he says that he did enjoy it. 'Yes, I did. I did. Because it was the plan, and the plan had worked.

'Fränk came back to the bus and said to me, "How did it go?" He didn't realise I had won; he thought there were still riders from the break ahead of me. He didn't hear anything on the radio. In the mountains you don't really hear the radios. But when I told him, he hugged me. Then he said, "That means I'm second!" We were one–two: that was nice.

'My dad was there as well. And I enjoyed it when Stuey came back; to see his face, because he was the first one I told the plan to.'

The other story of the day was the carnage behind. Eighty-nine riders finished outside the time limit. They should have been thrown off the race, but the race jury relented. It had been an epic day, the kind that Henri Desgrange would have liked, though he might not have approved of the special treatment for the stragglers.

*   *   *

It wasn't quite enough for Schleck.

The next day, a short stage to l'Alpe d'Huez that included climbing the other side of the Col du Galibier, saw a resurgent Contador try to salvage something from his Tour. He went on the attack early, Schleck followed, Voeckler was caught in no man's land, and Evans seemed to be having all kinds of difficulty, changing his bike, though perhaps the real problem was in his head: he seemed to be panicking. On l'Alpe d'Huez, Contador and Voeckler paid for their earlier efforts and cracked. Rolland won the stage, Schleck rode into yellow and Evans did enough to ensure that the next day, on the penultimate stage, he would take the lead and hold it to Paris. Schleck, despite his 65km solo effort two days before, had not been converted into a time triallist: he was still lousy against the watch.

'I was cooked from the day before,' says Schleck of the Alpe d'Huez stage. 'I wish I had been stronger. I have this mentality that if I ride hard for 100km one day I can do it again tomorrow, but it's not really the case. That 65km into the wind: I really felt it the day after. I wanted to attack again but it wasn't possible. I was happy just to hang on.'

When I met Schleck to speak to him about his Galibier stage win, he was happy to relive it. He had ridden that day without fear. Crucially, he said, 'I wasn't afraid to lose.' Since then, it had all gone wrong: poor form from the start of 2012, then a crash in the time trial stage of the Critérium du Dauphiné, earning him more ridicule and, more seriously, a fractured sacrum, the large, triangular bone at the base of the spine, which separates the two hip bones. It put him out of the Tour de France.

Since then he has been a shadow of the rider who won the Tour's highest ever finish. At the time of writing it is becoming one of cycling's great mysteries: whatever happened to Andy Schleck after July 2011? He says he can't answer it himself, only expressing his hope that he will rekindle the fire in his belly, or locate the wings that carried him up the Galibier. His team director, Luca Guercilena, says that he regularly talks to Schleck about the Galibier stage, hoping to inspire in him a Pavlovian response, or at least to instil the self-belief that made that day possible.

'I don't see myself finishing my career without at least once ending with yellow in Paris,' says Schleck, perhaps more in hope than expectation. There is a hint of melancholy about him. But he has enjoyed reliving his famous stage win, he says. 'That was *agréable*,' he says. '*Très agréable.*'

Classement

1 Andy Schleck, Luxembourg, Leopard Trek, 6 hours 7 minutes, 56 secs
2 Fränk Schleck, Luxembourg, Leopard Trek, at 2 minutes, 7 secs
3 Cadel Evans, Australia, BMC Racing Team, at 2 minutes, 15 secs
4 Ivan Basso, Italy, Liquigas-Cannondale, at 2 minutes, 18 secs
5 Thomas Voeckler, France, Team Europcar, at 2 minutes, 21 secs
6 Pierre Rolland, France, Team Europcar, at 2 minutes, 27 secs

DAVID MILLAR

Chapter 19

REDEMPTION

13 July 2012. Stage Twelve:
Saint-Jean-de-Maurienne to Annonay
266km. Mid mountains

'We had two and a half weeks to go,' says David Millar, reflecting on the situation he and his team, Garmin-Sharp, found themselves in, just one week into the 2012 Tour. 'So we had to pull our heads out of our arses and find a new way of racing.'

The American team had almost been obliterated on one horrific day, when they appeared at the finish of stage six in Metz looking like a defeated army returning from the front line. So many riders went down that it was impossible to count, but an astonishing proportion of the tangled bodies and bikes were from Garmin. When they arrived back at their team bus, they were bedraggled, bloodied, in various states of agony and distress, their clothing ripped and in rags. The casualties included the team leaders, Ryder Hesjedal, who had just won the Giro d'Italia, and Tom Danielson. Millar was one of the better-off ones: all you could see was a deep, bloody gash in his arm. His team-mate, Johan Vansummeren, seemed to have left most of his skin on the road; his shorts barely concealed his modesty; his buttocks looked like bloody, raw steaks. It was one of those rare occasions at the Tour when the reporters, waiting like vultures by the bus, thought better of approaching the riders.

Instead, surveying the carnage, there was Allan Peiper. Peiper, slim and silver-haired, was leaning against the team car with his arms folded. He looked resigned, but it was worse than that, more like trauma. It was the worst day he had seen in thirty years at the Tour, he said. 'We've lost most of our chances for everything in the Tour de France. At this moment, I can't see what a successful Tour might be.'

All this from one crash. One story was that it was caused by one of Alessandro Petacchi's domestiques, who was helping the Lampre sprinter prepare for the finale. Petacchi had decided to remove his overshoes and handed them to his domestique, who removed his hands from the bars to stuff them in his back pocket, touched a wheel, lost control …

For Millar, it was 'the scariest crash I've been in … a perfect storm: a howling tailwind, going from a big road to a narrow road; 3km from a left turn. We were going so fast, 78kph when the impact happened. It was such a narrow road, we were so tightly packed, and it was that stage in the race when everyone is engaged. And all of a sudden there was a sea of bikes and people. It was like it was all falling from the sky in front of you. There is nothing you can do other than pile into it. And at that speed you're going to get hurt. That's what's scary. You were sliding into it. And you know it's coming from behind as well. We had been moving Ryder up the bunch at that point, and were grouped together: me, Christian [Vande Velde], Summy [Vansummeren], Tommy D, Ryder.'

Millar finished with blood still dripping from the wound on his arm. 'I didn't even notice my arm, I was so bashed and bruised all over: my legs, shoulders, knees. About 10km later I noticed the blood on my handlebars.'

It was a day that changed everything, that narrowed the scope of his team's ambition. Yet, paradoxically, it opened a door for Millar to try to do what team orders ordinarily denied him. It gave him freedom, *carte blanche* to ride his own race, get in a breakaway and try to win a stage, his first since 2003 (or 2002, if you go by Millar's own, edited palmarès), his first since his return, in 2006, from a two-year suspension for doping.

Getting in a break and winning a stage sounds so simple. But it is not just a case of picking a day. It is a common misconception, but as Millar explains, 'You have to try over several days. You need the combination of a good day, the right people, the right move. It takes a few days of warning up for. I'd say you need a good week of trying.

'I had been trying every day. I was chipping closer, getting my head around the effort needed, and the calculations you need to do. Most of the big breaks that had gone, I had been in, and they were getting a bit further every time. But it's a different style of racing, getting in breaks.'

Like pregnancy, sometimes it happens when you stop trying so hard. On the day in question, exactly one week after the carnage of Metz, going with the break was not Millar's priority. It was a tough stage: borderline mountainous. There were two category-one climbs early on that worried him. And it was because of these that he remained close to the front of the peloton. From this vantage point, he saw riders attacking, trying to get something to stick. Then he watched them come back, spent from the effort. Some would go again – they included riders Millar describes as 'big hitters', people like Alejandro Valverde, who seemed determined to get away. But it wasn't happening for Valverde, who excels on such tough stages. Then it dawned on Millar that riding close to the front, following the accelerations, wasn't hurting as much as it should be.

He began to think about attacking himself. But he felt so good that the prospect – and the pressure he immediately put on himself – did not make him nervous. Another positive sign. 'When you're on a good day, when you're super strong, you don't have to force it. You can wait. You can watch the break forming. You can see the race unfolding in front of you. You're lucid. You can relax.' He might have been in a minority of one, for it was almost two weeks into the Tour, and one of those hard, fast starts to a stage, when so many riders know that it isn't one for sprinters, or climbers, or overall contenders, but for opportunists. Trouble is, the Tour is full of opportunists. When they sniff a half-chance, the relentless attacking pushes the pace up, stretching the peloton in one long line.

Throughout the 'mayhem', Millar remained well placed. At six foot three he is one of the tallest in the bunch, which meant he could see over others' heads: he could watch what was happening; see whether any move was going clear. 'The break always forms at the point where everyone is close to breaking; when everyone is just getting to that point where they can't go again. When you're super strong, you can watch all that unfold, and you're just waiting for everyone else's wheels to fall off, basically.

'That's what I did. I waited until I saw some of the big hitters getting desperate, even Valverde – guys who wanted to be in that break. They all tried to go and I could see them die and come back.'

Millar felt almost detached; he became an observer rather than a participant, poised to act when he could see that the race had decided which combination of riders would go clear. He waited until he could see a hard-working cluster of riders at the front, and a gap opening. The peloton hadn't so much eased off as run out of gas. The expanse of daylight between break and bunch was expanding. 'Then I went,' says Millar. 'I bridged across the gap in about 200 metres. And thought: Ooooh.'

It was only eighteen kilometres into the longest stage of the Tour. To most, it felt like they'd already ridden one hundred. The group that formed at the front comprised nineteen riders and Millar took his place among them. It was all so effortless and easy. 'I was so good that day,' recalls Millar now, 'that I didn't realise what a good day I was on.'

Millar was thirty-five. This was the opportunity he had been craving for at least seven years; it could provide the platform to make the point he had been waiting to make.

*　　*　　*

I first met David Millar at the end of his début professional season, in 1997, though it's more accurate to say that I ran into him in a small bar in the old town of San Sebastián. The world road race title, won by Frenchman Laurent Brochard, had been held there that day. Now it was the final night of the championsips: party time. Millar, barely out of his teens, was wide-eyed and awe-struck as, one by one, some of the sport's biggest names entered the tiny bar. There was Bjarne Riis, who had won the previous year's Tour, wearing a leather waistcoat and cap, along with some Danish team-mates; there were top Australian professionals, including Henk Vogels and Stuart O'Grady. Millar drank whatever he was given, smoked the cigar he was handed, and then, after closing time, went swimming in the sea, losing a leather jacket and a mobile phone.

The following summer, when the Festina scandal revealed the systematic doping of the world's No.1 team, Millar was an obvious go-to guy for the British media. He was starting out on a career of immense promise; so what did he make of the sordid revelations, which overshadowed the 1998 Tour? He was sickened by them. When he went training and kids shouted 'doper', it made him angry and even ashamed to be a professional cyclist. He felt like stopping and explaining to them that not all of them doped. The thing with Millar was, he didn't need to to do this. He had a hinterland beyond cycling. He was intelligent; he could have gone to university, or art school.

Instead he became a cyclist, and his career developed. Then in 2000 it detonated. He won the first stage of his first

Tour, a time trial that was a little too long to be classified as a prologue, ahead of the reigning champion, Lance Armstrong. He had a few days in yellow, and his profile soared. After that, his trajectory faltered. He bombed at the 2001 Tour, crashing and eventually pulling out, but bounced back at the Vuelta a España, where he won two stages.

In 2002, on the eve of his third Tour, I went to interview Millar at the Dauphiné Libéré in Tournon-sur-Rhône in the Ardèche, close to where, ten years later, he would find himself in the nineteen-man break that formed at the start of stage twelve of the 2012 Tour (only 35km north, following the Rhône). But a decade before that, it was apparent that he was different from the wide-eyed twenty-year-old I had encountered in San Sebastián. He was still only twenty-five, but his exuberance – his boyishness – seemed to have gone, or was obscured. He had been bright-eyed and bushy-tailed; now he was dead-eyed and cynical.

For several days he had put off the interview, as though he didn't really want to speak. When we finally sat down, on the morning of a stage that would finish at the summit of Mont Ventoux, he barely made eye-contact. His attention was repeatedly caught by people passing, especially the pretty girls who perform podium duties. He kept his sunglasses on. And he kept hold of his bike, rather than propping it against something, as though he wouldn't be stopping for long. I mentioned the night in San Sebastián as a conversation-starter, but it almost ended it. 'I was young,' he said tersely. 'I've grown up. I have serious responsibilities now.'

He kept stressing how serious his life was. That he was a professional, and didn't have time for frivolity – no reading, no listening to music, no drawing or painting. 'Cycling is taking over a larger and larger part of my life,' he explained. 'Balance was important to me, and I always tried to keep that, but it's getting to the point now where cycling is taking over. It is my life one hundred per cent – nothing else. But it's the way you have to be if you want to succeed. You have to accept it, and you sometimes realise you have nothing else.

'All your other interests fade away. Everything else is lost; that's what's happening now. I'm kind of ready for it. I was younger, and I wasn't ready for it before. But it's all right now. You've only got five or six years at the top.

'Until recently, I was engaged and everything, and madly in love.' But not any more? 'No, we split up. That's just part of my life. I've done it: fallen in love. Still am in love. But it's my lifestyle, and my personality. I don't want anybody just wanting ... I'm not at home 180 days of the year, and when I am, I'm a mental milkshake.

'You've got to be very egotistical in this sport. You have to realise that you have to be horrible to people. You have to tell them not to come to races, because there's no point. I'm not going to see them. I don't bring friends to races any more. It's my job, and I just want to get on with what I'm doing. I don't want to be thinking that I have to go and see people. It sounds like I'm a selfish bastard, and it is kind of lonely at times.'

In the past, Millar had wondered whether he thought too deeply. Now, he said, 'I don't think any more. I've stopped thinking, stopped reading, stopped writing. I'm becoming very dull, but very good.'

Without any intended irony, the headline to our interview, when it appeared in the newspaper, was: 'Millar's summit clear and bright.'

* * *

Something *had* happened to Millar, as he would reveal some years later in his book, *Racing Through the Dark*. In fact, when we sat down in June 2002, that something had happened quite recently. His disappointment at the 2001 Tour – he pulled out on the stage to l'Alpe d'Huez – was compounded by the fact that he was now the Cofidis leader, and felt he had 'let the team down'. He felt that most keenly the night of his withdrawal, when he sat in a room in the team's hotel with a team-mate and directeur sportif and discussed his 'preparation' for the forthcoming Vuelta – preparation being a euphemism. 'I knew what it meant,' said Millar. 'The background white noise of the struggle to fight doping finally subsided. I walked into that hotel room an anti-doper; I walked out of it a seasoned professional ready to do what was required of me.'

Another version of this story is told by Millar's sister, Fran, who by now was acting as his manager. After pulling out of the Tour in 2001, he called her, 'bawling his eyes out; he was in the car after the stage crying. He said, "I'm not good enough to do this, I've had to pull out." I said, "Dude, you were getting shit-faced twelve days ago with Shari [his ex-fiancée] – you're not good enough because you haven't prepared properly and you've had a nasty crash."'

A couple of months later, when Millar won the first stage of the Vuelta, a 12.3km time trial in Salamanca, it was job done. He was relieved rather than euphoric. In the build-up to the race, he had injected EPO into his shoulder, twice, in the Italian team-mate's house in Tuscany. 'In contrast to my Tour win the previous year, all I felt was relief – unadulterated pure relief,' Millar would later write. 'I'd fulfilled my professional obligations – I couldn't have imagined doping and not winning.'

So it continued. A month after our stilted, awkward interview during the Dauphiné, Millar won a stage of the 2002 Tour. It was a road stage this time, not a time trial, and it was executed in clinical fashion. He was in a break of eleven riders, including Brochard, who had won the world title all those years ago in San Sebastián, and another Laurent, Laurent Jalabert. Millar and Jalabert had different objectives – the Frenchman seeking points towards the King of the Mountains competition – and they made an unofficial alliance. When, towards the end, Jalabert attacked, it was to tee Millar up, he said afterwards. Four riders went with Millar's counter-attack, including Brochard and David Etxebarria of the Euskaltel team. It says much about the hideous, perverse logic of professional cycling at this time that Etxebarria's team doctor, Jesús Losa, was by now working with Millar on a freelance basis, advising him on his doping, for a basic 12,000 Euros a year, excluding drugs.

At the finish in Béziers, Millar seemed in full command – of himself, his rivals, the sprint. 'I was feeling so strong,' he said afterwards. 'I've always said it's easy to be tactically perfect when you've got good legs ... I was just having such good fun out there, it was like a game of chess, watching which guy was going to do what. I was anticipating already from 60km out how I was going to win it, that's how stupid it was. It was one of those incredible days that only happens once or twice a year.'

Millar was fulfilling the terms of his contract with Cofidis, winning major races, but he could be erratic. His wins weren't 'dialled in', as Lance Armstrong (who was close to Millar, and in 2001 asked him to join his team) would later say of his Tour victories. Unlike Armstrong, Millar, even when pumped full of drugs, was fallible. He was beaten into second by Jan Ullrich at the 2002 world time trial championship. At the Tour prologue in 2003, he was leading and poised to win until he unshipped his chain close to the finish, handing the victory to Bradley McGee. 'At least a clean rider won,' Millar told McGee, who was taken aback, and compromised, by Millar's admission. Millar then won the final time trial of the 2003 Tour, in the rain in Nantes, appearing on the podium in low-cut jeans with a team baseball cap on back-to-front. A few months later, now with bleached blond hair, he won the world time trial title.

The net began to close early the next year. In January the police raided the Cofidis headquarters in northern France.

An investigation followed. Millar denied he was involved; when it was reported that he was, after testimony from his team-mate, Philippe Gaumont, Millar dismissed Gaumont as a 'lunatic'.

By late May 2004, when the whispers about Cofidis and Millar were becoming deafening, I called his sister/manager, Fran, to fix up an interview. To set the record straight. It was duly arranged. A phone call this time. A Saturday morning. Millar, at home in Biarritz, was about to go training. Again he was surly, clipped. I wanted him to say that he was clean, that the accusations by Gaumont and others were false. Not only did I want to hear it, I wanted to believe it, which might have affected what I heard, or what I thought I heard, during our conversation. At the time, it seemed clear: Millar dismissed the allegations as nonsense and said the whole situation was crazy, out of control. But when I listened back to the tape, all that was really clear was his anger at his accusers. On what he had actually done, and whether he had doped, he was vague, opaque.

Realising this was unnerving: it seemed as though by not telling me what I wanted to hear he was telling me what I didn't want to hear. I called back. Fran answered. Millar had gone out training. I told her that I wanted to check one thing. In 1998, when the Festina scandal was at its height, Millar said that the kids who shouted 'doper' at him made him feel ashamed about being a cyclist, and that if he ever felt he couldn't continue without doping he would walk away from the sport. Fran said she'd ask him whether he stood by those words. The answer came back. He did.

*   *   *

I met Millar again in June 2006. He was about to return from his two-year ban, which came after he was arrested in Biarritz in June 2004, a couple of weeks after our phone call. He was dining with the British Cycling performance director

Dave Brailsford, discussing the forthcoming Athens Olympics (Millar later said that his involvement with British Cycling, which had started the previous year, had encouraged him to believe that he didn't need drugs, and that he had resolved never to take them again). On the night of his arrest, his home was turned upside down and empty vials of EPO were found in his bookcase (so even if he had given up reading, he still had a bookcase). He then admitted to having used EPO.

As is always the case, the length of suspension was decided by the rider's national governing body. Yet Brailsford and the governing body stood by Millar and supported his attempt to return. And so we met, almost two years later, at the head-quarters of British Cycling, the Manchester Velodrome.

Gone was the bleached blond hair, the house in Biarritz, the £400,000 salary, the flash lifestyle. Millar was wearing a yellow short-sleeved shirt with the logo of his new team, Saunier Duval, and driving a modest car, a VW Polo. He was clean-shaven, his hair combed in a neat side-parting. He was twenty-nine. And he said he was excited; that he was going to the 2006 Tour, his comeback race, with 'illusions of grandeur'. He wanted to win the prologue in Strasbourg, though that would create quite a stir, given his past. 'No doubt it would,' he said, 'but I'm prepared for that; prepared for the repercussions. It's something I'll quite happily deal with, to be honest.'

Millar hadn't been sure he would come back. At the start of his ban he went off the rails, drinking too much, living a peripatetic, rootless life that at one point saw him stranded in Monaco having lost his passport. Throughout this period his sister worried about him. Then again, she had always worried about him. 'His twenty-first birthday present from me was a T-shirt that said "Fragile" on it,' she says. 'He is massively impressionable, very easily led. It's a charming thing. He wants people to be what he thinks they are. But they very rarely are.'

Offers of a contract for a returning doper weren't thick on the ground, but the Spanish team Saunier Duval provided Millar with a way back, once he had decided he wanted to return. In 2004 he hadn't even watched the Tour, he told me two years later. 'I think I was in bed that July, waking up at four every day. It was primarily a form of escapism, a way of handling the sky falling in and losing everything. It was a way to forget, and it worked a treat. I went through a few months of not thinking about anything, not knowing anything. Then I got my head out my arse and started thinking that two years wasn't that long.'

Millar said he wanted to be rehabilitated in order to become a spokesman for anti-doping. He was bursting with ideas. He had felt his enthusiasm return the previous summer, watching the 2005 Tour 'through the eyes of a child', as he put it. He wanted to re-invent himself; didn't want anything to do with the cynical, dead-eyed doper he had become. As he put it, 'As soon as you stick a needle in your arm it's not sport any more, is it?'

He wanted to win, again, on the big stage, at the Tour, in order to be able to say all that he had to say. Until then, he believed his role was limited: 'I can't do anything until I've redeemed myself; until I've come back and won races. Then I'll have a voice and can have an official role. Until then I'm *persona non grata*, and rightly so.'

He didn't win a stage of the 2006 Tour. Nor did he win a stage at the 2007 Tour, the 2008 Tour, the 2009 Tour, the 2010 Tour or the 2011 Tour – he started and finished them all, but he was restricted to a team role, helping leaders including Christian Vande Velde, Bradley Wiggins and Hesjedal.

He did win a stage of the 2006 Vuelta, a time trial, and promptly sent an email to UK Anti-Doping. Anything he could do to help, he said, he would. He was invited to speak at their conference in London the following March. When he appeared, he gave a presentation: 'I think there's a great lack of knowledge about why athletes dope,' he said. 'There are very few examples of athletes who've doped then afterwards been proactive in helping an anti-doping organisation, so I'd like to set an example to other athletes because we have to learn a lot more on a human level, a psychological level, about why athletes dope.

'When I was preparing my presentation and thinking of that key question – why did I dope? – I got to thinking, why did I *not* dope for so long?' Millar continued. 'It was an odd realisation. But that's maybe an area we should concentrate on.' Often, what influences whether an athlete dopes or not are their 'core values, ideals, ethics, but also their peer group and their belief in the system. If you don't believe in that system, if you think you're being let down, if you know that other people around you are doping, and you know they're getting away with it, then you start to lose faith.

'A lot of guys aren't in a position to take on this role,' Millar added. 'Some are jealous. I know a lot of guys in the peloton, friends of mine, who are clean, and have been clean for two or three years, but have skeletons in the closet.'

*   *   *

When Millar found himself in the break on the longest stage of the 2012 Tour de France, there were parallels with his win in 2002. Interestingly, that was a stage that he said he hadn't doped for, and so it remained on his CV (he took an airbrush to his palmarès on his team's website, removing his 2003 Tour stage win and his Vuelta stage wins from 2001, along with other victories. Only the 2003 world time trial title was officially stripped).

Millar had gone close-ish to a stage win on one other occasion, in 2008, when they finished in Barcelona and he led, alone, into the city, only to be caught on the final rise to the finish. But that was different, he tells me now. 'When I got away that day I was like, fuck, what am I doing away? I was riding on pure emotion. It was an impossible scenario; only the fact that it rained meant I was out front longer than I should have been. But this stage [in 2012] was different. I had a cool head. I was calculating.'

Once in the break he was working out his odds, which were shortening as the stage wore on. 'There were nineteen of us at the bottom of the first climb, and by the top we were less than half that. By the top of the next one, we were half again. We were never further than a minute up that whole time; it was about 100k before the elastic properly broke. We were going flat out up the climbs, on the descents, in the valley; it was fucking horrible.'

On the day's biggest climb, the Col du Granier, after only 80km, with the peloton still reluctant to let them get too far ahead, five riders emerged at the front: Millar, Jean-Christophe Péraud, Egoi Martínez, Robert Kišerlovski and Cyril Gautier. Millar was still surprising himself; he was still comfortable. 'I was going up the climbs easily. I couldn't understand why everyone was getting dropped. I actually felt the same as I did normally; I was just going a lot faster than normal. By the time I got halfway up the Granier, I realised I was one of the strongest there. I realised I had a strong chance to win the stage.'

This confidence was important. 'If you have self-doubt or you're not so good you'll try desperate tactics.' He drew confidence, too, from the company he was in. He had been checking out his companions in the break – you can tell, from the way they ride, who is just glad to be there, who wonders *why* he is there, who thinks he can win. The nature of this stage, with its tough climbs, acted as a filter. 'The guys still there after the two big mountains, I realised, were going to be climbers. And climbers are not going to beat me in a sprint. Then I made my decision: I'm going to keep the group together, not going to hesitate, whoever attacks I'm going with them, going to shut them down, till I get to the finish line.'

Millar didn't need to initiate any attacks; he didn't need to win alone; he would react to the others, only moving if they moved. Patience was the key. No heroics. 'It becomes a mind game. I think they realised, after I shut the second attack down, that I was very confident I'd win the sprint.'

Then again, he wasn't thinking much. 'When you feel that good, you're very lucid. You don't think, just act.'

The others, however, were thinking that they had to get rid of Millar. In the final 4km, there came a flurry of attacks, but they were testing the water, hedging their bets. Martínez and Kišerlovski both had a go, their accelerations coming to nothing. But when Péraud jumped with 2.7km remaining, he did so with a real sense of purpose – and Millar pounced. The others hesitated. This was the move. Millar bridged to Péraud and then led him through the final kilometre. He kept glancing over his shoulder, making sure Péraud wasn't winding it up, or shifting out the saddle, preparing to sprint. But there was no foxing, no cat-and-mouse stuff, because Millar was confident; he didn't need Péraud in front to beat him. At 200 metres to go, Péraud jumped. A half-second later, as he drew level, Millar jumped too. And side by side they sprinted.

Millar thought, *this isn't as easy as it should be*. Finally, he felt a sense of nervous panic. Péraud was fighting: he was strong, and fast. But Millar held him; then his front wheel edged in front. Inexplicably, Péraud glanced backwards. He was beaten.

Crossing the line, Millar sat down in the saddle, punched the air and yelled: 'Yesssss!'

*   *   *

He collapsed to the road and lay there, spreadeagled. 'That wasn't tiredness,' he says now. 'I was getting a moment of peace, because I knew I wouldn't be able to enjoy it for a while yet. I knew I'd have to be articulate, to put the win into context. I knew it was my time.'

After a stage, the day's winner is fêted on the podium, then walked into a pen. On the other side of the fence, peering through like prisoners, are the media, arranged in sections according to nationality and type – broadcast first, then print, then online, the order reflecting the unofficial hierarchy. Millar walked around them all, and said the same to each. 'I'm an ex-doper,' he told French, American, Danish, British, Australian and German TV. Then he said the same to the broadcast media, then to online, adding: 'But now I want to prove that it's possible to ride and win clean.'

This is what he meant by context. It was the opportunity he'd been waiting for, for seven years. In ninety-nine years of the Tour, no stage winner had introduced himself as an ex-doper. The fact that it was forty-five years to the day since the drug-induced death of another British rider, Tom Simpson, on nearby Mont Ventoux, added extra resonance. 'I think it's poignant that I win today because I'm an ex-doper,' said Millar. 'I made the same mistakes as Tommy made, but I'm trying to show that you can do it clean, and that cycling has come a long way in the last five years. So it's kind of full circle. I'm very proud to do it today because we mustn't forget Tommy's memory and because of what this sport's been through and where we are now.'

Millar says his post-stage speech was a responsibility rather than a choice. 'Whenever I do well I try to make it clear, and talk about my past. I don't want to forget about it or pretend it didn't happen.'

Had he not won, 'the disappointment would have been massive', he says. There had been a stage of the Giro, in 2007, that he looked certain to win – the scenario was similar: he was in a small breakaway, close to the finish – when his chain broke. 'That weighed on my mind.

'It was very similar to the stage I won in Béziers, but there was a difference. In 2002 I was very confident I would win. This time it was more that I was very determined to win.

I knew how rarely the stars aligned like that, and it was more a case of, "I'm not fucking this up; I can't lose." When I was younger it was, "I'm going to win, nobody can beat me." Being a thirty-five-year-old, I could appreciate how rare these days are; it's not just a case of being incredibly fit, and mentally astute, you also need a wonderful series of events to coincide to end up in a situation where you could win.'

For Millar's team there was relief, too. He had salvaged their Tour; in fact, he had defined what Allan Peiper, the team director, struggled to envisage when, at the finish in Metz, he said, 'I can't imagine what a successful Tour would look like.'

Seven days later, he found out that it looked like this: Millar slumped on the tarmac, giving interviews for two hours, repeating himself throughout; followed by more waiting for dope control – it would be ironic, in the circumstances, if we overlooked that. Which all meant that Millar did not see his team-mates until five hours later. There was no big celebration. 'All the emotion had gone by that point.' He missed dinner. 'I had a glass of champagne in the car on the way to the hotel.'

'*Millar: propre et fier*,' read the headline in *L'Equipe* the following morning. Millar: clean and proud.

Classement

1 David Millar, Great Britain, Garmin-Sharp, 5 hours, 42 minutes, 46 secs
2 Jean-Christophe Péraud, France, AG2R-La Mondiale, same time
3 Egoi Martínez, Spain, Euskaltel-Euskadi, at 5 secs
4 Cyril Gautier, France, Europcar, s.t.
5 Robert Kišerlovski, Croatia, Astana, s.t.
6 Peter Sagan, Slovakia, Liquigas-Cannondale, at 7 minutes, 53 secs

L–R: LAURENT FIGNON, GREG LEMOND, PEDRO DELGADO

Chapter 20

LA RÉSURRECTION

23 July 1989. Stage Twenty-One: Versailles to Paris 24.5km. Flat. Time trial

Greg LeMond awoke in Paris on Sunday, 23 July, the final day of the 1989 Tour de France, and wondered what the next twelve hours held in store. The previous evening he had told his soigneur, Otto Jacome, that he thought he could do it. 'That's the way to talk,' said Jacome. But now his mind fluttered between confidence and doubt; unsure whether to feel satisfaction at a job well done, or to dare hope that it wasn't finished yet, that there was still a slim chance.

Two decades on and LeMond sits in a café in Coventry, England, where he has been speaking at a conference, and shakes his head, as if his thoughts are still jumbled, as though he still cannot quite believe how that day unfolded. He is not the only one. He is recalling his return to the Tour, three years after becoming the first American winner, and the fact that nine months later he was shot and almost died in a hunting accident. It caused him to miss most of the next two seasons. When he did race, he was a shadow of the rider he had been. There was a fleeting glimpse of the old LeMond at the 1989 Giro d'Italia. But, overall, that race seemed to confirm that he was finished as a contender in three-week Tours.

LeMond went from the Giro to the Tour de France, for the first time since his win in 1986. 'I had no hope of anything. Zero. No expectations. My fitness was unknown. My mind was still in '86, my body was ... a mystery.'

Reports of LeMond's near-death in April 1987, when he was accidentally shot by his brother-in-law while hunting turkey, were no exaggeration. His shooting party had split up and he was hiding in bushes – dressed in fatigues – when he heard a gun go off. It was so loud that he thought it was his own. It took a few moments to realise that his back and side had been peppered with sixty pellets. His lung collapsed and he came within twenty minutes of bleeding to death; had a helicopter from the California Highway Patrol not happened to be nearby, he would have died where he was shot, in a field in California. When his wife, Kathy, went to see him in hospital, 'He was like a colander ... He had sixty holes and he was just dripping blood out of every single one.' Surgery removed lead pellets from his legs, arms, liver, kidneys and intestines. Some remained lodged in his heart lining, unreachable.

When LeMond returned to the sport and struggled even to finish races, then suffered in the *gruppetto* for much of the 1989 Giro, he seemed to suffer another kind of death, as an athlete.

*   *   *

'Was I confident?' LeMond repeats the question. 'No! No, no, no.' He laughs. 'I have to laugh. I wasn't even getting paid.'

It was a sign of how far LeMond had fallen: in 1989 he was riding for a small Belgian team, ADR, that didn't appear to have any money. 'I was supposed to get paid on 1 January.

January came, February came, March came, with no money. Then April came, with no money.

'They had also promised me a car. By March I said, "Where's the car?" I was taken to a showroom in Antwerp, and told: "Pick a Mercedes." I picked this 500. It never showed up.

'I was under financial pressure. I had a bike company, which my dad was running. My dad was driving me crazy and I wanted to end it, but I didn't know how to tell him. I felt like a boxer, supporting everyone around me. But having not been paid in January, February or March, finally in April, two days before Liège–Bastogne–Liège, I said, "Fuck cycling." And I got drunk. I needed relief from the pressure.

'I told the team boss, "There is no fucking way I am doing Liège–Bastogne–Liège." That was Friday, the race was on Sunday, so I went out, had a good time, had dinner with my wife, and I drank a lot of port. I had a hangover on the Saturday. I haven't drunk port again.

'José De Cauwer was the directeur sportif, and he was a great guy,' LeMond continues. 'But I said, "I'm not riding." And I didn't. I went back to the US and didn't ride at all for three weeks. I was going to quit. But Kathy said, "Give it this year."

'I turned up to the Tour de Trump [the US stage race backed by Donald Trump] with no training, and barely made it through. Then I showed up at the Tour of Italy, and on the first day I lose eight minutes. There's a combination of things affecting me. Allergies, iron deficiency, psychological pressure. The stress of not being paid really affected me.

'One day I lost seventeen minutes. I called my wife and, yeah, I broke down crying. I said, "I can't do this any more." I looked at Stephen Roche and said, "I can't believe I used to be that good." I wanted to quit that night.'

When LeMond phoned Kathy, at their European home in Kortrijk, in Belgium, she sought to reassure him. 'Take it easy,' said Kathy. 'Get through the Tour of Italy. Get to the end of the season. If you get to then and find you can't do it, you can't do it.'

*   *   *

LeMond had always been regarded as a curiosity. He was different, an outsider from beyond the European heartland, with his own ideas about training and diet. He had not grown up with the sport, surrounded by its myths and legends, absorbing its traditions and customs. 'There is a whole history I didn't know. I wasn't connected. I was parachuted in.'

Although LeMond won lots of admirers with his warm smile and effervescent personality, there were critics, perhaps those who were automatically suspicious of outsiders, who had a field day when it seemed that he might be finished. 'There were some mean-assed letters and articles that were very negative,' LeMond says. 'There was this myth that I didn't train. When I got shot in '87, there was an article in a newspaper in Belgium saying, "This is the guy who eats hamburgers, who eats ice cream, and he shouldn't have been hunting at that time." The implication being? That I got what I deserved? Well, I had broken my wrist at Tirreno–Adriatico in '87. I couldn't race for six weeks, so I went home, and I went turkey hunting.'

Six weeks after he was shot, LeMond rode his bike: just five kilometres. Four weeks later, he was able to ride his mountain bike for forty-five minutes. Having lost seventy per cent of his blood volume, he says that it took two months for his body to be fully replenished; it was at the height of hysteria about AIDS, and his doctors were reluctant to give him a transfusion. When he was shot, he weighed sixty-eight kilogrammes. His body fat was four per cent. When he returned to training he weighed sixty-two, with body fat of seventeen; his muscles had all but disappeared.

After three months, he was riding for up to two hours. Then, in mid-July, while Stephen Roche was succeeding him as Tour winner, he was admitted to hospital again, this time with severe stomach pain. Appendicitis. More surgery.

As he recuperated, LeMond agreed to join the Dutch team PDM for his comeback season in 1988, but their offer was on the condition that he raced in 1987. 'If you knew what had happened to me, that was insane,' LeMond says, 'but in September I showed up in Belgium to make sure I could get on the team next year, and I rode one criterium. One lap, and I pretended I had a flat tyre.'

Nineteen eighty-eight was another write-off. Once again, he was in hospital in July rather than at the Tour. While Pedro Delgado was succeeding Roche as champion, LeMond was having an operation for tendinitis in his shin. One of his team managers at PDM, Harrie Jansen, criticised LeMond's lifestyle: 'I told him he was not a professional, that he was acting like an amateur, not training enough, not taking care of his body.' He was, said Jansen, 'too fat, and still eating his hamburgers, his pizzas, his beers'.

Although LeMond was contracted to PDM for another year, they wanted to renegotiate his salary. On 31 December he signed for ADR, the small Belgian team sponsored by a truck rental company. They had declared their interest twelve months earlier, to which LeMond had responded: 'ADR! It's one of the weakest teams around and there's no way they could help me win a race, never mind the Tour.'

By May, five months into a season in which he had been racing without glory, and also without a penny of his $350,000 salary (with a promised $150,000 bonus if he won the Tour – as if), he was at breaking point when, in his hotel room in Italy, LeMond cried down the phone to his wife. It was the evening of the thirteenth stage of the Giro, which included the climb of Tre Cime di Lavaredo. He had finished seventeen minutes down. When he called Kathy he told her, 'Get ready to sell everything.'

'Give it this year,' Kathy told him, before boarding a plane to Italy to support her husband. 'Just get through the Tour of Italy.'

Finally, there was a sliver of hope; a glimpse of the old LeMond. On the final day, a 54km time trial into Florence, he was second to Lech Piasecki, the Polish time trial specialist, and over a minute faster than the overall winner of the Giro, Laurent Fignon.

LeMond? Second?

There were those who didn't realise he was still riding. 'It was just pure luck that I got better,' LeMond says. 'Literally, the day after I lost seventeen minutes, and phoned my wife in tears, it started raining. I now know what my allergies do to me; I get wiped out, 25, 30 per cent. I used to think I didn't race well at the Tour of Italy because I wasn't in shape. But in May the grass has all-time high pollen. When I raced the Tour of Italy I suffered so bad, my eyes were closed; you wouldn't even recognise me.'

At the time, LeMond told journalists that his improvement was down to iron injections from the ADR team doctor, Yvan Vanmol. 'I had three shots of iron,' LeMond says. 'Later, [Lance] Armstrong says I had EPO. If I took that, why would I announce it to the public? I had three shots of iron over the course of the race. I was anaemic. Otto, my Mexican soigneur, kept saying, "You look like a woman who's menstruating." I was grey.'

Whatever the benefits of the iron, LeMond felt better. 'Crying on the phone to my wife was like an emotional release. I did question what I was doing, but I started feeling a bit better, mentally. There was a day it snowed [stage sixteen, to the ski resort of Santa Caterina di Valfurva, which was cancelled] and we had to take the bus. That gave me a day of recovery. Then my legs started feeling good. I still didn't trust myself; didn't believe I had all my strength back. But the morning of the final day, the time trial, I told José I was going to pretend that I was in contention for the Tour of Italy and see where I was in comparison to everybody else.

'In a time trial, you don't put 100 per cent in if you're not in contention. So I had to sit there at the start and pretend I was in the lead, or second place.' LeMond smiles at the memory of his self-deception. 'It worked: I got myself really psyched up. I went flat out and got second place. I put a minute and 20 seconds into Fignon. That blew me away. I caught five people but I had no clue I was going to get second. I thought maybe top twenty.

'I didn't know what it meant. For two years I almost hadn't been able to finish a race. I didn't have any confidence. It was a day-by-day deal. And that was what I thought when I went to the Tour. My goal was top twenty, maybe a stage ...'

*   *   *

There were other factors that might have helped explain LeMond's performance in the Giro time trial. The fact that he started well before Fignon, and enjoyed more favourable weather, for example. Nonetheless, it rang a warning bell for Cyrille Guimard.

Guimard was Fignon's directeur sportif, as well as the man who had brought LeMond to Europe in 1981, travelling to Nevada to sign him for his team. That wasn't the kind of undertaking he would have made for any rider, but Guimard knew LeMond was a thoroughbred. He had been world junior champion and under Guimard became one of the youngest riders ever to win the world senior title in 1983. The following year he made his début at the Tour and finished third; the year after he was second, the year after that first. Few riders had ever seemed so blessed with so much natural talent.

Guimard thought that talent like that was unlikely to disappear. LeMond's performance in the time trial at the Giro sounded a warning that it had not. 'LeMond will be dangerous at the Tour,' Guimard warned. Fignon thought his director had lost the plot.

When the Tour started, LeMond was fourth in the prologue in Luxembourg, with Fignon second, in the same time. It was a strong performance, but it was overshadowed by a bizarre late-show by the defending champion and favourite, Delgado. After missing his start time, Delgado began the Tour two minutes 40 seconds down, then lost another two minutes with stomach trouble the next day.

Stage five, a long 73km time trial to Rennes, was the first major test for the overall contenders. LeMond won, and won convincingly. 'And I'm, like, wow,' he says. He was excited; but a voice urged caution. 'We hadn't hit a climb yet. I thought, well, maybe top ten and one more stage ... maybe that's realistic.'

Not only did LeMond win the stage five time trial, by 56 seconds over Fignon, but he took the yellow jersey. He also used a new type of handlebar. These were extensions that allowed him to bring his elbows together and stretch his arms over his front wheel: a position similar to a ski tuck. 'I didn't know if they would make a difference. I had just got them. I saw Davis Phinney actually pass me in the Tour de Trump earlier that year and thought, man, he looks more aerodynamic. And he had the handlebars. But I didn't use them until that first time trial. I had trained with them, but it was the first time I'd used them in a race.'

Now he was in yellow, leading Fignon by five seconds, but still LeMond's mind fluttered, as it has always tended to do, between confidence and doubt. Sure, he had won, but how much difference had the handlebars made? And the mountains were to come. To reporters, he said: 'I'm really surprised. Since the end of the Tour of Italy, I've noticed real progress ... I still doubt how well I can go, for example in the mountains. I'll be going into the unknown there.'

After nine days, they entered the Pyrenees. 'And I didn't get dropped,' LeMond says. 'I was riding top five.' He still led

Fignon by five seconds. Next day, he was dropped by Fignon towards the end of the climb to Superbagnères, conceding twelve seconds. Fignon was now in yellow by seven. But the rivalry between the pair was turning sour. LeMond noticed a change in Fignon, who, once in yellow, 'went overnight from being a humble guy to really arrogant'.

Fignon accused LeMond of always following, and not riding like a champion. That irritated LeMond, because on the second day in the Pyrenees he had seen Fignon reach out and hold on to a photographer's motorcycle, only for a few seconds, but enough to avoid being dropped on the climb. Later on the same stage, to the summit of Superbagnères, he had dropped LeMond. Next day, LeMond confronted him in the start village. 'Don't talk to me about not racing like a champion. I saw you hang on to that motorcycle, and if you consider that racing like a champion I'd be happy to tell people about it.'

From the Pyrenees they raced across the south of France to begin five crucial days in the Alps. The first was a mountain time trial over 39km to Orcières-Merlette. And the race swung back in LeMond's favour. Fignon suffered again the next day. He was dropped on the Col d'Izoard but caught LeMond on the descent, before being dropped again on the steep 2km climb to the finish in Briançon, conceding another thirteen seconds. 'I lost the jersey, took it back, lost it,' LeMond says, 'but I was happy just being where I was. I had very little team help. It was a sprinters' team. They did the maximum they could for me, but mainly I was by myself.'

By now, having proved to himself that he could stay with the leaders in the mountains, LeMond was starting to believe. But he couldn't turn off his thoughts at night. He couldn't sleep. One night, at 2am, he called Kathy at their home in Kortrijk, just to tell her he was too excited to sleep. 'We began to get greedy and think about the possibility of

Greg winning the Tour,' said Kathy. 'So I stopped sleeping at night, too.'

*   *   *

L'Alpe d'Huez: stage seventeen. LeMond, in yellow, and Fignon, trailing him by 53 seconds, were together as they reached the base of the mountain and began the twenty-one hairpins. Fignon attacked from the start, at hairpin twenty; LeMond countered. Fignon went again. 'It was life or death,' Fignon would later write in his autobiography, 'cut and thrust, blow and counter-blow ... To overcome LeMond, one of the world's great followers, you had to harass him mercilessly.' The relentless attacking was similar to Fignon's duel with Bernard Hinault on l'Alpe d'Huez in 1984, though on that occasion Fignon's superiority showed; now, he wasn't so sure.

But midway up the climb LeMond began to tire. He was paying for his efforts earlier in the day, and also the previous day, when he dug deep on the climb into Briançon. 'I felt great until the last five Ks and then ... I ran out of juice. Guimard knew me well, and José was starting to get to know me, and he could tell when my shoulders started bouncing up and down that I was in trouble.

'Guimard saw me rocking and tried to get up there to tell Fignon to go and attack. José knew what was going on; he was in the car and didn't let Guimard through. There was a car fight between the pair of them on l'Alpe d'Huez. Eventually, Guimard got through and said to Fignon, "Attack him now! He's finished." Fignon said, "I can't." I heard the whole conversation.'

Guimard was insistent, explaining later: 'When Greg sits down, stands up, sits down again, it's because he's cracked. And when he cracks, he really cracks.'

'I look back now,' LeMond says, 'and think, thank God

there weren't radios back then. Cycling's about bluffing. It's poker.

'I was trying to bluff, but Guimard could see me rocking and he knew. He went back up to Fignon. "You have to attack. You've got to go now!" At that point Fignon attacked and I just blew.'

There were four kilometres to the summit, and as Fignon rode away LeMond's head dropped. His strength seemed to vanish. It was as though he was pedalling through treacle. He was in the saddle, out, in, out, searching for an elusive rhythm. 'For five hundred metres, it's awful,' wrote Philippe Bouvet in *L'Equipe*. 'The yellow jersey is drowning in amongst the hordes of people.' Up until now, LeMond's strategy in the mountains had been all about bluffing. He simply did not know what he was capable of. 'I didn't have any confidence, so I thought if I followed him in attack I'd look strong.

'But I felt like shit on l'Alpe d'Huez.' By the top, with Fignon crossing the line one minute nine seconds ahead of LeMond, the overall lead had swung back to Fignon. Now he was back in yellow. He was resurgent. The next day, to Villard-de-Lans, he increased his overall lead to 50 seconds by winning the stage with a surprise attack. 'I had another bad day,' LeMond says. 'I had dug so deep.'

There was one more day in the mountains, to Aix-les-Bains. It wasn't as hard as the previous two. The only scare came when all the leaders, including Fignon and LeMond, overshot a bend on a roundabout coming into the finish town, where LeMond took the sprint to claim his second stage. It meant that, with no mountains left, Fignon still led by 50 seconds. Beyond the finish line, he tapped LeMond on the shoulder and told him: 'You raced a great race, Greg. I have to tell you, Guimard predicted this is how it would finish: me winning and you second.'

'That day, there was a truce,' LeMond says. 'I felt good, but I wasn't confident I could stay in the group. I spent the whole day at the back. The climbs weren't steep enough or hard enough to make a difference. After that I thought, if I can recover I have to put everything into the final time trial.'

The Tour would finish with a time trial for the first time since 1968, when Jan Janssen held off Herman Van Springel by 38 seconds: the closest ever finish.

*   *   *

The 1989 Tour represented a comeback for Fignon, too. When he pulled on the yellow jersey in Luxembourg, after the stage two team time trial, it was for the first time since 1984, when he won the second of his two titles. He hadn't suffered a near-death experience, like LeMond, but he had endured a series of injuries over the previous four years. Finally, though, he seemed close to his best. In Aix-les-Bains, where he congratulated LeMond on the stage win, he was confident the Tour was won.

Later that night, Fignon 'felt a sharp pain between my legs'. A saddle sore. Not an uncommon injury, and nothing to worry about. But after the next day's penultimate stage 'it hurt so much that I couldn't go and urinate at the dope control'. Fignon could not move without excruciating pain, and he didn't sleep. When he climbed on his bike the next day, he wanted to scream but tried not to even wince: he didn't want LeMond, or anyone else, to pick up any hint of the 'ferocious pain' he was feeling.

Yet, even with a saddle sore, all Fignon had to do was defend a 50-second lead. Over 24.5km, it shouldn't be too difficult. In the Tour's first time trial, over 73km, LeMond had beaten him by 56. This suggested that LeMond would need at least 50km to gain the 51 seconds he needed. 'One second a kilometre is possible,' said Paul Köchli, LeMond's former directeur sportif. 'Two seconds a kilometre is not possible.'

'Greg believes he can win,' Fignon said on the eve of the stage. 'But it is impossible. I am too strong in the mind and the legs.'

The day was warm, with a light breeze to blow the riders from Versailles into Paris, to finish on the Champs-Élysées. The 24.5km time trial was also slightly downhill. LeMond woke up not sure what to expect, but when he went out in the morning to ride the course he was reassured by how he felt. 'By the time I showed up for my time trial, my legs were fully recovered. I felt better than when I started the Tour.'

At 4.12pm LeMond left the start house in front of the Palace of Versailles, sprinted down the Avenue de Paris then settled quickly into his aerodynamic tuck: arms stretched in front of him, yellow teardrop-shaped helmet, rear disc wheel. Every few seconds he looked down at the road, then back up for five: a pattern he maintained all the way. At 4.14pm Fignon followed him out the start house, throwing his bike from side to side as he got up to speed, then sitting down, gripping the upturned handlebars on his time trial bike. The sight of a battling Fignon provided a stark contrast to the more fluid, certainly more aerodynamic LeMond. The handlebars made a noticeable difference. When LeMond tried them before the time trial in Rennes, warming up alongside a team-mate, Janusz Kuum, who was not using them, De Cauwer was struck by the difference. 'The air flows around LeMond, who is shaped like an egg, but it hits Kuum in the chest and slows him down as if his body was a parachute.' LeMond had won the time trial, of course; yet it hadn't shown the bars at their best. LeMond hit a bump in the road early on, knocking them marginally out of position, enough to affect his ride.

It wasn't just the bars. Fignon, in his yellow jersey and plain black shorts, shifted constantly in the saddle – no doubt a symptom of the saddle sore. He was bespectacled and bare-headed; when he dipped his head his blond ponytail fluttered in the wind. His only real concession to aerodynamics was two disc wheels.

Crowds lined the roads into Paris, Fignon's home city, and clustered on the bridges. There was an official time-check at half-distance, as they raced along the bank of the Seine. LeMond flashed through: 12.08. It was the fastest time by 20 seconds.

Fignon was next: 12.29. He was 21 seconds down. After five kilometers, he had been told by Guimard that he was six seconds down on LeMond, which shocked him. He put his head down and pressed hard, but the second time check confirmed he was losing ground, that his 50-second advantage was being eaten into. Now time checks started coming every kilometre. LeMond didn't hear any of them; he had told De Cauwer that he didn't want to know.

The Eiffel Tower reared up at the end of the Seine. Now the gap was 24 seconds. Still LeMond punched the pedals, head down, head back up, head down, head up; his upper body rock solid. Fignon had no rhythm; his shoulders rocked; he shifted in the saddle; he stood up on the pedals, swinging his bike to try to generate more power. When he sat back down, his head dropped between his shoulders.

Twenty-nine seconds.

Now LeMond was on the Rue de Rivoli, a yellow and purple blur as he sped past the Louvre Palace, through a shaded corridor of crowds and five-storey buildings, towards daylight, the vast, open space of the Place de la Concorde.

Thirty-two seconds.

LeMond raced across the Place de la Concorde, dwarfed by its scale, and began the gradual climb of the Champs-Élysées, up the left side to the Arc de Triomphe, where the riders would turn back on themselves to finish on the other side.

Thirty-five seconds.

LeMond hugged the left gutter, searching for shelter and the smoothest bit of the road. He maintained his speed;

he remained in the saddle. At the top he turned, stood on the pedals to get back up to speed. On the other side of the Champs-Élysées, still making his way to the turn, was Fignon.

Forty seconds.

Fignon was ragged, his face a mask of desperation and pain. He kept lifting himself out of the saddle, searching for power and relief. When he sat back down and his head dropped between his shoulders, it was with an air of resignation. He had three kilometres to hang on.

Forty-eight seconds.

Now it was downhill for LeMond: he thundered towards the finish, almost catching Pedro Delgado, who had started two minutes before him. He crossed the line in 26.57. It was the fastest time of the day; and at 54.545kph, the fastest time trial in Tour history.[8]

Fignon was still making his way up towards the turn. Out of the saddle, reaching down for his gear lever. Around the turn. He was a tiny speck in front of an enormous entourage: twenty motorbikes, ten cars, then an endless convoy of Tour vehicles. Searching for the smoothest bit of road, he veered to the left. Parking cones formed a funnel to the finish and Fignon appeared to bounce off them as he approached the line.

LeMond had collapsed beyond the finish line. He picked himself up, took a large set of headphones and listened to French radio commentary. Then he discarded them; he was edgy, impatient, tetchy and brushed off Kathy and his father, Bob. He stretched on to his tiptoes, trying to peer over the crowds, a large bottle of water in one hand, his head in the

---

8 LeMond's time trial into Paris in 1989 remains the fastest time trial over 10km in the Tour's history. It was beaten by David Zabriskie on the opening day of the 2005 Tour, but Zabriskie was subsequently stripped of that success after admitting to doping. LeMond is also the only American Tour de France winner.

other. As Fignon reached the 100m to go sign his time ticked over 27.47. The clock stopped at 27.55. He was third on the stage; never in his life had he ridden such a fast time trial. He had completed the 3,285.3km around France in 87 hours, 38 minutes, 43 seconds. He had lost the Tour.

By eight seconds.

*   *   *

'A day of insane sadness. A day of monstrous defeat. The only day in my life when a few seconds were an eternity.' Fignon never got over the disappointment, or that is the impression formed by reading his book, *We Were Young and Carefree*. It opens with an epigraph: an exchange with a taxi driver who years later said, 'Ah, I remember you: you're the guy who lost the Tour de France by eight seconds!'

'No, monsieur,' said Fignon, 'I'm the guy who won the Tour twice.'

Two decades on, LeMond says, 'I had dinner with Fignon recently and I really learned a lot about him. He really was an incredible athlete. He trained twice a week. Turned pro in '82 and in his second year he won his first Tour. That's genetics. He had real talent.'

They dined together not long before Fignon's death from cancer, aged fifty, in 2010. LeMond led the tributes. 'It's a really sad day. He had a very, very big talent, much more than anyone recognised. We were team-mates, competitors, but also friends. He was a great person, one of the few that I find was really true to himself. He was one of the few riders who I really admired for his honesty and his frankness. We talked about a lot of different things outside of cycling and I was fortunate to really get to know him when my career stopped.'

When they met for dinner, they discussed the 1989 Tour de France, of course. It was the race that, for very different reasons, defined both their careers. 'I lost the race in Briançon,' Fignon told LeMond.

'Bullshit,' LeMond told him. 'You lost the race because of Guimard.'

Guimard, says LeMond, had the opportunity to use the new handebars, but dismissed them. 'Guimard said the position hurt your breathing. It's bizarre; he was so far advanced aerodynamically; we had deep dish wheels in '82, aerodynamic helmets in '83. He had the option to use the 'bars, but he didn't.'

'I told Fignon, "If you'd used them, you probably would have won."'

Does LeMond really think so? *'Maybe,'* he says, but doesn't sound convinced. *Bicycling* magazine attempted to answer the question in November 1989, running wind tunnel tests that suggested the handlebars – ubiquitous from the moment of LeMond's victory – were worth a minute over the 24.5km course from Versailles to Paris. They also claimed LeMond's aero helmet gave him a further sixteen-second advantage over the bare-headed Fignon. Fignon's front disc was, they reckoned, worth five seconds. Perhaps, then, it is true: that the 'bars won the Tour.

Then again, as LeMond says, 'Everyone can say, "I lost it here, I won it here." I remember Delgado saying he would have won because he started five minutes behind after he turned up late for the prologue. But the tactics are always played out based on the situation. If Delgado is five minutes behind, you give him some time.'[9]

If Fignon never got over 1989, neither, perhaps, did Guimard. As a directeur sportif, he had won seven Tours with

9 Pedro Delgado, who conceded 2:40 by turning up late for the prologue, lost another two minutes-plus in the following day's team time trial. In Paris he was third, only 3:34 down. Without his mishaps, the closest Tour in history might have been even closer.

three different riders in fourteen years; Fignon's eight-second defeat was as close as he ever got to an eighth.

*   *   *

On the podium in Paris, LeMond grinned. To his right, on the step below, Fignon glowered. His eyes were red. 'It is the first time I have cried since I was a child,' he told reporters. 'When I saw Fignon, I knew he was disappointed,' LeMond said. 'What could I say to him? What could he say to me? I would have been devastated.' On the podium, LeMond did speak to Fignon. 'At least you won the Giro,' he told him.

Then LeMond told reporters, 'It's a miracle that I'm even racing. Two years ago I was almost dead … It was a strange feeling to see myself win the Tour de France. For sure that's the craziest thing that ever happened in my life.'

LeMond seems as bemused now as he did then. 'I dunno, it was funny. My team still hadn't paid me. And throughout that Tour I thought, you can't tell me to try harder. There was pressure to do well, but there was kind of a relief not to have to do it because of money.

'From the start of the Tour I thought, I'll sign for the team that comes up to me on the first rest day … and Roger Legeay came up to me in Rennes.' Legeay was the boss of the French Z team. 'He made me my first offer in three years, and I won the time trial in Rennes the next day. Of course, after Paris it was a feeding frenzy; all these people making offers.'

LeMond, who went on to win his second world road race title in the autumn, joined Z, becoming the best-paid cyclist in history when he signed a contract for $5.5 million over three years. He returned to the Tour in 1990 and again came from behind, reeling in the long-time leader, Claudio Chiappucci, to claim his third title. But, at twenty-nine, it was his last major win. He was seventh in 1991 – the first time he had failed to make the podium in five starts – and began to be dogged by health problems. He put that down to the lead pellets lodged in his heart lining; later, he wondered whether his career was also curtailed by others' use of EPO. 'What really hurt at the end of my career is that people looked at my performance and equated it to lack of training,' LeMond says. 'But I never took a week off.'

In retirement, LeMond seemed to become despondent about his health and disillusioned about his sport and its doping problems. When he went public with his suspicions about his successor, Lance Armstrong, he was labelled by some as bitter and jealous. His feud with Armstrong damaged his bike business and took a huge personal and professional toll. 'It was like the longest Tour ever,' he says.

Now that LeMond has been reinstated as his country's only Tour champion, he might feel vindicated. 'No,' he says. 'I actually feel incredibly sad. I kinda don't know how my life got so intertwined with it all, because I wasn't part of what was going on, but somehow I got dragged into it. I know a lot of people came to me and, for whatever reason, they wanted to tell me stuff about Armstrong, and what he was doing. At times I wish I hadn't heard it, and I'd be off fishing somewhere.'

Or riding his bike? 'I've been riding a little bit, but I've got the lead poisoning problem and my lead levels went up when I started riding again. I've got thirty-five pellets still in me. I feel like I'm dying every day. If I do a couple of days of exercise a week, I'm on a downer. My friends go out and train, for triathlons, or ski races, and I can't even imagine it. They're disappointed that I'm not totally into it, but they're guys who didn't do it to that extent when they were younger.

'I feel good at times. It's weird, I don't have to ride that often and ...' – he twists his hand to mimic revving a throttle, and the sparkle returns to his eyes. 'I'm heavy,' he adds. 'I gotta lose weight. But I do like to ride.

'Y'know, I finally got accustomed to saying, "I'm done with cycling. I don't need it." But I love it as well.'

The 1989 Tour is LeMond's life in microcosm: the uncertainty and optimism, the self-doubt and confidence, the setbacks and persistence, being dismissed and written off. Then the counter-attack, the comeback. And in the end, the triumph. 'Today has been the greatest moment in my whole life,' said a disbelieving LeMond as dusk fell on the Champs-Élysées on 23 July 1989.

Before the final time trial into Paris, most journalists had already written their stories for Monday's newspapers: 'Fignon wins third Tour.' The articles had to be trashed, but the new headline wrote itself: 'La Résurrection.' And a cartoon in *L'Equipe* summed up the miracle of LeMond. It depicted the graves of three late legends of the Tour: Italy's double-winner Fausto Coppi, and the Frenchmen, three-time winner Louison Bobet and five-time winner Jacques Anquetil.

'LeMond was almost dead,' says Bobet.

'Next year, we'll enter,' says Anquetil.

Classement

1 Greg LeMond, USA, ADR, 26 minutes, 57 secs
2 Thierry Marie, France, Super-U, at 33 secs
3 Laurent Fignon, France, Super-U, at 58 secs
4 Jelle Nijdam, Netherlands, Superconfex, at 1 minute, 7 secs
5 Sean Yates, Great Britain, 7-Eleven, at 1 minute, 10 secs
6 Erich Maechler, Switzerland, Carrera, same time

ACKNOWLEDGEMENTS

This book would have been impossible without the coopera-tion of the Tour de France riders who feature on its pages. I am grateful to the following, listed in order of appearance, who all agreed to be interviewed: Chris Boardman, Bernard Hinault, Graham Jones, Sean Kelly, Wilfried Nelissen, Marc Sergeant, Joël Pelier, Mark Cavendish, Lance Armstrong, Frans Maassen, Leo van Vliet, Bernhard Eisel, Iban Mayo, Urs Zimmermann, José Luis Viejo, Stephen Roche, Andy Hampsten, Freddy Maertens, Eddy Merckx, Luis Herrera, Claudio Chiappucci, Bobby Julich, Jörg Jaksche, Andy Schleck, Maxime Monfort, David Millar and Greg LeMond. Thanks, too, to Luca Guercilena, Hilaire van der Schueren, Brian Nygaard and Shelley Verses. And to colleagues whose help has been invaluable. I am particularly indebt-ed to Daniel Friebe, Lionel Birnie, Jan-Pieter De Vlieger, Raymond Kerckhoffs, Alain Laiseka, Klaus Bellon, Alasdair Fotheringham, Neal Rogers and Hector Urrego.

It was Iain MacGregor, an editor at Collins, who came up with the original idea for this book, and I am grateful to him, as I am to Rory Scarfe, who picked up the reins when Iain moved on, offering fantastic support and constructive feedback as my chapters began landing in his inbox. Thanks as ever to my agent, David Luxton, for his encouragement and calm reassurance. Finally, thank you for their loving support to my wife Virginie, and to the rest of my family, Brian, Jennifer, Robin, Peter, Iciar and Kena.

INDEX

Abdoujaparov, Djamolidine 35, 36–7, 38, 39, 40, 41, 44, 66, 212
Abilliera, José Luis 225
Abt, Samuel 1, 129, 130, 136, 137, 172
ADR team 56, 320–1, 323, 324
Agostinho, Joaquim 110, 111, 112, 119
Amstel Gold Race 94, 98
Andersen, Kim 289, 291
Anderson, Mike 256
Anderson, Phil 5, 211, 241, 243
Andreu, Frankie 81, 187
Anquetil, Jacques 110, 111, 248, 286, 338
Ariostea team 78
Armani, Luciano 116
Armstrong, Kristin 248
Armstrong, Lance 19–20, 22, 82–5, 186–7, 199, 309
  on doping 84–5, 247–8, 250, 254, 258, 324, 337
  doping charge 263–4, 266
  Olympics 1992 77–8
  TdF 1995 77, 78, 79, 81, 82, 85–9
  TdF 2003 247–9, 250–66
  TdF 2010 280–1
Arroyo, David 70
Astana team 71, 280
Aurore, L' 106
Auto, L' 2, 222

Baal, Daniel 185
Bahamontes, Federico 223–5, 284–5
Ballan, Alessandro 73, 74
Banesto team 157, 168
Baracchi Trophy 238
Barnes, Simon 201
Barredo, Carlos 70
Barteau, Vincent 133, 134–5
Basso, Ivan 260, 275, 280

Bauer, Steve 154
Belkin team 95
Bellon, Klaus 125, 128, 139
Beloki, Joseba 255
Beltran, Manuel 259
Bernard, Jean-François 145–6, 148–51, 153–5, 156–8, 174, 177
Bernaudeau, Jean-René 240
Berzin, Evgeni 16
Beyssens, Herman 239
Bianchi team 164, 192, 256
Bic team 116
Bicycling 335
Bittinger, René 25
blood transfusions see doping
BMC team 294
Boardman, Chris 1, 4–16, 39
Boasson Hagen, Edvald 68
Bobet, Louison 292, 338
Boifava, Davide 207
Bolts, Udo 184, 197
Boule d'Or team 238
Bourlon, Albert 52, 59
Bouvatier, Philippe 55
Bouvet, Philippe 329
Bouygues Telecom team 71
Bracke, Ferdinand 235
Brailsford, David 311
Breukink, Erik 79
British Cycling 66, 310–11
Brochard, Laurent 305, 308, 309
Brunel, Philippe 120
Bruyère, Joseph 115, 118
Bruyneel, Johan 71, 85, 261
Buckler team 92, 95, 98, 102
Bugno, Gianni 168, 170, 171, 172, 175–6, 178

Cancellara, Fabian 3, 73
Cannibal (Friebe) 109, 113–14
Carmichael, Chris 266
Carrera team 96, 165, 206, 207, 208

Casagrande, Francesco 187
Casar, Sandy 271
Casartelli, Fabio 48, 78–9, 80–2, 88
Casera-Bahamontes, La (team) 224–5
Cassani, Davide 153
Cavendish, Mark 65–8, 233, 244, 273, 277–8, 290
  TdF 2008 67, 273
  TdF 2009 63–5, 69–75
  TdF 2010 269–70, 273–6, 278–81
  TdF 2012 68–9
Cecchini, Luigi 250
Cervélo team 72
Chancel, Jacques 140
Chavanel, Sylvain 262
Chiappucci, Claudio 80, 97–8, 161–5, 166–79, 336
Chiesa, Mario 165
Chirac, Jacques 150
Ciolek, Gerald 72
Cipollini, Mario 36, 37, 38, 39, 233
Claeys, Paul 237
Clásica San Sebastián 77, 82
Clásico RCN 124, 125, 128, 129
Cofidis team 187, 191, 307–8, 309–10
Colombian Cycling Federation 126
Colotti, Jean-Claude 92, 97, 98–101, 102
Conconi, Francesco 178
Contador, Alberto 65, 72, 281, 285–6, 288, 289, 295, 298
Cooke, Baden 277
Coppi, Fausto 125, 131, 164, 171, 232, 256, 338
Cornillet, Bruno 40
Corredor, Edgar 127, 131
Courcol, Pierre 2
Coyle, Dan 249, 251
Critérium du Dauphiné 298

Critérium International 187
CSC team 249
Cubino, Laudelino 51, 52
Cycling Weekly 28, 117, 131, 243

Danielson, Tom 301
Dauphiné Libéré 8–9, 37, 108, 109, 124, 130, 251–2, 253–4, 266, 298, 306
De Cauwer, José 321, 331
de Gribaldy, Jean 55, 60
de Las Cuevas, Armand 15
De Muer, Maurice 111, 235
De Roo, Alain 238, 241
de Rooy, Theo 20, 98–9
De Vlaeminck, Roger 25, 32
de Vlieger, Jan-Pieter 38
de Vries, Gerrit 40
De Witte, Ronald 238
De Wolf, Fons 243n
Dean, Julian 274
Death of Marco Pantani, The (Rendell) 198, 200
Deferre, Gaston 116
Dekker, Erik 78
Delcroix, Ludo 29
Delgado, Pedro 148, 154, 155–6, 323, 333, 335
Delion, Gilles 166
Demeyer, Marc 233–4
den Bakker, Maarten 88
Desgrange, Henri 284, 298
Devenyns, Dries 293, 294, 295
Dombrowski, Joe 67
doping 21, 63, 148, 183–5, 188–9, 194, 208, 218, 236–7, 247, 249–51n, 258–9, 265, 272, 285, 303, 333n
   Armstrong charged 263–4, 266
   Armstrong on 84–5, 247–8, 250, 254, 258
   blood transfusions 250, 254, 258, 259
   EPO 83–5, 166, 177–8, 183, 188, 200, 212, 250, 265, 308, 311, 324, 337
   Festina scandal 183–5, 188, 189, 250, 305, 310
   haematocrit 177, 254, 258
   and Millar 307–8, 309–13
Driessens, Lomme 115, 232–3, 238
Duclos-Lassalle, Gilbert 25, 175, 211
Dufaux, Laurent 85

Eisel, Bernhard 73, 269–70, 275–80, 281
Ekimov, Viatcheslav 85
Elliott, Shay 5
EPO *see* doping
Equipe, L' 84, 108, 111, 120, 126, 133, 137–8, 157, 222, 317, 329, 338
Escartín, Fernando 191, 193, 196, 198, 200
Esclassan, Jacques 234
Escobar, Pablo 141
Escobar, Roberto 141
Etxebarria, David 309
Europcar team 287, 296
Euskaltel team 255, 257, 295, 309
Evans, Cadel 70, 270, 288, 289, 294–5, 296–7, 298

Fall from Grace (Maertens) 231
Fedrigo, Pierrick 280–1
Ferrari, Michele 84, 85, 178, 250, 252, 253
Ferri, Jaime Mir 221
Ferrigato, Andrea 86
Festina scandal *see* doping
Fignon, Laurent 123, 124, 166, 175, 177–8, 324, 325, 334
   TdF 1983 132
   TdF 1984 132, 133–6, 137, 138, 139, 140–1
   TdF 1987 147, 154
   TdF 1989 326–7, 328–9, 330–2, 333, 334–6, 338
Fischer, Dr 237
Flandria team 232, 237
Flèche Wallonne 84, 236
Flórez, Alfonso 126
Fondriest, Maurizio 212
Fontanelli, Fabiano 42
Fotheringham, William 108
Française des Jeux team 201, 277
Freire, Oscar 71
Friebe, Daniel 109, 113–14, 115
Freuler, Urs 242
Fuente, José-Manuel 120
Fuentes, Eufemiano 250, 251n
Fuglsang, Jakob 289

Gan team 5, 7-8, 12, 17, 40
Garde, Dominique 154
Garmin team 272, 274, 301
Gatorade team 168
Gaumont, Philippe 20, 310
Gautier, Cyril 314

Gayant, Martial 153
GC team 85, 97, 169, 258, 291
Gendron, Christophe 43
Gerdemann, Linus 289
Gewiss-Ballan team 84
Ghent–Wevelgem 45, 48, 49, 94, 276
Gimondi, Felice 176
Giro d'Italia
   1911 170
   1968 107
   1971 108
   1980 25
   1985 206
   1987 147
   1988 157, 208
   1989 319–20, 323–5
   1991 163
   1992 165
   1998 181
   1999 200
   2003 252n
   2007 286, 316
   2009 69
   2011 81, 285
   2012 301
Goddet, Jacques 2, 105, 107, 111, 138
Godefroot, Walter 182
GP Eddy Merckx 7
GP William Tell 224
Gran Fondo 162
Grand, Odélie 106
Great Bike Race, The (Nicholson) 216, 217, 218, 219, 222
Guercilena, Luca 289, 291, 294, 295–6, 299
Guimard, Cyrille 23, 27, 55, 116, 132, 133, 137, 152, 325–6, 328–9, 335–6

Half Man, Half Bike (Fotheringham) 108
Hamilton, Tyler 249–51, 254, 255, 258, 260, 263, 264
Hampsten, Andy 149, 155, 170, 172, 208, 209, 212
Haussler, Heinrich 73
Herrera, Luis 'Lucho' 54, 123–4, 129–31, 135, 136–7, 138–40, 141–2, 149, 154
Hesjedal, Ryder 301, 312
Het Volk 38, 46, 108
Hinault, Bernard 21–3, 60, 124, 130, 145, 146–7, 152, 248, 266, 286
   Liège–Bastogne–Liège 1980 24–5

Paris–Roubaix 25, 26–7,
  31–2
TdF 1980 21, 25, 27–31
TdF 1981 240, 242
TdF 1984 123, 132,
  133–8, 140
TdF 1985 54, 140, 146
TdF 1986 146, 207
TdF 1989 54, 58
Hincapie, George 74, 84
Hoban, Barry 80, 115
Hoogerland, Johnny 291
HTC-Columbia team 233,
  274, 276, 280
Hunger (Kelly) 147
Hushovd, Thor 72, 75
Huysmans, Joseph 115, 116

Iglinsky, Maxim 291, 292,
  293, 295, 296
Imboden, Heinz 154
Imlach, Gary 199
In the Crosswind
  (Zimmermann) 207
In Search of Robert Millar
  (Moore) 103
Indurain, Miguel 4, 6, 11,
  16, 39–40, 85, 97–8,
  157, 163, 178, 248
  TdF 1992 165, 166, 167,
  170, 171, 172, 173–4,
  175, 176
IOC 185–6

Jacobs, Jos 242
Jacome, Otto 319, 324
Jaksche, Jörg 183, 184, 193,
  195–6
Jalabert, Laurent 41, 185,
  200, 308–9
Jansen, Harrie 323
Janssen, Jan 330
Järmann, Rolf 85, 87
Jiménez, José María 191,
  193–4, 196
Jiménez, Giovanni 126
Jiménez, Patrocinio 127, 134
Jones, Graham 5, 22, 27,
  28, 30
Jules, Pascal 133
Julich, Bobby 182, 183,
  186–90, 191, 192, 193,
  194–5, 196, 197–202

KAS team 225
Keen, Peter 8, 9, 10
Kelly, Sean 21, 52, 147,
  167, 240, 243
King of the Mountains 27,
  54, 73, 127, 134, 163,
  167, 218, 224, 308

Kings of the Mountains
  (Rendell) 124
Kirchen, Kim 70–1
Kišerlovski, Robert 314, 315
Knetemann, Gerrie 241
Köchli, Paul 154
Kouchner, Bernard 185
Kuiper, Hennie 24, 29–30,
  32, 88
Kuum, Janusz 331
Kwantum team 93, 94,
  95

L.A. Confidentiel (Walsh) 249
La Repubblica 166, 176
La Vie Claire team 132, 134,
  136, 140, 149
Landis, Floyd 250, 263
Langarica, Dalmacio 225
Leblanc, Jean-Marie 2, 43,
  79, 185, 211
Leblanc, Luc 6, 13, 15, 191,
  192, 193
Leclercq, Jean-Claude 153,
  154
Lefèvre, Laurent 73, 74
Legeay, Roger 5, 7, 336
Lejarreta, Marino 154
Lelli, Massimiliano 85
LeMond, Greg 5, 6, 7, 12,
  40, 82, 83, 145, 147,
  266, 286, 320–5, 337
  TdF 1984 135, 140
  TdF 1985 146
  TdF 1989 56, 319–20,
  326–36, 338
  TdF 1990 162–3, 336
  TdF 1992 167–8, 175
  TdF 1994 336
LeMond, Kathy 320,
  321–2, 323–4, 327–8
Leopard-Trek team 287,
  289, 290
Letort, Désiré 115
Liège–Bastogne–Liège 25,
  83, 289, 321
Liggett, Phil 13, 16, 35, 148
Lilholt, Søren 52
Lino, Pascal 168
Lotus 'Superbike' 12
Louviot, Philippe 40
Louy, Xavier 128
Ludwig, Olaf 35, 41, 95

Maassen, Frans 92,
  95–101, 102, 103
Madiot, Marc 133, 201, 277
Maertens, Carine 230, 233,
  238, 239
Maertens, Freddy 36, 215,
  217, 220, 225, 229–44

Maini, Orlando 194
Manzano, Jesús 251
Mapei team 276–7
Marie, Thierry 3, 9, 59
Martin, Tony 73–5, 280
Martínez, Egoi 314
Massi, Rodolfo 190, 191,
  193, 196, 198
Mayo, Iban 19, 251, 252,
  253, 255, 257, 258,
  259–60, 261, 262,
  264–5, 266
Memories of the Peloton
  (Hinault) 30–1
Menchov, Denis 73
Mercatone Uno team 192
Mercier, Scott 265
Merckx, Eddy 21, 83, 93,
  106–7, 220, 231, 232,
  234, 248, 286
  TdF 1969 107
  TdF 1970 107–8
  TdF 1971 105, 107,
  108–21
  TdF 2011 297
MG-Technogym team 87
Midi Libre 45, 108, 226,
  231, 234, 239
Milan–San Remo 69, 73,
  94, 107, 108, 163, 277
Millar, David 5, 37, 70, 72,
  95, 270–3, 281, 301–17
  anti-doping 311, 312–13
  doping 307–8, 309–12
  TdF 2000 305–6
  TdF 2001 307–8
  TdF 2002 306–7, 308–9
  TdF 2012 301, 302–5,
  313–17
Millar, Robert 126, 127,
  131, 135, 137
Milram team 72, 74
Mínguez, Javier 51, 52,
  55–6
Molteni team 109, 114–15
Mondory, Lloyd 274n
Monfort, Maxime 74,
  289–90
Moser, Francesco 5, 25
Motorola team 78, 80–1,
  84, 96, 187, 188, 209–10
Mottet, Charly 40, 152, 153,
  155, 210
Mulholland, Owen 67, 152
Mundo Ciclistico (magazine)
  125
Muñóz, Pedro 226
Mura, Gianni 166, 168,
  172, 176
Museeuw, Johan 20
Nardello, Daniele 190

Nelissen, Wilfried 35, 36, 37–9, 40–9
Nicholson, Geoffrey 216, 217, 218, 219, 222
Novell team 95
Novemail team 35, 37, 40–1
Nulens, Guy 40
Nygaard, Brian 289, 291

O'Grady, Stuart 73, 287–8, 289, 292, 305
Obree, Graeme 5–6
Ocaña, Luis 108, 109–21, 134, 216, 218, 219, 220, 225
Ochowicz, Jim 81, 209, 210, 211
Olympic Games
   1972 30, 224
   1992 5, 7, 9, 11, 77–8
   2000 264
   2004 311
ONCE team 96
Outschakov, Serguei 86
Ozols, Dainis 78

Panasonic team 37, 56, 92, 93, 98, 101, 102, 130
Pantani, Marco 80, 252n
   TdF 1998 181–2, 185, 190–4, 196, 197, 198–9, 200, 201
   TdF 2000 253
Paolini, Luca 68
Paris Match 108
Paris–Bourges 37
Paris–Brussels 94
Paris–Nice 8, 22, 45, 108, 187
Paris–Roubaix 19–20, 25, 26–7, 31–2, 94, 107, 108, 277
PDM team 323
Peeters, Ludo 241
Peiper, Allan 280, 302, 317
Pelier, Joël 51, 52–60
Pélissier, Charles 234
Pellizotti, Franco 73
Peña, Victor Hugo 263
Pensec, Ronan 40
Péraud, Jean-Christophe 314–15
Petacchi, Alessandro 274, 275, 302
Peugeot team 234–5, 240
Pevenage, Rudy 30
Pezzi, Luciano 181, 198
Phinney, Davis 326
Piasecki, Lech 324
Planckaert, Eddy 95, 243

Planckaert, Walter 102
Pollentier, Michel 29, 233–4, 236–7, 238
Polti team 183
Porte, Dr Gerard 79
Post, Peter 28, 31, 37, 40, 46, 47–8, 92–5, 96, 101, 102–3, 130, 242
Posthuma, Joost 289–91, 292–3
Poulidor, Raymond 110, 176
Prudhomme, Christian 2, 26

Quintarelli, Sandro 165, 169–70

Raas, Jan 28, 29, 31, 92, 93, 94–5, 101, 102, 103
Rabobank team 71–2, 95, 103
Race Against Time, The (Pickering) 6
Racing Through the Dark (Millar) 307
Ramírez, Martin 124
Rebellin, Davide 78
Renault team 132, 133, 134, 242
Rendell, Matt 124, 127, 200
Rezze, Dante 78
Richard, Pascal 210, 212
Riis, Bjarne 63–4, 80, 81, 185, 189, 292, 305
Rinero, Christophe 191, 194, 196, 198
Riotte, Raymond 113–14
Roche, Nicolas 291, 293, 294, 295
Roche, Stephen 5, 147, 148, 149, 151–4, 155–6, 172, 175, 177, 321, 322
Rodríguez, Martin Emilio 124
Rolland, Pierre 292, 296, 298
Rooks, Steven 96–7
Roscioli, Fabio 165
Rubiera, Chechu 261
Ryckaert, Eric 184

Saeco team 233
Samaranch, Juan-Antonio 185–6
Sánchez, Luis León 70, 74
Sánchez, Samuel 295, 297
Sastre, Carlos 270
Saunier Duval team 311, 312

Saura, Gabriel 219
Saxo Bank team 63, 295
Scheldeprijs (race) 277
Schepers, Eddy 151, 152–3
Schleck, Andy 63, 73, 281, 284–90, 291–9
Schleck, Fränk 19, 20, 73
Schleck, Johny 109, 115, 119
Sciandri, Max 85, 87
Scolastico, Vincenzo 178
Secret Race, The (Hamilton) 249
Sergeant, Marc 38, 40, 41, 42, 43, 92, 93, 95–102
Serrano, Marcos-Antonio 191, 193, 196
7-Eleven team 149, 208–9
Sherwen, Paul 40
Silin, Egor 293, 294, 295
Simpson, Tom 3, 5, 10, 80, 148, 316
Sky, see Team Sky
Sonolor team 113
Spencer, Jeff 251, 254
Stapleton, Bob 70
Stevens, Julien 115
Sukhoruchenkov, Sergey 126
Super Ser team 216, 218, 221, 222, 225
Superconfex team 95, 233
Syer, John 9, 11
Système U team 55, 152

T-Mobile team 276, 277
Tafi, Andrea 88
Talen, John 52
Tapie, Bernard 132, 140n, 149, 150
Team Sky 68, 69
Teka team 134, 225
Telekom team 41, 182, 191, 195
Three Days of De Panne 277
TI-Raleigh team 28, 29, 30, 31, 92, 93, 94, 242
Tirreno–Adriatico 322
Torres, Pedro 216, 218, 219
Toshiba team 145, 149, 152, 154
Tour de l'Avenir 126, 141
Tour of Belgium 108, 236
Tour of Britain 7
Tour of Corsica 22
Tour of the European Community 166
Tour of Flanders 32, 107, 230, 234, 236
Tour de France (TdF)
   1910 273

1911 283
1930 234
1947 52
1952 131, 171
1964 110
1967 1, 3, 80, 148
1968 3
1969 107
1970 107–8, 234
1971 105, 108–13, 134
1972 120, 125
1973 120, 218
1974 120, 234
1975 124, 225
1976 216–22, 225, 232,
    234–5, 237
1978 21, 236
1979 21, 25, 225
1980 20–1, 25, 27
1981 231, 239–43
1982 32
1983 127–8, 132
1984 101, 123–4,
    129–40, 206
1985 22, 53–4, 140, 146
1986 54–5, 140, 149, 208
1987 98, 145–6, 147–9,
    151–7
1988 110, 323
1989 51–5, 56–9, 141,
    319, 326–36, 338
1990 95–6, 98, 162–3, 336
1991 4, 37, 163, 207,
    210–12, 336
1992 91–2, 97–102, 164,
    165–77
1993 5, 39
1994 1, 3–4, 11–16, 35,
    39–44
1995 77, 78–82, 85–9
1996 63
1997 264
1998 181–2, 183–6,
    200–1, 202, 305
1999 36, 254
2000 250, 252–3, 264,
    305–6
2001 250, 253, 256, 306,
    307–8
2002 256, 308, 313
2003 251, 254–63, 264,
    251n, 266, 309, 313
2004 19
2005 2, 333
2006 230, 250n
2008 2, 65–6, 67, 270, 273
2009 65
2010 269–72, 273–6,
    278–81, 286
2011 283–4, 285–6,
    287–98

2012 60, 68, 69, 273,
    301–5, 313–16
2013 36
2014 26
Tour of Lombardy 107
Tour of Murcia 8
Tour of Poland 215, 216,
    224
Tour of Qatar 106, 277
Tour de Romandie 22, 274n
Tour of Switzerland 37, 206,
    234, 251, 274n
Tour de Trump 321, 326
Tygart, Travis 247, 263, 265
TVM team 185

UK Anti-Doping Agency 312
Ullrich, Jan 182, 250, 251,
    253, 309
    TdF 1998 186, 189–90,
    191, 192, 193, 195–7,
    199, 200n, 202
    TdF 2003 256–8, 259–61,
    262, 263, 264
Union Cycliste
    Internationale (UCI) 3,
    177, 183, 212, 258
Urrego, Hector 125, 126–8,
    129, 142
US Anti-Doping Agency 263
US Postal team 187, 247,
    250, 265

Valverde, Alejandro 303,
    304
van der Schueren, Hilaire
    95, 99, 102, 103
van der Velde, Johan 29
van Impe, Lucien 111, 112,
    119, 219, 220, 235
van Looy, Rik 232, 233
van Poppel, Jean-Paul 56,
    95, 233
Van Springel, Herman 330
van Vliet, Leo 29, 31, 92,
    94, 95, 103
Vande Velde, Christian 302,
    312
Vandenbroucke, Jean-Luc
    27, 46, 241
Vandersteen, Willy 38
Vanmol, Yvan 324
Vansummeren, Johan 301
Velo (magazine) 177–8
Verlinden, Gerry 29
Verses, Shelley 145–6, 149–
    50, 151, 156, 157
Viejo, José Luis 215–26
Vinokourov, Alexandre 255
Virenque, Richard 80, 167,
    185, 200

Voeckler, Thomas 71, 287,
    289, 296, 298
Voet, Willy 183–4
Vogels, Henk 305
Voigt, Jens 275
Vona, Franco 170, 174
Vuelta a Asturias 226
Vuelta Ciclista al País Vasco
    225
Vuelta a Colombia 125, 128
Vuelta a España
    1970 109
    1977 216, 220, 225
    1987 141
    1994 39, 41
    1996 187
    1998 199
    2001 306, 308, 313
    2006 312
Vuelta de la Juventud 129
Vuelta a Navarra 224
Vuelta a Toledo 224

Wagtmans, Rini 105, 112,
    115, 116, 117
Walsh, David 249
We Were Young and Carefree
    (Fignon) 124, 334
Weinmann team 37
Werner team 116
Weylandt, Wouter 81
Wheelmen (Albergotti &
    O'Connell) 250
Wiggins, Bradley 68, 69,
    73, 312
Willems, Daniel 241
Winfrey, Oprah 84
Woodworth, Pete 7
WordPerfect team 95
World Anti-Doping Agency
    186
world championships 54,
    177, 224, 240
world road race
    championship 31, 82,
    215

Yates, Sean 68, 167

Z team 59, 96, 205, 336
Zor team 225–6
Zabel, Erik 70, 78, 85
Zabriskie, David 333
Zimmermann, Urs 206–13
Zoetemelk, Joop 21, 28,
    29, 30, 31, 108, 110,
    111, 216
Zubeldia, Haimar 257, 258